KIM Basinger

LONGER THAN FOREVER

BY

RON BRITTON

WITH IAN MARKHAM-SMITH
& LIZ HODGSON

BLAKE

KIM Basinger

LONGER THAN FOREVER

Published by Blake Publishing Ltd,
3 Bramber Court, 2 Bramber Road, London W14 9PB, England

First published in hardback in Great Britain 1998

ISBN 1 85782 3257

British Library Cataloguing-in-Publication Data:
A catalogue record for this book is available from
the British Library.

Typeset by BCP

Printed and bound in Great Britain by
Creative Print and Design (Wales), Ebbw Vale, Gwent

1 3 5 7 9 10 8 6 4 2

Contents

Biography

IAN MARKHAM-SMITH has been a journalist, writer and broadcaster for more than 30 years. Originally from Farnham, Surrey, he has worked for numerous publications including *The Sunday Telegraph*, *Daily Mail* and *Sunday Mirror* newspapers in Britain.

In addition, he has held positions on the American magazines the *Globe* and the *National Enquirer* and the prestigious *South China Morning Post* in Hong Kong. He was also Editor of Hong Kong's leading social magazine *The Tatler*.

For many years a freelance, he has covered affairs in Europe, Africa, the Far East and North and South America. His articles appear in newspapers and magazines around the world. When not writing about the activities of celebrities and international events, he is also a widely published writer on wine, food and travel.

Based in Los Angeles, California, he spends most of his time between America's West Coast, the Far East and France.

LIZ HODGSON is a well-known and respected journalist whose articles appear in newspapers and magazines around the globe.

Originally from Wingate, County Durham, she has held positions on the *Sunday Mirror* and *Daily Mail* in Britain and the *South China Post* in Hong Kong. She has also edited a number of consumer and general interest magazines in the Far East.

A specialist on the entertainment industry and celebrity circuit, she also writes about human interest, travel, wine and food. She has homes in Los Angeles, London and Chamonix, France.

Acknowledgements

This book could not have been possible without the friendship and trust that exists between the authors.

And, although this is an intensely personal story, it would never have been told without the help and understanding of a small group of friends, some of whom asked not to be identified. We owe them our deepest and most heartfelt gratitude.

First we would like to thank our publisher, John Blake, without whom this book would not have happened. His confidence in us and his support have been very much appreciated.

We would also like to thank: Alan Aldaya, Wensley Clarkson, Rosalia de Guzman, Forrest D. Concannon, Albert Coombes, Robert J. Harbottle, Barry Kernon, Edward Nachtreib, John Polsue, Jack Roth and Sherry Snyder.

Lastly, no author can write with confidence and authority without the benefit of a good research library. Therefore our most sincere thanks go to the staff of the Academy of Motion Picture Arts & Sciences in Beverly Hills, California.

Ron Britton,
Ian Markham-Smith
& Liz Hodgson

Prologue

Kim Basinger spent more than 20 years trying to make it to the top in Hollywood, and with her Golden Globe and Oscar-winning role as a high-class hooker in *L.A. Confidential* she finally arrived at the summit. But the road was never an easy one, and there were plenty of twists and turns along the way.

Although she is a woman who appears to have it all — great natural beauty, international fame, a handsome, successful husband and an adored young daughter — Kim has paid her dues, as they say in Tinseltown.

A country girl from rural Georgia, the middle child in a family of five, she battled crippling shyness throughout her school days to fulfil her lifelong ambition to be an entertainer. With the encouragement of her parents, when she emerged from a gangling adolescence as a golden beauty, she entered a local beauty pageant which ultimately snagged her a job as a model for Breck Shampoo. She went on to become one of the highest-paid models in New York. But that was not enough for Kim.

Like many other good-looking girls before her, she was hungry for the bright lights of Hollywood. Packing her dogs and her actor boyfriend into her Jeep, she drove across country to try her luck. Bit parts in popular television series such as *Starsky and Hutch*, *Charlie's Angels* and *Vega$* quickly came her way, due, in part, to her stunning appearance. Thanks to the money she had saved from her modelling days, she was able to avoid the sleazy, soft-porn work many struggling actresses take to pay the rent.

After starring in a couple of made-for-television movies, and a mini-series version of *From Here to Eternity*, in 1979 she landed her first feature film, *Hard Country*, starring Jan-Michael Vincent. She also landed her first husband, make-up artist Ron Snyder. They fell in love on the set and married the next year and, at her request, he changed his surname to Britton ...

Hard Country flopped, as did her second movie, *Mother Lode*, which starred Charlton Heston, and to jump-start her career she did a sensational spread for *Playboy magazine*. That, coupled with her role as Domino in the controversial James Bond Film, *Never Say Never Again*, in which Sean Connery renewed his licence to kill, made her an international name, if not yet a star. And her steamy sex scenes with Mickey Rourke in the erotic epic *9½ Weeks* cemented her image as a sizzling sex symbol.

She starred opposite the hottest male stars in the world during the 1980s — Burt Reynolds, Robert Redford, Richard Gere, Bruce Willis — in a series of movies which did little at the box office. But she was able to steal scenes from her better-known leading men, and won critical praise even when her films were slammed. After bombs like *Nadine* and *My Stepmother Is an Alien*, it looked as if the stardom which had seem so certain in the early 1980s was going to fizzle out after all.

Then came *Batman*, which proved to be a turning point in her life, both personally and professionally. After being cast as Vicki Vale at the last minute, she fell for *Batman* producer Jon Peters and told Ron she was divorcing him. The affair with Peters did not last, neither did another fling with singer Prince.

She also hit the headlines for making one of the oddest business deals imaginable, 'buying' a small town near her birthplace in Georgia with great plans to build a film and recording studio — plans that were never fulfilled.

Making her next film, aptly named *The Marrying Man* — released in Britain as *Too Hot to Handle* — she fell in love again, with her handsome co-star Alec Baldwin. They allegedly behaved so badly during the making of that movie, turning up late for work, throwing furniture and telephones around, demanding Evian water for Kim to wash her hair, that she gained a sudden reputation as a prima donna. That, plus the fact that *The Marrying Man* was a flop, seemed to undo all the good her work in Batman had done, and she embarked on more films that went nowhere — *Final Analysis* and *Cool World*.

Then came perhaps her most famous film of all — famous because she never made it. She backed out of *Boxing Helena*, a bizarre and twisted saga of obsessive love, about a doctor who cuts off the arms and legs of his lover and keeps her in a box. The producers sued and won, and she was ordered to pay more than $8 million. The lawsuit was eventually overturned, but not before it had forced her into bankruptcy. Alec, who had stood by her throughout her court ordeal, finally got her to walk down the aisle for a second time and even offered to use his own film earnings to help pay off her debts. Kim made *Wayne's World 2*, *The Getaway* (again with Alec) and *Prêt-à-Porter* before backing out of *Kansas City* because she was pregnant.

She and Alec, who married in a romantic beach ceremony in New York State in 1993, became the proud parents of a daughter in 1995. Their joy at the birth, gruelling though it was for Kim, was overshadowed when Alec became involved in an altercation with a paparazzi photographer waiting outside their house when they brought their daughter home. Alec was charged with assault, but was acquitted in a jury trial.

Kim loved her new role as mother so much she was in no hurry to return to work and almost turned down *L.A. Confidential*. But she changed her mind and made a spectacular comeback to the big screen with the film that finally won her the acclaim of her peers.

Chapter 1

The first time I set eyes on Kim Basinger I knew I was looking at the woman of my dreams. Her stunning natural beauty just hit me. Everything about her was perfect. I didn't want to be seen staring at her but I simply couldn't help it. She had this gorgeous long, blonde mane of hair, perfect, unblemished skin and these amazing, pouty lips. A lot of women would kill for a peaches and cream complexion like hers. She was tall, just a few inches shorter than me, and I'm six foot. All my adult life I'd had an idea of perfection in my mind, but I never expected to find it. Now there she was, standing in front of me.

I knew I would be working with her for a couple of months and I was looking forward to it. After we spoke for a few minutes, during which she was very friendly and natural, I was sure I'd be making moves on her before long. How could I tell that we would be married in less than a year, and that my beautiful new wife would soon be one of the most famous women in the world?

Ironically, when we met, I was the seasoned professional in the movie business, a make-up man with 15 years in the industry, and she was just starting on her first film after a few television roles. It was a modern-day Western called *Hard Country*, starring Jan-Michael Vincent, who was then a Hollywood golden boy after the cult hits *White Line Fever* and *Big Wednesday*. It also starred Tanya Tucker. Kim was playing a Texas telephone operator who dreamed of moving to California to become an air stewardess and Jan-Michael was her redneck boyfriend who wanted to keep her at home.

As far as I was concerned, *Hard Country* was just another movie. I had no idea it was going to change my life so dramatically. I was just finishing work as the make-up man on

Bustin' Loose, with Richard Pryor and Cicely Tyson, when my friend, hairstylist Jan Brandow, recommended me for this new film. I always tried to line up my next job before I finished whatever film I was working on, so I could be sure there'd be some money coming in. Even though I had a long track record of film work, in that world you never know if you are ever going to work again.

So I went to be interviewed by the director, David Greene, an Englishman who had made *Jesus Christ, Superstar*. I had a great list of credits and a family history in the make-up business. My father was Marilyn Monroe's make-up man and even prepared her for her funeral. Greene said they'd be lucky to get me. In my usual cocky way, I replied, 'Yeah, you sure would be.' He didn't even bother to interview me, really. Within minutes he said, 'Let's do the movie.'

As I came out of his office, I ran into Jan, who said, 'There's Kim over there. Come on, I'll introduce you.' She was very relaxed and friendly when Jan told her who I was.

'Hey, that's cool,' she said. 'It's going to be easy. I don't care what you do to me as far as make-up goes.'

Just from that first look at her, I already knew I'd have to do very little work on her, because they wanted her to look plain. Now you can't make Kim look plain. All you can do is keep away from a high glamour look and let her own beauty shine through. Suddenly, this had changed from a routine job to a film I was excited about, even though it was going to be shot in some out-of-the-way parts of California.

When I got home that night, I phoned my best friend, Ron Lang, and told him I'd met the girl of my dreams. He asked what she looked like. I'd always had a thing about Brigitte Bardot, and he knew that. I said, 'You know what Brigitte Bardot looks like? Well, she looks like Brigitte Bardot — but prettier.'

I don't think Ron could believe what he was hearing. I've always been a ladies' man and tried it on with women I have worked with, and I've had a fair amount of success. I couldn't wait to start working with Kim and hoped something would happen, but I never dreamed how quickly we would become lovers and soul mates.

Kim and I hit it off the first night we started shooting *Hard Country* in Pasadena, California, an upper middle-class suburb of Los Angeles with some stunning old architecture. It was just before Christmas 1979, and the nights were cold. She was shivering so I gave her my jacket to wear, which she appreciated. Usually, the wardrobe people have a supply of jackets for times like this, because there's always a lot of standing around doing nothing when you're filming, but she preferred to take mine when I offered it, which immediately added an intimacy to our relationship. There was a vulnerability about her that appealed to me. She was definitely all woman but there was also a little girl quality to her.

The bizarre thing was, looking back, that jacket was lined with mink and had a mink collar. That's why it kept her so warm. Kim, who is a dedicated animal rights supporter, a vegetarian and totally opposed to the fur industry, wore it every night we were shooting and never thought about it. I'd had it made at a furrier in Seattle while I was making *Bustin' Loose*. It was just a bomber jacket, but because of the lining it had cost me something like $1,400.

As I was soon to learn, Kim prided herself on making men fall in love with her, which at times was ironic because, so often during our life together, she ended up falling out with her leading men. But she had a special way with directors, too, which often worked to her advantage because it meant she could manipulate them to adapt the focus of the movie that she was working on more towards her character. She developed this talent making *Hard Country*, her first film.

Jan-Michael Vincent was the star, but right from the start there was tension between him and Kim. He was arrogant and difficult to work with. Kim was always having rows with him and he'd make really crude comments about her having PMS. When I was making him up, he said things like, 'If this was real life, I'd smack her.' David Greene was so concerned about their on- and off-screen tensions that he ordered them to go away for a weekend together, to get to know the script and their characters better. It didn't help. They had a little fling, but after that she liked him even less!

Very quickly, she turned her attentions to Greene, asking questions about her role and making suggestions, and gradually the emphasis of the film swung much more her way. This was something I was to see time and time again in our years together. At the time, of course, I didn't know that. Kim and I were just friends, nothing more. Apart from anything else, there was a big age gap between us; I was 40 and she was 26 when filming started.

I was actually living by the Pacific Ocean in Redondo Beach, south of Los Angeles, with a girlfriend, Chris Filice, when we started shooting *Hard Country*. By the Friday before Christmas, when we were taking a break from work, I was trying to get my nerve up to ask Kim out, but I chickened out at the last minute. I was just going to ask her if she had anywhere to go for Christmas — I don't know what I'd have done if she'd agreed to go with me, when I had another woman at home. In the event, I think she went home to her folks in Georgia.

After Christmas, we moved to a location shoot at Bakersfield, a dull rural city in the Californian desert about 90 miles north of Los Angeles, and were staying in a motel. Kim started hanging out with the production crew, including me. She was never a prima donna, quite the opposite. Unlike so many actors and actresses, she preferred to socialise with the crew — the ordinary folks — rather than the other cast and production executives.

She used to go running on a local playing field during lunch breaks and she and I would play together on the swings. In the evenings, she would join a bunch of crew members for dinner. Kim always paid the bill, no matter how many people there were — or rather, I'd pay it with her money. We'd go to the Hungry Tiger, which served seafood, or to a Chinese restaurant. There wasn't a lot of choice in Bakersfield. Besides, you aren't around Kim very long before you know she's basically a vegetarian, although she will eat fish, and these were the only two places where we could guarantee there'd be something on the menu that she would eat.

Kim and I were becoming more friendly every day. She started getting me to pick up her *per diems* — the cash actors and crew get for subsistence when they are working on location — and asked me to keep her cash for her and pay for the dinners. Then she'd ask me to give her $20 or whatever. I was surprised by this, but it set the pattern for our years together, when I took care of the finances and even signed her cheques. Later, when I moved in with her, I was to discover that she was hopeless with money. I'd find cheques for thousands and thousands of dollars from her days as a model in her handbag and drawers at home, that she just hadn't bothered to cash.

Finally, one night, she had to give an interview to promote the film. 'Please come with me, Ron,' she asked me. I was happy to go along and we were soon sitting in a bar. She was drinking wine, probably not her favourite Pouilly Fuissé in a place like Bakersfield. Funnily enough, I didn't drink in those days — but I did do drugs. Later during the shoot of *Hard Country* I introduced Kim to cocaine, which made her talk incredibly fast. She was never a big drug user, but she did occasionally like coke.

The night of that interview I didn't realise then how nervous she got, but I wasn't complaining because under the table she was holding my hand! I was just a wallflower during the interview, but afterwards I walked her back to our motel. She had a first-floor room at the Bakersfield Inn and I walked her up the stairs to the door and we started necking.

We went inside and began making out on the bed. I soon had all her clothes off her, while I remained partly dressed. It was dark so I couldn't enjoy seeing the full beauty of her body, which I later came to feast my eyes on nightly. Although we didn't make love, we did everything but. I'd been through this kind of thing in the past with actresses and thought it would probably turn out to be just a one-night stand. But I decided to run with it as far as I could. The next morning there was a bit of tension between us when we met but it didn't last. We were both a bit embarrassed so we chatted while avoiding making eye contact for the first few minutes. That's pretty hard to do when you are trying to make someone up. Within a few minutes, the ice had been broken and we continued to talk as before.

I wasn't sure what was going to happen next, but that night we made love for the first time. We kept quiet about it, though, and never spent the whole night in each other's rooms throughout that entire first location shoot.

However discreet I thought I was being, there must have been a tone or a nervousness in my voice once when I was talking on the telephone to my girlfriend Chris. Somehow or other, I got myself into a situation where she talked me into inviting her up to the set for a weekend. I wasn't exactly sure what time she'd be arriving, so when Kim and I came in from filming a scene, we went to her room. I took her in my arms and we just started kissing. There was a knock at the door and we sprang apart in surprise. Kim walked quietly over to the door and looked through the spyhole to see Rick Provenzano, a hairstylist I'd got a job on the movie, and a girl.

'She's very tall with black hair,' said Kim, puzzled by the visitors.

'Oh, my God, it's Chris, my girlfriend,' I gasped. 'What are we going to do?'

I panicked and, almost without thinking, I ran to the window, opened it and jumped out, leaving Kim to deal with the couple at the door. I wasn't ready for a face-to-face confrontation. Unfortunately, I'd forgotten we were on the first floor. I hit the bonnet of a car on my way down, which broke my fall a bit, but still managed to twist my ankle. Then I hobbled to the production office, where we were all supposed to report when we came in from work, wondering what to do next. I'd been expecting Chris and had told people at the motel to let her into my room, so I phoned my own room and she answered.

'Hi, I've just got back,' I lied. 'I'll be with you in a minute.' Then I limped out, wincing from the pain of my ankle and tried to walk as normally as possible. That wasn't easy but I guess it was the price I was paying for being unfaithful.

That night, Chris, Kim, Rick, Jan Brandow and I all went out to dinner at the Hungry Tiger. I was sitting next to Chris, opposite the others, and you could already feel the tension between Kim and Chris. Kim was always fussy about her food. Being a vegetarian, she was always very concerned about what she was eating and she was also very health-conscious and aware about her diet. She asked for a salad without dressing but when the waiter brought it, he had obviously forgotten her request. Kim complained and insisted that he took it away and brought her a plain one instead.

When Chris and I got back to my room she made a really big thing of it.

'Why did she have to send her salad back?' she demanded. 'I'm sure she was just showing off.' I just shrugged it off and reached out for her. Chris, who worked for a telephone company and was as different from an actress as any woman could be, was still a very sexy and desirable woman. We had a really great night together ... but I couldn't help thinking about Kim in her room upstairs.

The next morning, Rick and I went to run at the local track and I really tore into him. I asked him what happened and he admitted that when Chris arrived and was looking for me, he had actually told her I was probably in Kim's room.

'What were you *thinking*?' I demanded. 'You knew Kim and I were back and that Chris doesn't know about us. Why didn't you just take her straight to my room?'

He apologised, admitting that he hadn't been thinking, and we dropped the subject. But I now realised why Chris was so antagonistic towards Kim. Right from the start, she suspected that something was up. Chris went back home that night, and I stayed in Kim's room.

Kim was a lot more than a beautiful woman. She was — and still is — a good actress as well. I could tell that right from the start. The cliché has always been that beautiful women can't act. I'd lived through that when I was a kid, with my father and Marilyn. Well, the thing about Kim was that she was real. She used all her own idiosyncracies to bring her characters to life.

One day, off the set, when Kim and Daryl Hannah, who was playing her younger sister, were talking to a horse and feeding it carrots, Kim started taking a bite from a carrot, offering it to the horse for a bite and then biting more off herself. Someone noticed her doing it and though it was great, and they ended up having her character do the same thing in the movie. Right from the start, I knew she was very good and I knew she was going to be very big. And by the end of filming, I could have picked her out of a crowd anywhere in the world.

I never realised at the beginning what a hot potato *Hard Country* would become for both me personally and the movie producers. For me, it was meeting Kim and the way that would affect my life for ever. For the producers, it was a struggle over getting the movie released.

Hard Country was supposed to be in the cinemas in the United States in October 1980, but just like my personal life, everything got confused. After we'd finished filming, the movie was granted a PG certificate by the authorities, which meant it was available to a wide family audience, but at the last minute the movie had to be pulled because of two little words — 'fuck' and 'fuck'. In those days, such language carried an automatic R rating under the rules of the Motion Picture Association of America's Classification and Ratings Administration, which determined which classification a film would get in the United States. R meant the film was only suitable for adults.

The film, which cost $7.5 million to make, had only been released in the cinemas for a few days when CARA executives discovered they'd been duped and that the copy of the movie they had viewed had apparently been doctored so as not to include any swearing. CARA director Richard Heffner announced that 'a significant difference between release prints and the rated print version of the film was called to the board's attention.' They had no idea that the movie included such swearing and immediately revoked *Hard Country's* classification. The row carried on for months, with the film's producers claiming it was all a 'misunderstanding'. It was almost another year before it was all sorted out and, by then, the film sank without trace.

Most of the critics thought the best thing about *Hard Country* was the music. In fact, the movie was based on a couple of songs that Michael Martin Murphy, a well-known country and western rock star at the time, had written in 1978. Michael swore that he never intended to make a movie out of his songs, it just happened.

He said, 'I was just trying to write one song.' But after he showed his material to his agents at International Creative Management, film agent Jim Wiatt became convinced that he had a movie in the making, and the rest, as they say, is history.

Hollywood was looking for movies about modern-day cowboys. It was at the time John Travolta was making *Urban Cowboy* and the television prime-time soap series Dallas was red hot with audiences. By coincidence, I had worked on *Urban Cowboy*. The guy doing John Travolta's make-up was an old friend — he was one of the people who had taught me the tricks of the trade — and he brought me in. In the movie they were doing a Mae West lookalike contest and he knew I'd worked with Mae on her last movie, *Sextette*, with Ringo Starr, Timothy Dalton, Keith Moon and Tony Curtis. So I spent three weeks doing all these gals up to look like Mae West.

Hard Country was supposed to be set in Midland, West Texas, but because of the budget, Bakersfield, a farming community noted for its cantaloupe melons, about two hours' drive outside Los Angeles and therefore easy and cheap for location shooting, was used, instead of taking the cast and crew more than 1,000 miles away from Hollywood.

The storyline had Jan-Michael's character, Kyle, as a guy who was content with spending his days working in a factory making fences and his nights at a local honky-tonk bar drinking and joking with his buddies. But his girlfriend, Jodie, played by Kim, was getting fed up with the small minds and lack of opportunities in Midland. When an old friend, played by Tanya Tucker, who had made something of her life by becoming a country and western star, came visiting, Jodie decided that moving to Los Angeles would be the answer to her problems.

However, to keep Jodie in Texas, Kyle took a better job as a mobile home salesman for his obnoxious brother Royce, played by Michael Parks. But when the brother tried to rape Jodie, instead of taking her side, Kyle blamed her and they split up. Jodie attempted to leave town to take up a new job with a Californian airline, but Kyle arrived at the airport to stop her. She refused to stay but after she witnessed Kyle being beaten to the ground by airport security guards, she rejoined him and together they drove off towards Los Angeles and a new life together.

One critic wrote, 'Oddly enough, the focus of the picture is on Jodie's blossoming feminism and her growing awareness of the insensitive dolts in the world around her. The men make sophomoric jokes about the women's anatomies and quarrel like boys.' To me, it wasn't odd at all. The focus was on Jodie because Kim had been working on David Greene and managed to persuade him to make her character more central to the film.

Greene was very taken with Kim. He told the British showbusiness writer Roderick Mann, whose articles used to appear in the *Sunday Express* in England and in the *Los Angeles Times*, 'She has beauty, intelligence and talent.'

Another critic, David Ehrenstein of the now-defunct *Los Angeles Herald Examiner* newspaper, also recognised that Kim was the central character in the movie. He wrote, 'Basinger gives it all she's got with a wonderful mixture of sweetness and spunk.' *Daily Variety* wrote, 'The real story here belongs to Basinger, terrific as the fiancée.' And *Cosmopolitan* called her, 'A dazzling, down-home edition of Julie Christie.' That was pretty good for Kim. Even though the plot left a lot to be desired, people recognised that she had given a good performance in her début feature film which would open doors for her in the future.

Even though Bakersfield wasn't exactly London or Paris and there was a lot of tension between Kim and Jan-Michael, making the movie still had its lighter moments.

In one scene, Bakersfield's Kern County Basque Club was converted into a fictional nightspot in Midland called The Stallion. It was supposed to be a bar similar to the famous Texas night club Gilley's, owned by country and western star Mickey Gilley, which was used in *Urban Cowboy* and sparked the whole mechanical bull craze that was all the rage in the United States in the early 1980s.

In this scene in *Hard Country*, Michael Martin Murphy was on stage shouting, 'Doesn't that feel good?' as the 300 or so cowboys crowded around the stage roared their approval, waving their hats, holding aloft long-necked bottles of Texas' famous Lone Star beer and, in a couple of cases, hoisting their girlfriends up on their shoulders.

'Well, I'm going to really make you feel good now,' Michael told the crowd. 'I'm going to bring on stage without doubt the finest country singer of a female nature anywhere in the USA!'

At that point, Michael faded into the wings and the crowd hollered and whooped it up impatiently and suddenly Tanya Tucker, dressed in a red Western shirt and black jeans, a black Western scarf around her neck and a sequined red bow in her hair, cantered on to the stage, where, under a 48-star flag, she launched into a rendition of her popular song *Texas When I Die*.

For that scene, 750 cases of Lone Star beer were imported into California from Texas. I don't like beer and thought it tasted terrible but everyone else was having such a good time that, after the scene was shot, Jan-Michael joined Tanya and Michael on stage and they gave an impromptu concert for at least another hour.

Kim was really into music. Since childhood, she always harboured a desire to be a singer, so this scene was great for her. Her character was supposed to be a member of the audience which suited Kim fine. While they were filming, she was singing along with Tanya to all the songs and really enjoyed herself. It was one wild night.

But any hawk-eyed movie buff watching the movie will have noticed that the cars and pick-up trucks in the parking lot outside mostly showed Californian number plates.

Jan-Michael had such a baby face that I decided he needed to grow a moustache to give his character the right look. One day, he confessed to me that whenever he went out drinking with his friends, barmen would always insist on seeing his identification as they never believed he was old enough to drink. After he grew the moustache, he went to a bar and wasn't asked for any ID. He was shocked and delighted. We had a good laugh about it.

I was already becoming very fond of Kim. When she spoke to you, she made you feel as if you were the only person in the universe. One of my fantasies had always been to do a slow dance with a beautiful woman singing to me. Kim did that spontaneously one night when we were playing music on a cassette recorder and dancing together cheek-to-cheek in her room. As we slowly circled in each other's arms, Kim's sweet voice was softly serenading me and I could feel her warm breath on my neck.

But I was also beginning to realise that she could be very possessive and jealous. I was doing the make-up for Cisse Cameron, a voluptuous little blonde who was playing Jan-Michael's sister-in-law. She gave me a photograph of herself in a bikini that I put in my make-up box. She wasn't trying anything on — actors and actresses often give their make-up artists pictures of themselves as mementoes — and, in any case, she was married to a bodybuilder and actor who was also in Bakersfield.

As soon as Kim saw the picture, she made me get rid of it and put a picture of her in its place. 'Why would you want to look at somebody else when you've got me?' she said. For a bit of fun, I pulled her incredibly long, flowing mane of hair over the top of her head and down across her face. I used her own hair to create the likeness of Leon Russell, the weird-looking musician with long white hair and a beard and thick black glasses. Then I took the picture of her that replaced Cisse's photograph.

In those days, I drove a Porsche 928. In fact, throughout all the time I was with Kim, I had Porsches. I had a border around my number plate that said, 'Make-up Men Do It To Your Face' and she made me give that up. As our relationship progressed, I was branded by many people in Hollywood as Kim's Svengali, but, in reality, it was Kim who was the control freak.

The first time I went to Kim's house was one of the hardest days of my life. We left Bakersfield early in the morning after completing our first location shoot and had the day free. I was going back to join Chris in Redondo Beach but Kim wanted us to spend the day together before we parted. The traffic was on our side and we were back in the San Fernando Valley before lunch so we went to a Mexican restaurant, the Red Onion on Canoga Avenue, near her home in Woodland Hills.

After lunch we went to her place which was just a couple of miles away in the hills south of the Ventura Freeway. Her home, halfway up a cul-de-sac called Don Juan Place, doesn't look much from the outside. It's not at all extravagant but inside it is much bigger than it looks with an enormous back garden and an Olympic-sized swimming pool. She also had an outdoor hot tub and she insisted that we got into it. I was very embarrassed because her maid was there, but Kim didn't care. She demanded that we strip off immediately so we were running around her garden in the nude.

As the day progressed, it got nearer and nearer the time I had to leave. I knew I had to be home by 6.30pm and I'd have to account for my movements all day. Nevertheless, Kim wanted us to stay together until the sun went down so we took a drive to Malibu and sat in the park next to Pepperdine University, watching the sun set over the Pacific. As we parted, I could see that Kim had tears in her eyes.

Shooting then moved close to San Bernardino, which is about 60 miles east of Los Angeles, nearer 90 from my home in Redondo Beach, but which was still regarded as a daily location. It was very frustrating for Kim and me, working all day together and going home separately at night. One night we just couldn't bear it. I called Chris and told her I was going to stay over because we were working late and starting early the next morning. Kim and I booked into adjoining rooms in a little motel, but spent the night in one bed. The next day, because I didn't have any clean clothes to change into, we went to a shopping mall and she bought me a tee-shirt with the word Michigan on it, for some reason. I remember wearing that for a long time. It was the first thing Kim ever bought me.

When it was time to go back to Bakersfield, we agreed that I would leave my car at her place and we'd drive up together in her black Corvette sports car. Kim was always very proud of that car because of the way she got it. Before landing her role in *Hard Country*, Kim had appeared in a number of television shows and television movies. Her last role before landing the female lead in *Hard Country* was playing the part of the hooker Lorene in a made-for-TV version of *From Here to Eternity*, which starred Natalie Wood.

At first, Kim hadn't been that keen on taking the role and had dragged out the negotiations. One day, she was on her way to the studio to have yet another discussion over the part and her money when she stopped to admire this shiny black Corvette which had been the pace car in an Indy race. It was on display in a car showroom just outside the studio. In a bid to get her to agree to play Lorene, the studio bosses told her that in addition to her money, they'd also give her a car. Kim replied, 'Okay, I'll play Lorene but I don't just want any old car. I want that car just outside your offices — the black Corvette in the showroom window.'

They agreed.

Driving up to Bakersfield was a nightmare. Once you leave LA and cross a mountain range, the terrain is a mixture of barren desert and mile upon mile of flat farming fields. Bakersfield is in the middle of that farming country and the weather can be very hostile, sometimes fiercely hot, incredibly windy or even intensely foggy. That morning, it was so foggy that we could only see a few feet ahead and the light from the car's headlamps bounced back off the impenetrable mist, dazzling us. It was like driving through a ball of cotton wool.

I'd arranged to meet Rick Provenzano and Jan Brandow so we could all drive in convoy. That route from LA through Bakersfield is popular with truck drivers heading up to the San Francisco Bay area and the state capital Sacramento. It was so bad that we tucked ourselves in behind one of these big rigs and stuck with him the entire journey. Nevertheless, I thought we were dicing with death. We were lucky we didn't do a James Dean.

When we returned to Bakersfield for the second shoot, we checked into the Holiday Inn because it was in a better part of town. Production executives had become concerned for our safety, because during the last few days of our first visit, someone broke into Director of Photography Dennis Dalzell's room and stole his watch, some money and, most importantly, his gun. I never did figure out why he'd taken a gun with him, but I guess he'd thought the place was more dangerous than we realised.

Kim had insisted we had adjoining rooms, with a connecting door. Soon afterwards, she told me she wanted me to move into her house after we'd finished filming so we could live together.

'Leave that other woman,' she told me. 'You are moving in with me at the end of this film.'

I was quite taken aback and protested, but not very convincingly because I wanted to take our relationship as far as I could.

I told her, 'I've been with Chris for some time now. I can't just walk out on her like that.'

But Kim insisted, and I was becoming very attached to her by this time. 'How long will it take you to sort yourself out?' she demanded. She wasn't taking no for an answer.

'Give me a couple of months,' I told her.

As it happened, I went home to Redondo Beach for a weekend and had the perfect opportunity to raise the issue with Chris. We'd been to the beach and had come home and made love, and she was talking about how happy we were together.

'Actually,' I said quietly, 'I'm not really happy any more.' I didn't want to hurt her. I always try to leave my women on friendly terms. Chris was really upset, though.

'I thought everything was cool,' she said. 'What do you want to do — move out or something?' Then she picked up a potted plant and threw it off the balcony.

She asked me what I was going to do, and I told her Kim had said I could move into the guest house at the back of her house until I got myself sorted out. I don't know if she believed me, but I didn't want to tell her the truth outright.

It wasn't until some time later — probably a few years — that Chris found out the truth, and she was less than impressed by my deception. For a time, I had kept in touch with her and never even told her that Kim and I had finally married. However, I'm pleased to say that, years later, we became friends again and are still in touch. In fact, years after Kim and I split up, she finally told me the truth about that fateful day in Bakersfield. When she arrived at the motel, the front desk had given her the key to my room, as I had told them to. As soon as she went in, she knew something was up. There were candle drippings — we often used candles in our bedroom. And she found a Polaroid snap of Kim, topless, so she knew something was going on. She must have been going through my drawers because I wouldn't have left a picture like that lying around for the maids to see. But Chris didn't have any hard feelings about it; she was able to laugh about it when she told me.

Hard Country finished on a set at Universal Studios and that's where the traditional wrap party was held. Kim had a trailer there as a dressing room, so we followed another Hollywood tradition and had sex in there, on the floor, before the party got going. I don't know if the trailer rocked — but I hope it did.

Chapter 2

Kim was wearing my ex-girlfriend's dressing gown with nothing underneath when she met my best friend, Ron Lang, and his wife, Linda, for the first time. They were stunned, but then, when they turned up on the doorstep, they were expecting to find me alone.

It had been very tempting to move in with Kim the night that Chris and I had the argument that ended our relationship. However, Chris was going out of town the next morning on business so I decided to hang on for an extra couple of days to enjoy life as a bachelor at the beach for the last time. I'd been living with Chris in the three-storey townhouse just a few streets from Redondo's sprawling, sandy beach for about a year, so moving out was a big step — especially as the ocean and sea breezes had always been an important part of my life. I was giving all this up to live with Kim in Woodland Hills, the ultimate in Los Angeles suburbia.

I invited the Langs over to stay the night and have a party, but Kim wouldn't have me being footloose and fancy free. She turned up on the doorstep first, with her overnight suitcase, and announced she was staying with me until I moved in with her. She went into the bathroom and took a shower to freshen up, but she hadn't brought a robe with her, so she helped herself to Chris'. No sooner had she wrapped herself in the pink cotton gown than the front doorbell rang. My friends had arrived.

Ron and Linda's jaws dropped as I introduced them to my stunning new lover, nearly naked with her long blonde hair still wet. They realised at once that my affair with Chris was over, but it wasn't a problem. Kim is an actress, a total pro and, even though she is intensely shy and private, she can put people at ease with her charm straight away. They took to each other immediately and formed a friendship that was to last for years. Linda even ended up working for Kim years later.

I didn't have any furniture, just a few clothes, so it was easy moving in to Kim's place. Even though I had told her I'd need two months to get myself together, in the end it only took me two weeks. I'd been dating Chris for about three years. Before I moved in with her, I had lived in a rented apartment overlooking the beach by Malibu pier. I'd had to go away to do the make-up on *Jaws II* and because the film took a lot longer than expected, almost a year, Chris had got rid of my furniture on my behalf, handed the keys back to the landlord and moved my remaining stuff into her place. We actually bought it together. She had sold another house and used the money she got from that as a down-payment. Then I paid the mortgage, about $1,900 a month. By the time we split, our investment had actually worked out to about 50-50, so I signed my share over to her. I was pretty guilt-ridden about leaving her, so that made me feel a bit better.

It felt strange locking the door at Redondo Beach for the last time, but I was looking forward to my new life with Kim, even though I wasn't exactly sure what it would bring. All I knew was that I would do anything for her. I was determined to take the relationship as far as I could.

My first night living with her was almost my last — I thought I was going to die of a heart attack, or worse. I woke up in the middle of the night and needed to go to the bathroom. Although I'd been to Kim's house before, I wasn't completely familiar with the layout and I was groping my way in the dark, trying to get my night eyes. Suddenly, in the dim, early-morning light, I saw a wizened old man staring at me from a rocking chair. I almost jumped out of my skin with shock. I didn't know what to do about the intruder. He appeared to be armed with an axe, and although I'm a big guy and have always kept myself in shape, I didn't fancy my chances tackling him. He didn't move or say anything and, after a couple of moments with my heart pounding in my chest, I reached out for the light switch.

Immediately I felt stupid. I was looking into the eyes of a life-size, six-foot-plus, carved wooden Indian brandishing a tomahawk, sitting in the corner of Kim's living room. I had never noticed it before, but was only too glad I hadn't made a fool of myself by trying to wrestle him to the ground. Kim had had him for years, and called him Chief How.

No sooner had I moved into Kim's house on Don Juan Place than she started talking about getting married. It wasn't so much that she was hinting that she wanted me to propose to her, but rather while we were talking, she would casually slip in, 'Of course, when we get married ...' or 'After we're married, we'll do this or that.' Her assumption from the very beginning was that in the very near future we would be man and wife, although I did not know if it would ever happen.

I was 41 years old and I was very flattered that she was paying me so much attention. That's what overwhelmed me; that I could score with this girl. I would become anything she needed, I was so amazed at my good fortune. I would have said 'yes' to anything she asked me at that time. I was going to make sure the relationship kept flowing. It all sounded good. At the same time, I didn't altogether trust Kim not to meet someone else a couple of months later. Of course, I was right in the end, but it was years ... not months. To be blunt, I'd dated too many married women to believe in forever.

Right from the start, Kim made it clear that she, who was destined to be a superstar, did not want to be associated with an artisan, a humble make-up man. Even when we were making *Hard Country*, before I'd agreed to move in with her, she was bugging me about quitting the business. Once I was living in Woodland Hills, she asked me again if I would be willing to give up my career and she would take care of both of us. I found it easy to cope with that, even though she was just a 26-year-old up-and-coming actress. In any case, I wasn't that enamoured with the business. I didn't go to work because I loved it. I went to work because I had to work. I never woke up in the morning looking forward to going on to the set, and I was always content to do just two or three films a year, working for about seven months, and then bumming around on the beach playing volleyball with my mates for the rest of the time. If I'd won the lottery, I wouldn't have gone to work the next day. I made good money in those days, well over $100,000 a year, and because I earned my money working in the movie industry, which all my friends thought was very glamourous, everyone thought it was wonderful. I always told people it was the wildest job you could imagine, the most unusual job there is and probably the most exciting — but then people would ask what I actually did and I couldn't explain it. People thought it was for art's sake but, in reality, it was mainly for money.

Kim did not object to me working completely, though. One day she asked, 'Why don't you get another job?'

'What have you in mind?' I asked.

Her astonishing reply was, 'Oh, I don't know. Chairman of Ford or something like that.'

I didn't actually think my professional background — a year in the US Navy Coast Guard service after high school, a degree in maths and business statistics from UCLA and, of course, my film work — actually qualified me for a top executive job in the auto industry, but that was just the way Kim was.

The reality of our life in those early days was that, after we finished work on *Hard Country*, we needed to make some money. We actually went on unemployment pay for a while — about $120 a week each. It's hard to imagine Kim being so broke she had to go on the dole, but we had to make ends meet. She'd bought her house for a good price but she still had the mortgage to pay. Even in those days, however, she was too proud to go and stand in line for a pay out — so I had to do it for her. It's all different these days; you don't have to queue up but can collect the money through the mail. And, of course, there's not much prospect of Kim ever needing to do that.

We were blissfully happy together. Initially, it had been lust that drew me to Kim, but by now I was falling in love. One day, Kim said to me, 'Do you love me? Will you love me forever?'

'Longer than forever,' I replied.

It was just something that came to me at that moment. I was lucky. That was the clincher for us. She liked it very much and it became a big catchphrase for us. It was our phrase. Everything we ever bought after that we had inscribed LTF ... The three dots were very significant to us because they were a sign meaning infinity. The love was going to last longer than forever and then some.

Everything about Kim was flawless to me. First there was the look, a look that I had painted in my mind a thousand times before I ever saw her. On top of that, she had such a good heart and was so sweet. She was a great date; she would concentrate on you, put you at the centre of her universe and really make you feel special. We were drawn together because we felt we were struggling, that it was the two of us against the world.

Our plan was that Kim was going to become a superstar, and the first years were hard. But looking back at the end of our marriage, I realised that those days were actually our happiest.

When I first met Kim, I was wearing a gold chain, a gift from Chris, around my neck. Kim couldn't bear any reminders that I'd ever been involved with anybody else and she made me get rid of it. She bought me a new one, and gave me a lucky charm to go with it — a gold disc inscribed with a heart containing a cross, which was a private symbol she had, and 'LTF ...' engraved on the back.

I also used to wear a gold bracelet that was given to me when I was doing a film called *Little Miss Marker*, which starred Walter Matthau and Tony Curtis. *Little Miss Marker* was played by a five-year-old girl, Sara Stimson, who had been discovered in a talent contest, and I was doing her make-up as well as Walter's. During the filming, she lost her two front teeth, as little girls do, so I had to make her two false ones on a plate which I fitted every morning. We became close friends, and I also became very friendly with her mother, a divorcée who was with her on the set. I was already living with Chris and this was another infidelity to her. At the end of the shoot, Sara's mother gave me the bracelet. So, of course, when Kim found out where it came from, it had to go, but again she bought me a replacement.

Funnily enough, after Kim and I split up, a new girlfriend made me stop wearing the jewellery Kim had given me and bought me still more. I guess I'm just lucky finding girlfriends who like buying me gold jewellery.

It wasn't just jewellery and gifts from girls Kim didn't like. She made me get rid of a lot of personal things that were reminders of the past. She seemed to want the two of us to live in a cocoon of our own and erase what had gone before. I'm sure she did the same with Alec when they got together, and I know she destroyed all the pictures she had of the two of us together. She didn't even have many mementoes of her own, and those she did have were mainly back home with her family in Georgia. She did have a lot of antiques, however, that she bought in little shops on the spur of the moment. When I moved in, I told her I thought the place was cluttered. It took me six or eight months to talk her into it, but eventually she did sell some of the stuff. She let it go for next to nothing, which I guess was my fault, but at least we had room to move.

Being broke was getting us down, so when Blake Edwards offered me a job as make-up man on *S.O.B.*, starring his wife, Julie Andrews, I immediately said 'yes'. I'd worked with Blake before — in fact, the first feature I ever worked on was Blake's *What Did You Do In The War, Daddy?* — and he was a good friend. My father was head make-up man on that picture, and had worked a lot with Blake.

Kim used to visit me on the set and Blake took to her immediately. He even told her that if he'd known her earlier, he would have cast her instead of Bo Derek in *10*, which had been his last film. In retrospect, that was very funny, because John Derek is always regarded as the Svengali who created Bo and, in years to come, I was to be accused of playing the same role in Kim's life. As it happened, Kim would eventually make two movies for Blake — *The Man Who Loved Women* and *Blind Date*.

When I took the job on *S.O.B.*, Kim decided to have a lot of work done on her house. The house had just one master bedroom and a guest room and separate maid's quarters. She wanted the bedroom extended. In addition, the back yard was enormous so we decided to have a second building placed there, in which we put a gym, and a studio where she later recorded music. We moved out while the work was being done and I rented a little beach house at Paradise Cove in Malibu and she moved in with me. It was a little red cottage which had been featured in lots of television shows, including *The Rockford Files*, *Charlie's Angels*, *Harry O*, *The A Team*, *Hart to Hart* and *Dallas*. There was a lot of night shooting and I could just walk down the beach to the set. Kim used to join us sometimes and she became very friendly with Blake's daughter Jenny, an actress who had a part in the movie. We also worked on a set in Culver City and, when we were filming there, Kim drove down every day so we could have lunch together. Kim was very nervous and agoraphobic in those days, and she needed to see me to reassure her that she could cope with the day. Her agoraphobia was a major problem for her, but one which I eventually would help her get over.

S.O.B. was not all work. It had its lighter moments, and its sad ones. Richie, an electrician on the show, had a racehorse which had not been performing well. He had had trouble with his legs, so Richie was giving him DMSO, which was a very popular pain reliever for sore muscles in those days, for people as well as horses. He even brought some on the set and Blake and William Holden, who also starred in *S.O.B.*, which turned out to be his last movie before his tragic death, both tried it and said it made them feel great. It has a garlic residue that leaches through the skin, so it also had the unfortunate side-effect of making them stink.

Anyway, the day came when Richie was going to run his horse in a race at Hollywood Park and he said he had a good chance. I've always been a gambler, with a particular weakness for the horses, so I asked Kim if she'd like to go to the races. There was another make-up man working with me, and he could cover for me while I took a few hours off. I went round all the crew, including Blake, and collected money to put on Richie's horse. Kim drove down from Malibu and picked me up from the set at Culver City and we went to the race course, near Los Angeles International Airport, with Richie and his children. He was in the middle of a divorce and he had custody of his five kids that day. The kids loved Kim, of course. She was always great with children and animals. There was something appealing about her that made them trust her instinctively. I would see this over and over again, when she was forever rescuing animals and chatting to poverty-stricken kids we were to meet on our travels around the world.

At the track, I put all the money I'd collected, several hundred dollars, on this horse and, much to our delight, he won. We were all cheering him on madly from the stand and we were so excited when he flashed past the winning post. It was thrilling enough to be there with a winner, but it was even better when I realised the winning payout was 22–1! That meant a lot of money for everyone who had chipped in on the bet. Before I could even think about collecting the winnings, we all rushed down to the winner's circle — Kim, Richie, the kids and me — to meet the horse when he came in, with steam rising from his sweat-slicked flanks. We all had our picture taken with the horse and Kim was loving every minute of it. And, of course, even though people didn't know who she was, they were looking at her, because Kim was such a beautiful woman and was so happy and excited.

Then the atmosphere changed. One of the children burst into tears, crying uncontrollably. Kim didn't understand what was going on at all.

'What's the matter?' she asked gently, and Richie told her that the horse had been claimed. In the horse-racing world, that's life.

'What do you mean, it's been claimed?' Kim asked.

Richie explained that in a claiming race, people could bid on horses before the race, and then 'claim' their thoroughbred afterwards. Whenever you enter a claiming race, you are effectively putting your horse up for sale at a fixed price. Someone had paid the money for the horse before the race and now it belonged to a new owner.

Kim said, 'Oh no, that can't happen. You can't do that to this little girl.'

But Richie shrugged his shoulders and said, 'It's too late, the horse is gone.'

Kim couldn't believe it. She pleaded with him, 'Is there nothing we can do? Can't I buy the horse for her?'

She would have done it if it had been possible, even though we didn't have any money. It was traumatic for her and for the kids. They cried all the way back home in the car, and she tried to console them through her own tears.

Nobody else was shedding tears over the day's events, however. I was the most popular man in Culver City when I went back to work and handed out the winnings!

Another win on the horses also enabled me to buy the first gift I ever gave Kim, though, to be honest, it was as much for my benefit as hers. We were always pretty adventurous lovers, and I decided to enhance our sex life with a mirror over the bed. So while the builders were working on the house and we were down at the beach, I commissioned this huge $1,000 mirror, as big as our king-sized bed, and had it fitted to the ceiling. It was very heavy, in a big wood frame, so I made sure they fixed it firmly enough to withstand an earthquake, since we lived close to a fault-line. We spent a lot of happy hours under that mirror. I also had mirrors put on the headboard and both sides of the bed. After I moved out, I learned from the housekeeper that Kim had had them taken down and destroyed. That was such a pity. I think her new husband, Alec Baldwin, might have got as much pleasure out of them as Kim and I did.

The ponies also let me buy his and hers, stainless-steel Cartier watches for us in the early days.

Kim wasn't really a great fan of horse racing. But soon after we were married, Hollywood Park decided to have an experiment with Friday night racing, under the lights. Before then, the meetings had always been in daylight, Tuesday to Saturday when I was a kid, then Tuesday to Sunday when I was a little older. Kim was invited to go to the opening night as a publicity stunt. We went along and were put in a special section, and I had to wear a jacket and tie. We left after the fifth or sixth race because Kim really wasn't interested. Walter Matthau was there, along with all the big shots who went racing all the time.

I used to go to the track sometimes without Kim and would bump into Walter. On one of the movies I worked on, he had a fall and his close friend, Dr Robert Kerlan, who was a well-known sports doctor who took care of a number of professional teams in LA, was in charge of him. Dr Kerlan had a box at Hollywood Park, where I used to sit and run into Walter there as well. Dr Kerlan was partially disabled and I used to go and place his bets for him sometimes and bring him back the tickets. Walter knew Kim because she went to Hawaii with me on the final weeks of *Buddy Buddy*, and he always called her Daisy Mae, which is from the cartoon *Li'l Abner*. Kerlan was into pretty girls too, so he and Kim became pretty good friends!

Walter had season tickets for the Lakers, the top LA basketball team, right on the court — and that was a hot ticket in those days. The Lakers then had stars like Kareem Abdul-Jabbar, who appeared in the film *Airplane*, and Magic Johnson, who was to shock the world by announcing he was HIV-positive. Every once in a while, Walter gave his tickets to me and I took Kim to see a game. Dr Kerlan would be there, too, sitting in the middle.

At one game, I remember the first half was over and the players had to walk right past us to get to their changing rooms. One player called Jamaal Wilkes, a black guy from UCLA, saw Kim and just stopped and stood there as if to say, 'Who's that?' Nobody knew who she was but she was so gorgeous. And at that time, a lot of stars used to follow the Lakers. One night, Jack Nicholson was sitting on the court right opposite us, next to Lou Adler; Dyan Cannon, who had been married to Cary Grant, was there as well.

Even though Kim repeatedly said she didn't want me to work, the fact was that I was getting more work lined up than her and it was hard to live on unemployment pay. Those early days, the days of discovery, were probably the happiest we spent together. We were on an even keel and we needed each other. Kim was just sorting her career out and she was at the bottom. We weren't wealthy but we knew she was going to make it, and that then the fact that she would be a movie star and I just a lay person, so to speak, would make it more difficult.

Kim was still talking about getting married. Finally, one day, when she asked me again, 'We are going to get married, aren't we?' we decided to go for it. I had been married briefly in my twenties and it hadn't worked out. But I wasn't going to let this relationship go. We went and had blood tests, which are compulsory in California, and took out a marriage licence. But Kim didn't want to go ahead and arrange anything formal. We kept ourselves very much to ourselves and didn't run around with any friends from the film industry, and she didn't want a big, elaborate affair. Kim also didn't ask me to sign a pre-nuptial agreement, even though her business advisers told her she should and I offered to sign anything they felt would be fitting. We were both convinced she was going to make a fortune in years to come, but she felt a pre-nuptial would be unlucky for the future and that was great for me as things turned out in the end. That decision brought us even closer together at the time, but was to cause her problems when, years later, she demanded a divorce.

The one thing she did want was to get married on the 12th of the month, because 12 is her lucky number. She had even told me, when we first got together, that I was her 12th sexual partner! And we did write out our own vows, to use when the time came. In California you can use any wording you like, and you can get married at home, in a church or just about anywhere else. There are lots of ministers who will perform any sort of service you want.

One day we were walking along Ventura Boulevard, the wide, main street that runs the length of the San Fernando Valley, and we looked in the window of an antique shop. There was a silver ring in the window that Kim admired, and I went back later and bought it. It had a French engraving inside which was almost the equivalent of our 'LTF ...' Next to it was a gold necklace, a chain with two hearts on it, inscribed 'Je t'aime sur tout quand je te l'exprime le moins' (I love you most when I express it least). They weren't expensive, no more than $250 for the two, but we didn't have much money and I wanted to be able to give Kim a present when — if — we ever got married.

The marriage licence, which we got on 14 August , was valid for three months. So we had three 12ths to choose from. The 12th of September 1980 came and went. But the following month we were sitting quietly at home on 12 October, which was a Sunday, and Kim suddenly said, 'Well, we'd better go and do it.' It was already early evening and we had never really discussed the practical side of getting married. So I grabbed the *Yellow Pages* and looked under Wedding Chapels, and found The Chapel in the Canyon just a couple of miles away. I telephoned them and they said they were closing up. I begged the minister, Dr Lawrence White, to stay open for us and told him we'd be there in just a few minutes. 'I'll make it worth your while,' I told him and I did give him a big tip.

When we turned up it was 10.00pm and they were getting ready to lock the doors. They opened up again and then we realised we needed a witness. So the minister called in his son, who was watching television, and he helped us out. For years afterwards, Kim would recall, 'The kid was eating hamburgers and got ketchup all over.' Kim's long hair was still wet because she'd just got out of the bath.

The chapel played a tape of Johnny Mathis singing 'The 12th of Never', instead of 'Here Comes the Bride'. We weren't really dressed for a wedding; Kim was in a red dress and white tennis shoes and socks and I was wearing a cream camel jacket with an open-neck black shirt and matching trousers. I rarely wore a tie. On the way out of the house, we had plucked a single flower from our garden and we each held it when we posed for our wedding pictures. Unfortunately, the minister had locked up as soon as the brief ceremony was over and gone home so there was nobody there to take a picture of the two of us together. As a result, we could only take a Polaroid picture of each other standing under the wedding chapel's sign. Most people have lavish albums full of wedding pictures with family and friends, especially movie stars. We had just two pictures as mementoes, not even a picture of me kissing my lovely bride.

That evening, I gave Kim the ring and the necklace. In fact, she never wore the ring. I understood that. She was an actress, after all, and if she wore it to work she would only have to take it off and give it to someone to look after. I wore a ring. She bought me a cheap gold band inscribed with 'LTF ...' and the date. Later, she bought me a thicker ring, also inscribed, and I wore that instead. I still have them both.

It was the maid's day off and there was no one to celebrate with so we went home to be with our children ... Kim's dogs. The animals were the most important thing in Kim's life. She would say, 'People who don't love animals are deficient in their souls,' adding, 'Dogs have souls, too, you know. All animals do.' We opened a bottle of Kim's favourite Pouilly Fuissé white wine, went to bed and made love under our mirror.

As soon as we started living together, Kim wanted me to change my name. It was all part of her wanting to distance me from my past and from the make-up business. To please her, just before we married I changed my name from my family name of Snyder to Christian. We'd been watching *Mutiny on the Bounty* starring Marlon Brando and Clark Gable. I fancied the name Fletcher Christian — the handsome hero that Gable had played — so I thought Christian would be a fun name. As a result, our marriage certificate showed my name as 'Ronald Snyder (AKA) Christian'. But my life as Ron Christian wasn't to last long — two weeks to be precise.

I awoke on the first morning of married life to be told by Kim that she thought I should change my name again. From her days as a top model in New York, she had acquired an enormous amount of luxury matching luggage which had her initials, K.A.B., Kimila Ann Basinger, engraved on each piece. 'Therefore,' she said, 'I think it would be better if you had a family name which started with a B so that it won't disrupt the luggage when we travel.'

Kim was confident that very soon she was going to be an important movie actress who would be travelling the world, and she was right.

I was speechless, but was happy to go along with whatever she wanted, with whatever would make her happy and keep us together. I guess I've always been someone who could think on my feet and, in a flash, my mind went back to one of my childhood crushes — the actress Barbara Britton. She played Mrs North in a top American television series, *Mr and Mrs North*, a detective show that also starred Richard Denning and was a sort of *Thin Man* for the 1950s. So I asked, 'Okay, how does Ron Britton sound?' She thought that was cool and from that day on I became Ron Britton. I never told her I got the name from a woman I had lusted after when I was about 13.

But as she took over my life and dictated what I would and would not do, in reality, from that moment on I was Ron Basinger, pronounced BAY-SING-ER, as Kim would always insist.

Chapter 3

Kimila Ann Basinger was born in Athens, Georgia, a mid-sized town about 60 miles east of Atlanta, in the heart of Georgia's farmlands, on 8 December, 1953. She was the middle child and the oldest daughter in a family of five children. Her father Don was a frustrated former musician. He had studied at the American Conservatory of Music in Chicago, Illinois, and had tried to make it as a professional musician playing the trumpet with swing bands at the end of the 1930s and early 1940s. But America entered World War II in 1941 and he went off to serve his country. When he returned from the services, musical tastes had changed radically and there was no work for him. He went back to his roots and to studying, eventually taking a business administration degree at the University of Georgia, which was and still is headquartered in Athens.

As things turned out, both of Kim's parents came from Hartwell, Georgia, a tiny community just down the road from Athens.

Cupid's arrow struck when Kim's mother Ann, a one-time model and would-have-been actress, walked into a Hartwell drugstore. Don Basinger, who was home at the time, was taken aback by the beauty he saw on the other side of the store and announced, 'You see that girl over there? That's the girl I'm goin' to marry someday.' Impetuosity obviously ran in the family, for despite being a few years older than Ann, he did just that. Kim said, 'He ended up having five kids instead of the career he wanted.'

In fact, both her parents scrapped their ambitions of having careers in the spotlight for the sake of their marriage and their children. Her mother had been a model for Florida seaside resort holiday postcards, a Breck hair-products model in New York and also a former professional swimmer who had performed with Hollywood Golden Age darling

Esther Williams. But all that ended when Ann, then known as Ann Cordell, met Don.

For his part, to support his family, Don took a job in management at a financial company arranging loans in Athens.

'My mom and dad were not together very much,' Kim told me. 'Living together is one thing. *Being* together is another. They should have divorced years ago. They were never suited for each other. It's amazing to me they even had five kids.'

Eventually, they did split up around the time Kim and I were getting together.

Kim explained, 'My mom had a lot of chances to do a lot of things, but then you get married and you bog yourself down with kids, and if you're a perfectionist, which she is, that doubles the problem. She was very smart, very energetic and could have had a great career. Like a lot of women of her generation, she's a little bitter. I think she looks at me now and says, "I could have done that."

'The neighbours always thought my mom was wild. She wore short shorts and mowed the grass in her bathin' suit top and was always real brown. She could have been my sister. She was the kind of mom who ran with you in the woods and picked pumpkins and loved Christmas. She's like a child in the *Twilight Zone*. But I always just loved her so.'

It was sad because that smothering relationship was just one of Kim's childhood tragedies that came back to haunt her and cause her grief in her adult life. Kim and her mother, the woman she admired so much, were eventually to have a bitter wedge driven between them, one which caused them both irrevocable heartache.

Apart from her mom and dad, most of Kim's family were farmers and, as a result, Kim spent much of her childhood on a 250-year-old working farm, where the relatives grew corn, cotton and butter beans. In addition, Kim said, 'There were dogs, cats, horses, mules, donkeys, pigs, goats ... anything that could breed together did.' I am sure that it was from those early days that Kim developed her deep and true love of all animals.

She said, 'Animals have taught me practically everything, and if I could accomplish one thing in this world, I'd like to change the definition of the word animal. It has a connotation that implies they're beneath us, yet animal intelligence is phenomenal. Animals listen — people in life do nothing but talk. They teach you to listen, which is rare for folks. You can get an education listening without paying a cent. Just keep that mouth shut. Animals remind me of *Candid Camera*; they're so natural and are better than any acting school ... they never fake it. What you get is true grit. I learn from it all. Isn't being "real" the highest compliment for an actor?'

Candid Camera was a long-running television show which used hidden cameras to film ordinary people having practical jokes played on them so viewers could witness their spontaneous reactions. It was very popular in the United States and went on to be franchised around the world.

Kim remembered, 'My family was very liberal at a time when the South was very conservative. We were taught to appreciate every living thing and care about the outdoor animals.'

Despite her links to the farm, Kim actually grew up in suburban Athens in a typical Southern brick-built house surrounded by lawns and palm trees on respectable, middle-class Chestnut Lane, just a few minutes away from the University of Georgia, which dominates life in the town. Everything in Athens revolves around the campus and academic life.

Every Sunday, the Basinger family put on their best clothes and attended church. Kim sang in the rafters with the Methodist church choir and on Saturday nights she attended choir practice. However, after she started high school, her attendance at both trickled off to nothing. After church came Sunday lunch, which is, after the sermon, the most important event of the week for God-fearing Southern folk. The Basingers had no television in the early days, so after the meal the family would improvise by putting on a show. Music was a tremendously important part of life in the Basinger household and it has had a huge impact on Kim's life. Kim said, 'One of my earliest memories of my parents was watching my daddy and mom jitter-bugging in the kitchen.'

At those Sunday early evening *soirées*, each member of the family had a responsibility to entertain the others. There were no exceptions, so Kim used to stand up and do her turn by singing. When she was very young she wasn't the slightest bit dejected when her skits for the family drew sceptical reviews. Neither did she mind the school playground snickering that met her declaration, 'I'm gonna be the biggest movie star and singer in the world.' But as she grew older, her near-crippling shyness developed.

As time went by, the family got a black-and-white television set and the impromptu family concerts subsided into evenings watching the popular shows of the day. Kim was always fantasising. She'd make up imaginary endings for programmes and would escape into her own dream world. She would also spend hours writing songs, poetry and stories.

Kim was a true daddy's girl but that caused her a lot of pain. The highlight of each week for her was time spent with her father.

'I loved to watch my daddy's face,' she said. 'He'd hug up against me on the living room floor, and we'd watch TV together — the *Miss American Pageant*, or a movie. The humour he got out of everything was just so joyous. I thought, "If I could ever make him laugh ..." So we got dramatic together.'

She took to singing to him, especially 'Wouldn't It Be Loverly?' from Lerner and Loewe's musical *My Fair Lady*, which would later help her win the Junior Miss Pageant which launched her career.

Kim recalled, 'I used to walk around pretending to be an actress, acting "emotional". I used to go to my daddy and say, "Kiss me, like they do in the movies," and he would get terribly embarrassed. I must have done it 'til I was 12 or 13. Ever since I was two years old, I knew I wanted to perform. I wanted to sing, dance, act. Everything. From day one I remember saying to my daddy, "I am going to be the greatest actress." I knew the dreams were going to come true. And they did. I also knew it wouldn't be pleasant getting there and it wasn't.'

Although she desperately sought the attention of her father, Kim admitted, 'He was pretty unconnected to us. I don't think my daddy thought any of us could do anything, except my brother. I just kept saying, "I'll get outta here, I'll get outta here, I'll get outta here." I talked myself into my own little cult. I was crazy about my daddy and crazy about music. But he never wanted any of us, especially his daughters, to do anything serious with music. He was intensely creative but frustrated, and I think he just didn't want me to get hurt like he'd been hurt. But inside my heart, I was saying, "I'll show you, I'll show you." '

In the perverse way that the human mind has of dealing with internal conflict, Kim turned in on herself and became increasingly shy. She would while away the hours with one of her few friends, dreaming of becoming an actress and having her girlfriend be her dresser.

As a child, Kim would feel ill if loved ones went away. 'I'd fear for their safety,' she said, 'I was a bundle of nerves.' She even stopped herself from treasuring favourite toys because she was so afraid of losing them. She felt lost in the crowd of her family and became more and more withdrawn. 'It didn't help that my mom and dad fought a lot before separating,' she said.

Her brother Mick recalled, 'Kim had special friends, playmates she would invent in her mind. She wasn't particularly good-looking. She wore braces on her teeth and had puppy fat. But she always knew she wanted to be famous. She'd say, "Mick, I'm gonna be a star and go to Hollywood." There was a town called Bogart a few miles up the road and, like any big brother, I would tease her and say, "No way! The closest you'll ever get to Hollywood is The Bogart Community Theatre, Georgia." She would run off crying, saying, "I *will* be a famous actress, I *will*." '

Kim, who was nicknamed Dodo by her brothers and sisters, was always aloof, a dreamer, a detached observer of life around her. She said, 'I'm a very old soul, a million years old. As a small child, I wanted to know everything and see everything. Early on, I made this deal with God: "Just let me see everything," I told him. I wished I had eyes all around my head, ears open 24 hours a day. I wanted knowledge and wisdom — I didn't care about anything else. I never was interested in all the Barbie dolls that we had at our house. I always thought, "I want to wear the clothes, not have her wearing 'em." I was the one with the doll's head on the end of a pencil.'

Kim excelled in gymnastics and diving, studied ballet for 15 years, played piano and guitar but was never a communicator.

'Physically, I was always so uninhibited,' she said. 'As a gymnast and diver, I was confident about my body. So I didn't want to talk — I could do it with my body. Just let me keep my mouth shut. I had a lot of problems and I never opened my mouth. People thought I was bitchy or stuck-up. But really I was petrified.'

Kim took to crossing off each day on the calendar with an X. 'Are you going to mark your whole life away?' her mother asked her.

To many, her childhood might sound an idyllic way of life, a life full of traditional, wholesome family values, a family that prayed together, ate together, and entertained each other. But Kim was desperately unhappy. It was quite common in the South for extended family members to be taken in by more affluent relatives. In the case of the Basinger family, in addition to Kim's older brothers Mick and Skip and younger sisters Ashley and Barbara, two other children would also often live with the family and Kim felt stifled and lost surrounded by so many people.

Continuing conflicts in her family life developed deep psychological problems within her.

'My parents were very, very young and had their own

problems,' she said. 'They had five kids and we had two that were with us, so we had seven kids. If you put me under the scrutinising eye of a psychologist, he would say, "This child was never allowed to be a child, because she was too involved with her mother's and her father's and everybody's problems in the house." '

A few years into our marriage, Kim told me, 'I've always been a loner and I still am. I've never really had close friends. As I grew up, my sisters became my best friends. When I was a teeny girl, I was really grown-up. I missed out on a lot of childhood things.' Perhaps nobody gave Kim the kind of personal attention she needed as she was growing up. I know during the time we were together, she needed a lot of attention from me.

Kim was particularly close to her sister Ashley. She confided in me that because their mother was so preoccupied with the whole family and her own personal problems, it was Kim, rather than her mother, who was mainly responsible for bringing up the youngest Basinger daughter. Ashley was regularly getting into trouble when she was a small girl. On one occasion she cut off all her hair and Kim had to stick up for her. Just like Kim, she was an outcast at school.

Within her family, Kim was perceived as too responsible and slightly daft. Kim said, 'They thought I was crazy. They thought maybe I should go for tests. They said, "Maybe she's autistic — we don't know what she is. I remember my mother sitting me on the bed and telling me, "Darling, you think so deep, you are not really being a child." My own mother was actually quite frightened of me. This went on for a good three years, then they took me to clinics and did the tests. But it wasn't anything physical.'

To compensate for her problems, Kim immersed herself in her music. She said, 'I loved music. I could imitate anybody as a kid. My biggest love in the world is music.'

There were always contradictions about Kim. She desperately wanted to be a star, yet she was desperately shy and inhibited about drawing attention to herself. Although she sang with the Methodist church choir, the idea of performing on stage before strangers paralysed her with fear. In junior school she was so frightened of speaking in class that once, when she was in the fifth grade, she fainted when her teacher called on her to answer a question.

Kim said, 'Ever since I was a teeny, teeny little girl, I was very intuitive. Almost scary intuitive, almost too much for my own good. It can scare the hell out of you. As a child, it made me much more nervous, to the point where I couldn't breathe. For instance, I hated school, hated goin' in every way, shape and form. School scared me every day. I was the shyest person in the world. They never called on me to read aloud because if they did, I would faint — pass out, I was so afraid. I'd break out in a sweat and turn purple in the face. I would start shaking so much I couldn't read a word. So every summer my mother had to call up my new teacher two weeks before school started and tell her never to call on me.'

For Kim — the dreamer — childhood was not all fantasy. The day her father took her to enrol for her first school, Alps Road Elementary School, she said, 'I remember when my daddy took me to register for school. We stayed about four hours and I remember asking him, "You mean we have to go back there again on Monday?" I thought that was it, this was school, now let's get on with it. My father looked at me and said, "You have to go back there for the whole year." Like every day! I just absolutely, totally hated school. It was like a prison to me. I just could not stand the structured, absolute disciplined way of having to deal with life. I was gone.

'I knew exactly what I wanted to do — I wanted to be in showbusiness; I wanted to sing. I just knew it was all going to happen. I wanted everything yesterday. I wanted to be the greatest there ever was. I had it down to a phrase: "I want to fill Wembley Stadium". Two nights, three nights. That was how big I thought I had to be in order to make myself heard and understood.'

Every time Kim got on the bus to go to school was a trauma for her. Kim suffered from separation anxiety. This became very obvious during the school holidays in the summer of 1962. She became so attached to her mother that returning to class was a tremendous strain for her.

Kim said, 'It was hard to return to school that fall. We were two women all summer long having Cokes at an old-fashioned soda parlour, like in the afternoon. I didn't want those Coke days to be over. I just couldn't understand why I had to go to school and leave her.' That fear continued right through her years at Athens Junior High School.

Kim's anxieties never left her in her youth. She said, 'Fear was a great friend of mine as a kid. I know this sounds strange but I feared getting attached to something because I might lose it. They were childlike fears that grew up with me until I had a fear of fear.'

Throughout her childhood, the fears and paralysing shyness that consumed Kim led people to consider her difficult and withdrawn. She now thanks her father for helping her overcome her anxieties and for helping her launch her acting career, even though she also blames her parents' problems and her strange relationship with her dad when she was a young girl for her psychological terror of appearing in public. She also blamed him for indirectly or directly being responsible for many of her other complex psychological difficulties.

Ironically, although Kim was much closer to her mother in her formative years, as she has grown older, she has developed a close relationship with her father while abandoning Ann. That became blatantly obvious for all the world to see during Kim's acceptance speech years later when she won her Oscar for *L.A. Confidential.* and thanked her father, but not her mother. Don is now one of her most ardent fans. He even went to see *9½ Weeks* — probably her most controversial and outrageous movie — more than a dozen times. 'Daddy helped me make my dreams come true,' she said.

Kim could never understand what her mother wanted out of life. She said, 'I guess she wanted a family because that's what she ended up with. But she must have had dreams at one time.' It was a tragedy, as Kim and her mother had been great friends for many years.

Kim once told me, 'We are each other's best friend.' But it would always end in tears. I don't think they ever really understood each other. Kim would end up crying because she felt that she'd failed to meet her mother's expectations. There would be terrible rows on the telephone. Kim would end up slamming down the telephone and then bursting into tears, complaining to me that her mother didn't understand her.

Kim confided, 'She was a great protector. I was different from her. As a girl, I kept to myself and observed. My painful shyness caused me a lot of trouble in school. When you're debilitatingly shy, even to speak scares you. You listen a lot and, because you don't talk, they think you're a stuck-up pig. I hid a lot. It was fear that made me so shy. But although I hated it, it has helped me to become strong. That fear and shyness was the most real feeling I ever had. It was constant. It made me so much stronger because I had to face it and beat it.'

Then Kim would reveal some of the true hurt that she had experienced from her father while she was growing up, for those family concerts were not always the joyous occasions they were made out to be.

She said, 'On meeting Daddy, you would think that he was somewhat conservative because he holds everything in. But basically he's just wild. However, my father and I weren't close. There were rare times when my father used to get in front of the piano, and I'd sing and play one song and then he'd play another. Then, maybe right in the middle of a song, he'd just get up and leave without a word. He'd get up and take his iced tea and leave and go to the kitchen or wherever. And I knew it would be for ever before we'd ever get to do that again. So I couldn't enjoy those moments for thinking about the way he was going to cut it off.

'My father never once said to me, "I love you". As a child, I just couldn't please him enough. I think my father never thought anybody could do anything. He never complimented me, ever. There was a lot of silence in our house. Children always read something terrible into silence.'

In her more reflective moments, Kim said to me, 'There's nobody to blame, just my perceptions as a little girl that formed me. I liked to collect problems and make them mine. I put too much on myself as a child. And I think Mom and Dad's relationship really hurt me. Their fights with each other were really tough on me.'

To make pocket money, Kim went hunting for old Pepsi bottles to get the refunds on the empties. She said, 'The bottles were crusty with dirt, and you'd find a hornet's nest or that the bottom chipped out when you washed them. That's the way the South is; full of old Pepsi bottles and characters from the country store, lots of odd memories are present always — you pick them up like little dimes.'

Rummaging for rubbish was a habit that stuck with her. She genuinely enjoyed it. After we were married, she loved going home to Georgia to poke around junk yards. Our house in Woodland Hills was full of antiques, most of which I thought were junk. Whenever we'd be away on location, Kim would go looking to buy old things.

In her formative years, Kim didn't show the beauty that would eventually place the world at her feet. As a girl, once she'd shed her puppy fat she was a bit lanky and gangly. She towered over the other girls in her class and felt awkward because of her height. She suffered all the usual teenage problems but did not handle them well. For her, they were more intense.

However, by her final years in school, she had developed into a stunning beauty. Nonetheless she was known as 'Miss Untouchable' and most of the boys avoided her at school. Alex

Allen was her former boyfriend at Clarke Central High School, the boy who lived next door to Kim's family and the lad that her mom wished she'd marry. It's not hard to see why ambitious Kim didn't want any of that. Alex became a car salesman while Kim went on to become one of the best known beauties on the planet.

Alex said, 'I just can't believe her reputation now. She used to be so much of a prude, like she was afraid of sex. Kim was one of the prettiest girls at school but very strait-laced. I'd love to say I was the first guy to make love to Kim. But in those days, she just wasn't that type of girl. She was very shy, very sweet and very naïve. The nearest thing we ever got to sex was petting on the banks of the Oconee River. Even then we ended up in a patch of poison ivy and we were both covered in rashes from head to foot.'

Poor old Alex. After we were married, when Kim and I went back to Athens to visit her folks, we hired a car and went back to all those old haunts so that we could have sex for old times' sake.

Ugly duckling Kim had grown into a beauty by the end of her adolescence. As she grew older, her face became extraordinarily attractive, with large, intelligent-looking, deep-blue eyes. She had high cheekbones, a wide nose and a sensuous mouth that, when relaxed, seemed to be permanently pouting. But it was those luscious lips — the ones that helped establish her as an extremely photogenic model — that caused her so much grief as a girl.

The other children at school did not take to her. They interpreted her shyness for standoffishness and snobbery. As a result, as so many young kids can be cruel, they looked for anything to fault, anything they could find to make fun of, anything they didn't like. In Kim's case it was her lips. Those lips that most men would die to kiss became the focus of ridicule. We are talking about the deep South of the United States, an area where people still belong to the Ku Klux Klan and where segregation was regarded as a God-given right — if you get into the boonies today it still is regarded that way by many!

Kim was growing up when Martin Luther King Jr was still struggling to gain acceptance. So how did those children attack Kim? They called her 'Nigger Lips'. It became a taunt that was to hurt her as deeply as a knife being plunged into her chest … a taunt that would reduce her to tears and cause her grief for years to come.

She said, 'I was called such derogatory names because of my lips, that in school pictures I'd pull my lips in. I really felt I was ugly. Kids used to make fun of my thick lips and I was always so big no one would see the rest of my face. As a kid, I had a terrible name at home. They called me Nigger Lips. I went to school with my hand over my mouth. My lips were a curse. I had a strange prettiness that wasn't accepted. I was too tall and so uncomfortable around the more boisterous and outspoken girls that my palms were sweating whenever I was in their company.'

I don't know if it was because of that hurtful nickname or because of Kim's inbred love of music, but recalling her school days, Kim said, 'One of my greatest school memories was the way the black girls danced in the bathroom and in the halls, so alive and free-spirited. I grew up on soul music. I was a dancing little creep. A lot of people say to me, "Are you country? Do you like country?" I never grew up with country music in my life. I never heard of country music until I moved to New York. I learned about black music.'

As she grew into a beautiful young woman, so boys started noticing her. But when boys called, hoping for a date, Kim would lock herself in her room. Once, though, a boy called Charles Birch had a crush on her and gave her a floppy-eared dog with The Georgia Bulldogs — the name of the football team of the University of Georgia — embroidered on it, and she kept it for years in her room.

When she wasn't dreaming of being a famous star, Kim's other ambition as a child was to become a country doctor, but she was never academic. Her hatred of school ran so deep she said, 'I thought it stunk. I felt like a caged tiger, I couldn't concentrate. I almost didn't pass anything. It's pretty hard to fail study hall, you've just got to show up. I was put in the D class with some of these guys who I ended up loving; they were just hanging on the outskirts of life. There were the hoodlums, there were the absolute extinctions — they made paper airplanes, they played games. And I was a cheerleader.

'My parents thought I was crazy. But I never was a rebel. I just did things my own way. I've just always believed you can get *anything* you want in this life, anything you want. Don't tell me it cannot be done. There's no such word as impossibility. So they thought, on that note, I was a crazy woman, crazy little girl, crazy. Because people are so socially structured to follow a pattern. My pattern was figuring out how I was going to get out of there.'

Kim never saw herself as a rebel; she regarded herself as a non-conformist.

But she could also be inconsistent. Despite her obsession with escaping her roots, she said, 'Anyone who comes from the South kind of understands about the South. I love the South. I really do love it, even the parts I'm not from, like New Orleans or Texas.'

In some ways, Kim was a professional Southerner. She was always a small-town Southern belle who wore her upbringing like a badge. When I first met her, her Georgia accent was very prominent although she tried to suppress it as her career progressed. Nevertheless, the moment she picked up the telephone to talk to one of her sisters or her mother, it would immediately come back to haunt her.

'Southern women are very strong willed and intuitive,' Kim said. 'But sometimes bein' Southern can be incredibly strangling. I was determined to beat that rap. Ever since I was born, I said, "This is bullshit." I didn't want to have anythin' to do with it. I knew I was goin' to California. I didn't know how I'd get out; I just knew I would and as long as you know that, you will.'

It was ironic that, as a youngster, Kim was obsessed with 'goin' to California' because her first feature film role was playing a Texas gal longing to head to the west coast in *Hard Country*, which was where we met.

Everything about Kim was a contradiction. She was always very proud of her family name although she tried to play that down in her early days in Hollywood. Most of the world never used to know, and some still don't, how to pronounce her name. When asked about it, Kim would tell interviewers, 'It's like my uncle told me one time. He's a farmer in Georgia. I love him with my heart. He used to put us in a truck and take us to country stores to pick out 25 cents worth of candy. Well, he had about four names, and we said, "What should we call you? Jack or ..." And he said, "I don't give a shit if you call me Jack, Uncle Jack or Jackass." '

But it wasn't true. Kim cared desperately how people pronounced her name. In private, she took great pains to make sure everyone around her knew they had to pronounce her last name with a long 'a' and a hard 'g'. She'd be as mad as hell if people pronounced it wrongly.

Chapter 4

When Kim was 16, her life was turned around for ever and she first gained the strength to conquer her fears. Oddly, in view of what she has said about her father, it was Don who played a pivotal part in the transformation from pitifully shy wallflower to sexy superstar. In the 1970 Athens Junior Miss Pageant, Don Basinger saw an opportunity for his oldest daughter to display her talents to the world. Kim was shocked. Her father was not a man to push her into anything, yet on this occasion he persisted. He pushed and he pushed. She said, 'My daddy made a bet with me. They had these Junior Miss Pageants and, in addition to being good looking, you had to have a talent and I was a good singer. So Daddy said, "I'll make a bet with you that if we find somethin' for you to sing and you do it, you won't faint, you won't die up there." Now, I had no desire to go through this pageant except for the talent part.'

After Kim had seen the Audrey Hepburn musical *My Fair Lady*, she had learned to sing 'Wouldn't It Be Loverly?' for her father and imitate Eliza Doolittle's cockney accent. She went on, 'So Daddy helped me find a piano player and helped me rehearse it for about three weeks and I entered the pageant.'

After steeling herself for a public performance, when the big night came Kim was convinced she was doomed to failure. She was suffering from bronchitis, but she was determined to soldier on regardless. Ironically, because she had dropped out of the Methodist church choir by this time, most of her high school friends had no idea that she could sing.

'It was just the scariest, the greatest night of my life,' she said when she told me about it years later. 'Even if I think of my accomplishments as an actress, nothing could have been quite like the thrill of having made it through that whole song, that I got through it without dying! Well, everybody was in the audience and nobody had ever known that I could even open my mouth, much less sing. I was a senior in high school and I never talked at all. Before I sang, I prayed, "Please help me, God, just to get through this song. I don't care if I win." After I did it there was no applause, just silence. You could have heard a pin drop. They were all shocked that I could open my mouth. Then they stood up and started clapping. It was magical. And I won. I won the whole pageant. But I didn't care about the applause, I wanted to find the curtain to get off the stage, because I was back into reality.

'I know I'll accomplish everything I want to, but nothing will be as exciting as the night that I finished singing at the Junior Miss contest and did not die.'

Kim progressed to the Georgia state pageant in Atlanta but did not win the Junior Miss title. However, the Breck hair products company was sponsoring the event and Kim snagged the Miss Breck award, in part at least, because of her long, blonde mane of hair.

She said, 'There was a lady from Breck in the audience who asked me if I'd ever modelled. 'Course, I said no, never really having thought much about modellin'.'

Having won the Miss Georgia Breck award, Kim was invited to compete against girls from all the other states in the 1971 national Miss Breck contest in New York, and she won. As part of the contest, the girls were each asked to name the two people they'd most like to meet. Kim said, 'Everyone said Martha Washington or Eleanor Roosevelt ... somebody dead, what good is that gonna do 'em? So I called my daddy and said, "Who should I say?" '

Kim's father told her to 'tickle them'. He advised her to say John Lindsay, who was then Mayor of New York, and Eileen Ford, head of one of the most prestigious modelling agencies in Manhattan and one of the most influential women in the glamour business — who, by good fortune, was in the audience that night. Kim said, 'So I did, and I was invited to a party at Mayor Lindsay's and met Eileen Ford, who asked me to sign with her agency that summer.'

However, although Eileen was destined to become her springboard to fame and fortune, Kim was not sure modelling was for her. She refused to sign a contract on the spot, and even when Eileen wrote to her parents to ask them to encourage her, she said she would have to go home to think about it, whatever her mom and dad said. Eileen, someone who was not easily impressed by young girls, was struck by Kim's beauty and freshness and desperately wanted the Southern belle and former cheerleader to join her stable of angelic-looking beauties, who at that time included Kim Alexis and Patti Hansen, Rolling Stone Keith Richards' wife.

Later on, Kim was to get to know all the other models. She was always amazed at the way they ate. She told me that the models used to purge themselves a lot. They would eat ice cream and all the other treats they wanted and then they'd just get rid of it by vomiting. The practice revolted Kim. She always remembered that one of Patti Hansen's favourite snacks was peanut butter sandwiches made with plain old Wonderbread. 'Patti had to have her peanut butter and Wonder,' Kim used to say.

The trip to New York to accept the Miss Breck title eventually helped her make up her mind. Kim's mother Ann accompanied her daughter to the Big Apple, where they stayed in a hotel overlooking the Ziegfeld Theatre. Kim told her mom that one day her own name would appear on the Ziegfeld marquee. Her mom dismissed this as a girlish fantasy, but years later, when she co-starred with Robert Redford in *The Natural*, it did.

'I didn't know if I was ready for New York,' said Kim, who didn't forget the model boss' offer. 'There was just so much of it. I didn't have enough eyes to take it all in. All the buildings, the limousines on 5th Avenue. All those big yellow taxis! We didn't have anything like that back home. It was the most worrying thing I'd ever seen. I didn't know if I could live there.'

Finally, after a restless summer back home — and a listless few months at the University of Georgia — Kim knew she was prepared for the change.

'I had Daddy call Eileen and tell her I was ready to come live with her,' she said. She was just 17. It had not been easy for Kim to reach her decision. She had gone through a lot of anguish and soul searching. As she did when she entered her first pageant, she struggled with her fear of appearing in public, of strangers, of rejection, before accepting the offer. Her fears of being on show, of meeting new faces and of being put down by thoughtless people who didn't know her haunted her throughout her time in Manhattan, and time and again would cause her grief.

'I was really itchy back home,' Kim told me, recalling how she reacted to returning to Athens after being in New York for the first time. 'I said to myself, "I've got to get out of here or I'll be trapped." '

She asked her father to lend her $500 to help her get started in

Manhattan. He did and he gave her a little locket. Inside was a message in his handwriting, 'Today a star, tomorrow a superstar. Good luck. I love you. Daddy.' The words 'I love you' meant more to Kim than anything money could buy.

Her daddy also gave her a bible and a piece of advice. In the bible he wrote, 'God will always be your co-pilot.' For advice, he told her that whenever she felt nervous or threatened she should sing a little song to help relax herself. It was some tune they both knew from the Broadway musical *Sidewalks* of *New York* which went 'East side, west side, all around the town ...' He told her that at the same time she was singing, she should do a little soft shoe shuffle dance. And she did. It was very sweet. Whenever she felt tense, Kim would revert to being this little girl and go into her routine as her daddy had told her.

Dick Darose, who runs a hardware store in Athens, dated Kim during her last year in Georgia. He drove her to Atlanta's Hartsfield International Airport when she embarked on the journey that was to change her life for ever. Dick recalled, 'She was real nervous. She kept asking me if she was doing the right thing. When I watched her going towards the plane, she turned and smiled and gave a little wave. She looked so much like a little girl.' The good old boy had romanced Kim for several months and knew that she was sexually inexperienced as she boarded that plane. He said, 'She was a virgin before she left Athens. Kim was a very down-home country girl. She wore very plain clothes — skirts and ankle-socks and no make-up. She didn't try to be sexy like many of the girls, showing a lot of leg with mini-skirts and high heels. I remember our first kiss on her back porch. She was very shy, very squirmy. She seemed embarrassed at getting close to a boy. She was always a "Goody Two Shoes". That's why it amazes me when I hear about her today — it's like once she left Athens, she shed her inhibitions and went wild and crazy.'

Dick was astonished to discover that Kim had experimented with drugs with me. He said, 'I have to remind myself that this is the girl who wouldn't even touch a glass of beer when we were dating.'

One of Kim's few school girlfriends also remembered her as a shy wallflower. Rene Padget said, 'When I see Kim on screen, it's like night and day compared to the mousey girl she was.'

Even Kim, who liked to boast to the press that she learned about oral sex in the fields that surrounded Braselton, the Georgia town she 'bought' in 1989, used to say, 'My boyfriend was the idea of getting out. That was his name. Getting Out. Bye Bye was his name.'

Kim was always capable of glossing over her sad childhood. She'd say to me, 'I was 17 when I said to my daddy, "Can you lend me $500?" and I was gone. My family was a very nice bunch of folks, and they'd kept me sheltered. It wasn't until I got on the streets of New York that I started growing up, when I realised what a "hurtable" business modelling is — *hurtable*.' The next moment she'd be telling me how sad her family had made her.

No sooner had Kim touched down at New York's La Guardia Airport to start her new career, than that golden hair of hers, hanging to her waist, was spotted by Bill Mathis, the New York Jets football player. She used to giggle about how he tried to strike up a conversation — edging over, very shyly, quite red-faced and talking so fast that she could barely understand what he was saying to her. Mathis offered her a ride into the city but she told him that the last words her family had said were, 'Don't get into a car with anybody!' Shifting from foot to foot as he stood there in the airport arrivals area, he explained he was from Georgia himself and he actually *knew* Eileen Ford, the head of the modelling agency that was going to represent Kim. 'I am a very respectful man,' he said. 'I swear to God I know everybody in New York. You can trust me.'

She was glad of Mathis' offer of the ride into town but had an unexpected welcome awaiting her at Eileen's home. She remembered, 'When I got there, nobody was home. I beat and beat on the door and, finally, a Finnish gal named Suby came down the stairs. She couldn't speak a word of English and I couldn't speak from fear, so we made perfect room mates. However, reality hit me at about five that afternoon. I just broke into tears ... called Daddy and Mama on the phone and just said, "God, I'm here." '

Meeting Mathis at the airport was a stroke of luck for Kim. He introduced her to other players and they became the centre of her social life in the early years. She used to hang out in sports bars with Mathis, Tucker Frederickson, Frank Gifford and Joe Namath. Kim became particularly close to Namath, who has always been one of America's gridiron greats and a man who prided himself on scoring big both on and off the football field. Before he met Kim, the superstud New York Jets quarterback had had a fling with late rock singer Janis Joplin, who died from a drugs overdose in 1970. Kim, who was obsessed with the idea of getting into the music industry, would have been impressed by that. Namath wasn't a man to be intimidated by anyone on the sportsfield but Kim sure managed to intimidate him in the bedroom one night. He'd been drinking and Kim said he couldn't perform. It wasn't very impressive for a sportsman like Namath not to be able to rise to the occasion. Kim thought it was funny. All the players were very protective of her and would phone her up and say, 'Has anybody attacked you?' I hate to think what would have happened to anyone who had!

Within two weeks of arriving in the Big Apple, Kim was firmly establishing herself as a popular and busy model. She had repaid her father's loan after just three days. It wasn't long before she was one of the world's leading cover-girl models, earning $1,000 a day. Her healthy good looks were perfect for the early '70s. The camera loved her blonde locks and sensuous features, a product of Swedish, German and Cherokee Indian ancestry. As a Breck Girl she met all the *Vogue*, *Mademoiselle*, *Glamour* and *Seventeen* magazine editors and quickly became the darling of the cover-girl world.

Kim said, 'When I walked into *Vogue* — pretty scary, let me tell you — Polly Mellen, one of the magazine's executives, let out this shriek: "Will you look at this girl?" she screamed to anyone who'd listen. And it gave me such confidence to think she thought I was pretty. The legendary photographer Francesco Scavullo met me, and the next day I shot a *Cosmo* cover. I had no idea what *Cosmo* was.'

After staying with Eileen Ford for a while, she moved into the Barbizon Hotel. That was a women-only place where a lot of models started out when they came in from out of state. Kim told me there were always a bunch of Arabs hanging about, wanting to run with the models. But Eileen was like a second mother to her, and protected her from that side of the modelling world. Kim was ambitious but she was still a naïve country girl and she never really got used to New York and was never truly happy there. But she did like the money.

She said, 'I hated New York. It was filthy. I was scared and lonely. I wasn't close to anybody. I didn't run around with the modelling crowd. I soon moved out of Eileen's to the hotel and then I got my own apartment. I lived alone. The only thing I loved was the money. I thought it was crazy what you got paid.'

New York was a considerable culture shock for a kid from the country. She recalled, 'What a change ... riding the subways, and the fumes from the buses, and the night life.' The night life, however, was the one thing she liked about the city, apart from the money. But there was a backlash to that, as far as I was concerned; she had her fill of partying in Manhattan and, as a result, we never went to Hollywood bashes because Kim would say she'd done all that when she lived in New York and was tired of it.

It must have been fate — something she always believed in — that during her first week in New York, Kim was chosen to be in a commercial that was to be filmed in Los Angeles. She said, 'They took me to California — the place I'd always wanted to go. They took me out to Malibu and I couldn't believe it. I said, "This isn't the place. This isn't the place where they have surfboards and girls in bikinis and tons of cars. This isn't where the Beach Boys live." ' Then Kim would laugh. It was a memory that was to keep her going and fire her ambitions throughout her time back East.

That visit to Malibu also gave Kim ammunition for, what I've always felt, was her first lie to me. In my younger days, I was a keen volleyball player who had even tried out for the American team for the 1964 Tokyo Olympics but lost out because of an injury. After Kim and I met filming *Hard Country*, she told me that when she'd been out visiting the West Coast on that first trip, she had been up in Malibu and had seen me playing volleyball on the beach and had never forgotten me. It was flattering, but I'm sure it was pure fantasy from the imagination of my lovely Georgia Peach. It would have been pretty amazing if she'd carried that memory with her for so many years, but Kim was good at having these flights of fancy that she later came to make herself believe.

Throughout her time in New York, Kim was a restless spirit. She took an apartment on East 68th Street but she didn't like it so she moved to 64th and she didn't like that either. She moved again, this time to Greenwich Village. She said, 'I bought a floor of a building and lost a lot of money but it didn't matter because I could make it so easily. I didn't know a damned thing about money. And all the time, I was just running around in circles — taking acting classes, playing guitar in Village cafés and battling with Eileen, who wanted me to go to Europe. I was determined not to be a model.'

Kim had no conception of how much money she was making. She would just put all her cheques in her purse and only use the money when she needed it. She said, 'I didn't even have a bank account. I walked around with $25,000 cheques. I went to buy a TV one day in this hardware store and I gave the guy this $25,000 cheque. He said, "You're walking around with a cheque with your name on the back of it, endorsed?" He led me to the Bank of

America. Thank God for people like that.' After that, Kim said, 'Models get paid through the mail and the agency will send you a cheque, so I just carried tons of those envelopes around in my handbag all the time. Once, I carried a $25,000 cheque around for a week. Finally, I'd get to the bank and hand 'em over and say, "Put 'em in my account". I never had money and money had no importance to me.'

Even when we met, she still had the habit of carrying uncashed cheques all over the place with her. I used to find them in her handbag and rush to the bank. She spent her money on make-up and junk and presents for her family and more junk.

Kim was desperately lonely when she was first in New York, and even though she had longed for years to escape from small-town living, she still yearned for the familiar family routine.

'The Southern part of me desperately wanted to be back home where life was nice and cosy-comfortable,' she said. 'I would fly home three times a week to eat lunch with Mama and Daddy.'

Her mother flew to New York regularly to console Kim and keep her company. And Kim would phone home in tears when she was rejected for a job — something that Eileen Ford insists rarely happened.

Her mother Ann, a former Breck Girl herself, actually went back to work, thanks to Kim, during those early years in New York. The company thought it would be a good gimmick to launch an advertising campaign using a former Breck girl with a current one, so two generations of Basinger women appeared in commercials to promote the shampoo. Later, Kim graduated from being a Breck daughter to a Breck bride, appearing in adverts as a gorgeous blonde in a wedding dress. This was a very prestigious modelling assigment. Many former Breck girls are famous today, including Cybill Shepherd, Christie Brinkley, Erin Gray, Jaclyn Smith and Brooke Shields.

Ann wasn't the only family visitor who Kim had in New York. Her sister Ashley, who was always very close to Kim, suddenly turned up unexpectedly at her apartment. Ashley was having boyfriend trouble and had run away from home and hitch-hiked all the way from Georgia to Manhattan to see Kim and ask her advice. Kim took her in, let the family know she was OK and then set about showing her youngest sister the sights of the big city before sending her home. They spent a girlie week together, giggling and having a good time.

Kim always enjoyed being with Ashley so she once invited her to go on an exotic holiday down to Zihuatanejo on Mexico's Pacific coast. Unfortunately, after a few days in the sun, eating spicy foods and drinking fruity cocktails, country girl Ashley got an awful stomach bug and became terribly sick. She had a severe bout of food poisoning and Kim thought she was going to die. So Kim, who could always manipulate men, found some rich guy staying at the hotel and luckily — or more likely, calculatingly — latched on to him. She fiddled with her hair and licked her luscious lips poutingly and, before too long, she had him wrapped around her little finger. She managed to persuade him to get them flown home so that Ashley could get medical attention back in the United States. The guy was only too pleased to oblige to get himself into Kim's good books.

Despite making a fortune by normal standards, enough to let her live a life of pampered luxury, Kim hated the feeling that her livelihood required her to be inspected like a piece of meat 24 hours a day. It was a very unsatisfactory life for her. She told me, 'I felt the highest level of frustration I've ever felt in my entire life. I couldn't live as a basket case all the time, feeling whether people loved me or hated me depended on the way I'd look tomorrow morning. I just couldn't breathe very well.'

Although she was adept at showing off her face and figure for the camera, the old insecurities were never far from the surface. She never understood why she was such a popular model. 'I just copied the other girls, went to Bloomingdale's and bought the same make-up and clothes they did,' Kim said. 'I was probably the worst model that ever lived.' She did, however, have her reasons for putting herself through such purgatory. Modelling was a road to another place. It was a lot better than waiting for a train full of talent scouts to come through Georgia looking for someone like her, the way casting people had hunted down newcomers as a publicity stunt for *Gone With the Wind* nearly 50 years earlier.

She used her spare time to take acting classes and, despite her shyness, to perfect her singing by performing in seedy Greenwich Village clubs. She said, 'I wanted to follow in the footsteps of Bob Dylan and Joni Mitchell in Greenwich Village but those days were over. I sang in little dives and played small parts in rep holes, off-off Broadway, where there were rats running across the stage in the middle of the performance.' In a desperate attempt to put herself at ease, Kim would ask her audiences, 'Do you know what it's like to be scared shitless? Well, I am right now.' She added, 'Then they would laugh and I felt like, "Now I can do this." I was always proud of myself that I did that.'

One of her proudest possessions was a guitar she told me she had bought from Bob Dylan. I don't know how they got together, but she met him one night backstage and ended up taking home his musical instrument to play with. She bought the guitar for $5,000 and it was one of the things which took pride of place in our home. Kim was a very good guitar player. She bought me a guitar to match hers although she didn't pay as much for mine. But I didn't mind, I don't even play the guitar.

She also enrolled as an apprentice at New York's Neighbourhood Playhouse, determined that her destiny lay in singing and acting. She didn't particularly enjoy the lessons, saying you've either got the talent to act or you haven't. But the lessons did give her more self-confidence and taught her to get outside herself and into another character. 'I was so shy and out of my mind that acting classes were just something that made me get up on Wednesday night,' she said. 'It was basically a bore. It was totally to get confidence, that's all it was. Basically, you have it or you don't. I don't think you learn that. You have to love looking at yourself. And me, I enjoyed not being myself. I loved being funny and a clown and jumping up and down acting the fool.'

To gain more experience and confidence appearing in public, she appeared in a small revue put on in a church on the West Side and also took additional acting classes from world-famous coach Sandy Meisner.

Kim's singing was improving to the extent that John Mace, her teacher at the Vocals Arts Foundation on 125th Street, wanted her to be an opera singer, or at least to think about Broadway, but the only music she really cared about was black music, soul music. She said, 'I was totally into it.'

Despite herself, Kim had quickly become a top model appearing in Revlon, Maybelline, Cover Girl, Yamaha and Clairol advertisement campaigns and posing for most of the world's top magazines. Her face promoted a whole range of products.

'Kim was one of the nicest girls we ever had,' Eileen Ford recalled. 'She was one of the most sought-after models in the world and she worked hard for whatever she got. She certainly got any job she ever went out for. She was very, very big. She was the all-American girl. She always had a certain voluptuousness that translates to film. She was the most angelic girl who ever stayed with me — totally innocent about the ways of the world. She could have been nominated for sainthood.'

According to Eileen, Kim would often read from the Bible, but

Kim always laughed and denied it. Kim said, 'Eileen saw hundreds of models, some of the wildest ones ever, and I can understand where she's coming from. She remembers me as a little girl who got off a plane from Athens. A lot of people think of Southerners as people who go to church every Sunday and eat fried chicken and go around with greasy fingers. But there are a lot of crazy, talented people in the South, hungry people who want to get out and go to places like New York to make their dreams come true.'

As things panned out, with Kim becoming one of the sexiest and most outrageous women in the movie business, it is also ironic that Eileen remembered that when Kim was young in New York 'she was against anything that was suggestive'.

It was during her early days in New York that Kim developed one of her many concerns for the welfare of animals that would eventually turn her into an activist campaigning for their rights and well-being. She was walking across Central Park one summer's day and she saw some horses pulling carriages. It is quite a familiar sight. They are a world-famous tourist attraction. Kim said, 'One of them fell. He was dying of the heat on the streets of New York. And I went, "What is this?"' From that moment on, Kim was totally opposed to using horses to pull carriages. Years later, she and her second husband, Alec Baldwin, held a protest against the treatment of the Central Park carriage horses in Manhattan. She is ardently against those horses being used to give tourists rides.

Unfortunately for photographers and the advertising executives, modelling was never going to be part of Kim's long-term future. It just wasn't her style. Besides, she said, 'I hated it. I never felt comfortable with it. I just never understood it, I guess. I was just biding my time. I worked way uptown and lived way downtown. I kept to myself. I didn't fit in with the crowd. I just went to work, went straight back home. If you didn't know me, you never would have thought I was a model. I wasn't happy. I was frustrated. I still wanted to be a singer. I used to take my guitar down to the Village and sing at open mike nights. It was scary but it was exciting. But I had to do them. I had to do something. I still had all my dreams. I just didn't know how to make them come true.'

Gradually, she gravitated to people who could help her get involved in showcasing her musical talents in her spare time. Meanwhile she kept modelling, making a lot of money, and hating it. She told me, 'To make a long, long story short, I just quit. One day, I just woke up and said to myself, "I'm leaving." '

Even as the hottest face at the hottest agency, she said, 'I learned what it means to be rejected over and over again for no good reason that I could see. The only thing that kept me going were the goals I had in my head from my childhood. You get tired of seeing yourself on the covers, you sure do, and just when you think that at least your parents are thrilled, they tell you, "Oh, I didn't notice, hon."'

Kim yearned to throw in the towel as a model. She said, 'I wanted to be an actress — I didn't want to be a model. I felt suffocated as a model. I hated it with a passion. I got hurt very easily. I mean, I'd come in weighing 8st 3lb (115lb) and 5ft 7½in tall and I'd be told I was 10lb too heavy. And at that time I wasn't eating a damn thing.' She hated being pinned and tucked. She never felt like a pro. She said, 'My hands just wouldn't stay down. I couldn't just look into a camera; I found no peace in a still camera. I needed to really express myself.'

Sue Charmey, then her booker at the Ford agency, who later went on to be president and co-owner of Faces Model Management, became one of her closest confidantes during those unhappy but useful years. One night, Kim went to Sue's East Side apartment to meet someone from the music industry who might help her. Sue recalled, 'She sat there and peeled the polish off her nails in nervousness. He was not overly impressed with her because she just wasn't selling herself. She just wasn't ready for it.'

Although Kim didn't mingle much with other models, she found a soulmate in Sue. The two used to spend evenings gossiping about men and work. 'I had a wild boy in the Village,' Kim said. 'He was sort of Mr Greenwich Village. He'd walk around there and he knew all the poor people — I was amazed. He taught me a lot. I wrote so much stuff in the Village, just walking down there and just living around at night. But it was lonely. Real lonely.'

Finally, that old devil shyness bared its awful horns again, and she found herself standing at street corners while the traffic lights changed three or four times before she could muster the courage to cross. 'I used to imagine the newspaper headline,' she said, shuddering and laughing, at the same time — 'MODEL GOES SPLAT ON 6TH AVENUE. Some girls liked to be looked at, but I just couldn't stay perfect all the time.' Unbeknown to her, Kim was beginning to develop agoraphobia, a terrible illness that manifests itself into a fear of being outside which was to haunt her for years to come.

After five years, she had gained a considerable degree of financial and personal independence. One morning, Kim woke up, telephoned Sue and quit. 'Eventually, I rebelled against modelling,' she said. 'I never could find a reason to like it. I was terrible at it, too, that's the funny thing. All the time I was doing it, and being successful, I knew I'd wake up one morning and never model again. And that's what I did. I woke up and I went and bought a Jeep and I drove it to California with my boyfriend.'

By the time Kim left Manhattan, the prim and proper Southern belle cheerleader had become both sexually active and experienced. She had an English boyfriend who had become a top male model in New York. His name was Tim Saunders and she'd say, 'He came from some place in England called Goring-on-Sea.' She told me she was crazy about him, but his mother hated her when they met. Just as she had won her first beauty pageant thanks to her impersonation of Eliza Doolittle, Kim enjoyed any excuse to mimic people, and Tim's mother became one of her victims.

'In those days, I used to chew gum,' she said. 'You know, it was really gross. His mother, who hated me, used to say ...' and then Kim broke into a perfect English accent ' "... This *gel* does nothing but blow bubble gum balloons. Quite, quite *ghaastly*." '

Years later, when she had established herself in Hollywood, Kim lured Tim's maid, a black woman from Harlem called Doris Gilmore, away from him to work as our housekeeper in California.

Tim was history, and Kim was living with soap opera TV series actor Dale Robinette, who had been offered some work in California, when she finally decided to quit. She bundled her two dogs and a cat into the Jeep and she and Dale sped off, heading west across country to California. Kim would say she went off with 'no prospects, no nothin' '. She made Dale stop the car as they crossed the Brooklyn Bridge so she could pitch her modelling portfolio — which had been her life and her source of income — into the East River. It wasn't the first time and it wouldn't be the last that Kim just turned her back on part of her life as if it had never happened.

To help ease her pain and self-doubt in New York, Kim had written pages and pages of songs, poems, childhood memoirs, scripts and treatments. One unproduced screenplay was called *Eggs in New York*. It was about a wealthy and glamorous New York couple who were trapped in their chic routines. So they ran away, just like Kim and Dale.

When she arrived in California, she moved into a hotel. She said, 'I wasn't Rockefeller's daughter but I had enough money to last a year-and-a-half. I lived in a Howard Johnson's. I used to help the woman who ran the place feed the chickens.' Later, she lived in a Holiday Inn.

For a while, after Kim and Dale split up, he got his friend Joanne Carson, the ex-wife of talk show giant Johnny Carson, to put her up. She stayed in the house where, years later, outrageously gay author Truman Capote, who wrote *Breakfast at Tiffany's* and *In Cold Blood*, died. But Kim moved out rather quickly after she and Joanne — whom Kim said was sad, doped and drunk at the time — were swimming naked in the pool one day and Kim interpreted Joanne's actions and conversations as coming on to her. She told me, 'I thought maybe Joanne wanted a lesbian relationship and I wasn't interested.'

Agent Martin Gage vividly remembered the day in 1976 when Kim strode into his LA office and announced that she wanted to be an actress. He said, 'Dale Robinette was a client of mine and he brought her in. She was wearing a loose rag dress and rubber thong sandals. Her hair was pulled in a rubber band and she had no make-up on. I thought, "Oh, my God, she's gorgeous!" And that was it. Within two weeks, I'd booked her on *Starsky and Hutch*.'

Kim would insist that she just tagged along to auditions before eventually trying out herself. She said, 'I had to be pushed into them. My boyfriend kept urging me on. He said, "Just do it. Don't worry." He helped me out of myself. I needed it. Everybody does, I think.'

On one occasion, Dale took Kim along when he went for an audition. He didn't get the role but she got a part in the production! However, during her early years in Tinseltown, Kim felt the stigma of having been a model stuck hard to her. She said, 'I'd hear, "Oh, models can't even walk, and if you think you're gonna act, forget it." All they saw was this pretty, blue-eyed blonde, and I resented it. I knew inside that this silent girl had so much more than what she looked like.'

Throughout 1977 and 1978, Kim paid her dues in television commercials, TV guest shots — *Charlie's Angels*, *Vega$* — and playing one of the title roles in the short-lived and forgettable cops and robbers series *Dog and Cat*. It was a light police drama that was only on the air for a few months. She played rookie officer JZ Kane who had been paired with a veteran cop. Lou Antonio played her partner and became one of the few Hollywood people she socialised with after work. Her first real break came in 1978 with *Katie: Portrait of a Centerfold*. The television movie's subject was just spicy enough to generate a lot of publicity ink in the American press and Kim bathed in it.

In the movie, she played a girlie magazine model from a small town, which wasn't stretching for her. Meanwhile, she was giving herself a crash course in the movie business. 'She'd run behind the camera and say, "Oh, can I look in?" ' said the show's executive producer Frank Von Zerneck.

Kim turned down a starring part in the hit series *Charlie's Angels*, although she did make a guest appearance in one episode. Kim was offered the part that eventually went to Cheryl Ladd when she replaced Farrah Fawcett after the first season. Kim turned the role down even though she knew the series was a massive hit because she simply did not want to be committed to a long-running series. She said, 'I could have been the Angels' little sister. But it was a mess. I did one segment, "Angels in Chains", and it became a classic *Charlie's Angels*. But I knew I wanted to do film and I wanted to sing. Real simple.'

In 1979 she played the part that Donna Reed had in the classic movie *From Here to Eternity* in a mini-series remake by the giant American television network NBC which starred Natalie Wood and William Devane. But when it turned into a weekly series, Kim refused to sign a long-term deal again and rejected the role. She was beginning to realise she had to start playing hard to get. 'Kim instinctively knows whom to meet and when,' Gage remembered.

Television simply wasn't the movies as far as Kim was concerned. She said, 'That's what I'd made up in my mind to do, so I took the view to stop doing TV. I sat by my phone. I had some high and dry times. I'll tell you, sitting at home in this town with nothing to do can make you suicidal. You need to call on all your stick-to-it-ive-ness, your spirits and tenacity.' As Kim was to prove to herself, and to the world, she had more than enough tenacity to get her through those lean times and make her dream of becoming a movie star come true.

Chapter 5

It was early winter in California as I drove my Porsche north, towards the ski resort of Mammoth, with Kim sitting in the passenger seat. Once again I had been offered a job — another Walter Matthau film called *First Monday in October*, and since she wasn't working, Kim came along with me to stay in a ski lodge and keep me company during the long, five-hour-plus drive. We almost didn't make it. While we were speeding along the virtually deserted highway, I felt Kim's hand wander on to my lap. I wasn't complaining. I also didn't realise how far she intended to go. She unzipped my fly and then, to my surprise, I felt her breath as she started to perform oral sex on me as I drove. It was pretty difficult to concentrate on driving straight, I can tell you, especially as her head kept knocking the steering wheel. I'd always known Kim was an adventurous lover with a wild fantasy life, but that was something completely unexpected. You could say it really blew my mind. We'd only been married a few weeks and I was loving every minute of it. We kept the sizzle going after we arrived in Mammoth, even though it was freezing cold. We enjoyed fooling around and, one evening, Kim ran outside in her bra and pants, and I snapped a picture of her standing in the snow. Later in our relationship, when I had stopped working, she made up photo albums of pictures I had taken of her during our adventurous love life — mainly nude or topless shots — for me to look at while I was waiting at home or in her trailer. She called the albums 'goodies' and that picture from Mammoth was in one of them.

After shooting in Mammoth we moved on to Washington DC, shooting near the Watergate Hotel and the US Justice Department, and again Kim came with me. She was afraid of the dark and hated being alone at night, so we had a deal that we would stay together all the time. *First Monday In October*, a comedy about the first woman appointed to the US Supreme Court, wrapped on 9 January, 1981. We left the bitter cold of the capital behind us to return home to Los Angeles briefly, and four days later we were on our way to the tropical paradise of Hawaii for the event which would put Kim firmly on the map — her spread in *Playboy* magazine.

Until this time, Kim was best known as a model for beauty products with her face appearing in all the glossy women's magazines. That helped pay the bills, of course, but it was very frustrating for Kim. She'd taken a huge gamble on leaving her successful modelling career with the hope of making it big in Hollywood, and after a promising start her acting work seemed to have fizzled out. So when *Playboy* came calling, we discussed it at great length and decided it could only work to Kim's advantage, even though her agent and publicist were advising her against doing it. We flew to New York to discuss it with the writer, Bruce Williamson, who had known of Kim from her modelling days.

Eventually, Kim said, 'To hell with the consequences. If we're wrong we'll just sell the house, pack up the dogs and haul ass.'

In addition to her career being at a standstill, there were rumours of an upcoming actors' strike, which would have meant less work for everyone for as long as it lasted. And, of course, we needed the money.

Although *Playboy* proved to be such a turning point for Kim, she almost backed out of it on several occasions. When we got to Los Angeles International Airport to check in, I learned we were only flying business class. I'd always insisted on flying first class when I was working, and even went first when I was paying for it myself. There was no way I was going to let Kim do anything less. She may have been an unknown — *Hard Country* still had not been released because of the row over its rating — but I knew she was going to be a big star and expected her to have star treatment all the way. I rushed to a public telephone and called *Playboy*. I told them we were not getting on the plane unless they arranged for us to be upgraded. It was a gamble on my part because they could have called the whole thing off — but then I've always been a gambler. They were surprised, but I insisted, and we ended up at the front of the plane. This was a role I was to get used to playing — Kim's hard man — as she became a bigger star. We would very often arrive at a hotel somewhere and I would insist on a better room, or even check out altogether if the place was simply not up to our standards. On this occasion, when we boarded the plane we found we were the only people in first class. The flight attendants spent most of their time working business and economy class because they didn't have much to do for us, so we took advantage of their absence to join the Mile High Club.

As our relationship developed, I would discover time and again that Kim got a thrill out of having sex in public places where we could be at risk of being caught out, or at least watched from a distance.

Our first destination was the Big Island, Hawaii itself, to shoot on the famous black beaches at Hilo. *Playboy* flew in a load of clothes for her to choose from, which seems bizarre considering the whole point of *Playboy* is the nudity. However, Kim ended up choosing one of her own dresses that she had brought with her, a flowing, romantic, gauzy thing. It was completely destroyed by the end of the photo shoot. The black beaches aren't really covered with sand; they are covered in volcanic deposits which are as sharp as glass. Hawaii Big Island is one huge volcano. It is not at all made up of dense jungle as many people imagine. Some of the other Hawaiian islands are much more like that. But the Big Island isn't. It's rocky and surrounded by a really rough ocean with huge waves lashing the coastline. I remember there was a sign on one of the beaches saying 'No Swimming. Sharks', but it wasn't a place where you'd want to go in the water anyway. Sitting and lying on the beach and rolling in the edge of the surf cut the dress to ribbons. Kim was very upset about that but *Playboy* never replaced it.

At first, the shoot went smoothly and Kim was comfortable baring her breasts, which is something she had never done during her modelling days in Manhattan. But when we moved on to Kauai, the lush green island where *Jurassic Park* was filmed, there was a problem. The art director in charge wanted total nudity, and for some reason Kim was reluctant. It had been discussed right from the start that she would do full-frontal nudity, but I think in the beginning, in her own mind, she hadn't actually admitted this to herself. Although she was an actress and model and used to performing for the camera, there was always the shyness in her and this was a big leap for her. She also thought she could get away with semi-nudity, scantily clad in lingerie and so on, because she wasn't your normal *Playboy* picture girl who was a complete unknown. She was already an actress. So when it came to the moment when she was supposed to take everything off, she froze.

She had a big blow-up with the photographer, Richard Fegley. She came and sat in the car with me to talk it over.

'I think I'll just go home,' she said, close to tears. 'It's not going to work, it's just not going to work. I can't do it, I don't want to do it.' But we couldn't afford to throw away $40,000 for a few days' work. I talked to her for a long, long time.

Eventually, Richard came and joined us and we talked the thing around and around as we sat in the car overlooking this most idyllic ocean scene. I don't know whether it was the sound of the Pacific Ocean hitting the sandy beach, the tranquil look of the deep blue sea stretching into the horizon as far as the eye could see or Richard and me persuading her. Richard assured her they would be the best pictures ever taken of her; they would be really special. And she would also get to approve every single picture the magazine eventually used. Finally, Kim said, 'OK, I'll do it.'

Girlie magazines in those days weren't as brash and revealing as they are now, of course. And *Playboy* in particular has always been very tastefully done. There was certainly nothing gynaecological about it. But Kim was worried about how she would look.

Obviously, she had done plenty of modelling before she became an actress. But she was a clothes and hair and beauty model and topless wasn't her thing. As far as I know, she had never done any nude scenes in her acting work; she certainly didn't in *Hard Country* and I can't imagine anything very revealing in the American television work she had done in the 1970s. Ironically, in her television film *Katie: Portrait of a Centerfold*, which co-starred Don Johnson, Tab Hunter and Fabian, she had played a girl from a small town who posed nude for a magazine — just like she was now doing in real life. Her character was supposed to be naked, but that was in the days when they didn't actually show nudity on screen on television. It was so tame that even the video guides you can now buy that list every glimpse of suggestive flesh could not find a single frame to highlight.

Despite Kim agreeing to pose totally nude in front of Richard, he was concerned that I'd talked her into it against her wishes. Even then for some reason people thought I controlled her, though actually it was much more the other way round. She talked to him for about an hour, with Richard reassuring her it was all going to be tastefully done. After that there were no difficulties at all. In fact, she was really into nudity by the end of the shoot.

There's one stretch of coastline on Kauai, the Na Pali Coast, which is very beautiful and really private. They shot parts of the classic Rodgers and Hammerstein musical movie *South Pacific* there. The only access was by helicopter, which flew us in and dropped us off, then returned to pick us up. We did a lot of shots on the beach and in the water, with Kim running naked along the beach and the cameraman and his assistant up in the helicopter. It really was like a little piece of heaven, just the four of us and the pilot there surrounded by that beautiful scenery, with the plaintive cries of the seagulls and the sound of the heavy surf hitting the rocks filling the air.

On another day, we went to the top of the volcano on Hawaii Big Island to shoot. It reminded me of something out of the Raquel Welch movie *One Million Years BC*. It was a live volcano so there was smoke and steam in the air, and it was a tricky and potentially dangerous place to fly. The pilot warned us as we landed, 'You know, when I say we have to go, we have to go ... instantly.'

They took some pictures and then it was time to go. Kim remembered what the pilot had said and jumped into the chopper stark naked, because there was no time for her even to grab a wrap. It was very funny, really — Kim in the front seat next to the pilot, totally nude, with the rest of us all fully clothed in the back. After that, when we were flying to all these private beaches, Kim never bothered to get dressed between takes. It was too much trouble to pull clothes on for a flight of a few minutes when she'd only have to take them off again. I think the pilot had worked for *Playboy* before, fortunately, so he didn't have too much trouble concentrating on his job.

In the end, it all worked out very well and the pictures were great. The spread didn't appear for a long time — two years — but when it did, it was sensational. Kim has always called it her 'silent movie' because all sorts of people would meet her after it appeared and say, 'I've seen you in something, I know I have. Your face and name are so familiar.' And Kim would know they meant *Playboy*. Maybe some people were embarrassed to admit that's where they'd seen her, or thought it might be embarrassing for her to be reminded of it, but I'm sure others simply didn't realise that's where they had seen her. But it was such a wonderful layout that it certainly registered with a lot of people.

One other big advantage for Kim was that, before it was published, the *Playboy* people introduced her or showed her pictures to a lot of men they considered true connoisseurs of beauty, and they were all overwhelmed by her. Legendary French film director Roger Vadim — who, of course, was once married to the goddess of my younger days, Brigitte Bardot — said, 'She has this quality — absolutely indispensable for a *beautiful* actress, which is not to *know* that she's beautiful.' Top British-born hairdresser Vidal Sassoon said she had the most sensual lips in the business, while Italian movie icon Federico Fellini called her a 'galactic New Woman' — whatever that means. *Playboy* also showed the layout to my dad, Allan 'Whitey' Snyder, but, of course, I've got to admit he was probably biased!

The spread didn't appear for two years, because nobody could agree on the cover. We looked at so many pictures. I wasn't there when they eventually chose the right one. And as things turned out, by that time Kim had been cast as Domino in *Never Say Never Again*. *Playboy* also got Sean to say nice things about her in the film, which was her first big break.

'Having rehearsed with Kim, filmed with her and seen the early results, I can say she's terrific, the kind of totally professional actress I enjoy working with,' he said. Kim was delighted that he took her seriously rather than regarding her as decoration. As a kind of postscript to *Playboy*, Kim wore a one-piece bathing costume with a lion's face on the front which she had been given by the magazine in the final scenes of *Never Say Never Again*.

Thanks to this double exposure, in print and on film, 1983 was the year she finally became an international star.

Later, Kim said, 'I needed a film and it did exactly what I thought it would do — it made a lot of noise and I got calls off the wall to do films. I don't have any regrets. There are several things I'd do differently but at that time in my life I made the best choice I could. I remember struggling with the choice because I am in no way an exhibitionist. I am basically a shy girl. I like to underplay things. I am not comfortable running around in the nude. At the time, I had to reckon with the fact that it was just nudity. Now what is nudity? We're all born into this world naked. So I went through all this stuff in my head. Then finally I just said, "What is it, man? I am what I am. I take a shower every day and that's the end of that." '

I knew full well that after she overcame her initial reservations about baring all, Kim was very comfortable in the nude. In fact, clothes were totally unimportant to her. Despite being a former model who had worn some of the most beautiful clothes in the world, Kim really did not care what she wore. At home, we had enormous walk-in wardrobes full of designer clothes that she'd never even put on. Many of the garments still had the price tags and other labels attached. She gave a lot of them away to her sisters and was happy to wander around at home wearing white sweat suits, pyjamas or dungarees.

Not everybody was happy with *Playboy*, however. The cosmetics company Revlon had paid Kim $40,000 for a series of adverts which she shot over three days in March 1982, for Ciara perfume. The people at Revlon didn't know anything about the *Playboy* shoot and they were far from pleased when the magazine was finally published shortly after their adverts began to run in magazines they considered more 'respectable'. I also don't think they were thrilled that *Playboy* ran a series of small photos of their adverts to go with Kim's layout, even though it must have been good publicity for them. They claimed she had something in her contract with them that prohibited nudity. Their Vice-President, Roger Shelley, said, 'She has harmed herself by associating with *Playboy*. We are deeply upset and disappointed.'

But Kim didn't care; she was on her way to the top. She called it a 'tempest in a make-up pot'. And while she would do modelling in the future, she could pick and choose assignments and knew she was wanted because of who she was, not because she was a beautiful but anonymous face. In fact, when Kim was getting a lot of publicity for *Playboy*, Revlon came back to her and asked if they could run some of the adverts again and she turned them down flat.

'Now everyone's talking about me, noticing me, and suddenly they like me again,' she said. 'Well, too bad. I don't need Revlon now. I never did like working for them and I'm glad that phase of my life is over.'

Perhaps Kim was lucky that the Revlon adverts had already been published when *Playboy* came out. In *Katie: Portrait of a Centerfold*, her character was dropped from a prestigious perfume advert because she had posed in the nude.

The spread caused a stir back at Kim's home town in Georgia. Her father accepted it without any trouble, but her mother was very upset. But then Kim and her mother always had a volatile relationship, so it didn't take much for them to have a row. Most of the time, I could never work out why they were upset with each other. Kim told me it took ages before her mother would go to her local grocery store after *Playboy* came out because she was so embarrassed bumping into friends who had seen her daughter naked. She was a religious woman and disapproved of a lot of 'Hollywood' ways. Everybody in Athens seemed to know Kim was famous — but not everyone realised quite why. One Sunday, the minister at the Methodist church the family went to stopped one of her sisters and said, 'I heard Kim's on the cover of a national magazine. What magazine was it?' She was embarrassed and stammered for a couple of minutes before blurting out the truth. Kim was pleased when she heard that; she wasn't ashamed of what she'd done and she didn't want her family to be. I don't know how the minister reacted, though.

Playboy was also a bone of contention between Kim and me when it was finally published. She was very proud of it and thought the pictures were beautiful. But she cut her pages out of the magazine and told me I wasn't allowed to look at the other photo layouts or even read the articles or cartoons! She still had this obsession that as long as I had her, I shouldn't even look at anybody else. Throughout our relationship, her attitude was, 'You've got me so you don't need to look at another woman. You've already got the best there is.'

Returning to our normal life after the *Playboy* shoot was a bit of an anti-climax. Although we were confident it would eventually boost her career, we still had to make a living while we waited for it to be published. We had nothing lined up apart from a quick trip to Dallas to do publicity for *Hard Country*. That film seemed so long ago and it was almost impossible to believe it would ever be released. We were supposed to stay in Dallas overnight, but as soon as Kim had made her appearance we decided to fly straight home.

Then I was offered yet another Walter Matthau film, *Buddy Buddy*, with Jack Lemmon and Klaus Kinski. It was directed by Billy Wilder, who made *Some Like It Hot* with Marilyn Monroe and, coincidentally, Jack Lemmon. By another coincidence, my father had done Marilyn's make-up on that film. It was being shot in Riverside, California, near where Kim and I had enjoyed a surreptitious night together on location for *Hard Country*, and then *Buddy Buddy* moved to the studio in Culver City.

While we were shooting there, Walter had a freak accident. He was playing a killer who had to make an escape by jumping into a laundry chute. He was supposed to fall two storeys on to a cushioned platform, but the bottom section had not been finished and there was no padding on the platform. He fell through the chute and landed heavily on the platform and fell off. The crew called the paramedics and there was a big panic because he had had a heart condition some time earlier. He was rushed to hospital to be checked out, and he was fine. But when shooting moved to

Hawaii for some scenes, he insisted on taking his old friend Dr Robert Kerlan along as his personal physician. Kim was back collecting unemployment pay and beginning to wonder if she would ever work again, so she went on location with me, of course.

We had a fun time back in Hawaii. One day, Kim went down to have a walk in the ocean and while she was there she found a large log that had floated on to the beach. She had time to kill so she wrote a message across the trunk in sand. It took her hours to do it. It read 'I LOVE RON'. As a surprise, she brought me down to the beach to see her handiwork and I took a picture of it with her straddled across the log in a casual blue zip-up top and tiny white shorts.

While we were there, we took off to Kauai for a few days. I rented a house on the beach for us. At least, it was advertised as a beach-front property, but when we got there it was two blocks back from the ocean. Kim had twisted her ankle a few days earlier and thought it was too far for her to walk. In addition, it had no character and she hated it. We had already paid the rent but I had an idea. 'You're the actress,' I said. 'Start limping!'

We told the people we'd rented it from she had turned her ankle on the steps of the house and that I had to get her back to Oahu, the main Hawaiian island, (though it isn't the biggest in the chain), for medical treatment. I made such a fuss that they thought I was planning to sue them, so they refunded our rent and we caught the next plane out.

In June 1981, Kim was offered a made-for-television movie called *Killjoy*. She did not want to do it because she wanted to leave television behind her, as she had left modelling, so she saw *Killjoy* as a step back. She had done television films before *Hard Country*, of course, such as *Katie: Portrait of a Centerfold* and the mini-series of *From Here to Eternity*. But when she moved to Los Angeles in 1976, she had set her sights on a proper film career and just as she had regarded modelling as a road to something else so she had seen television acting as no more than a route to get her into feature films. However, cash was very tight and her business manager warned her she would risk losing her house if she didn't make some money quickly. All the renovations we'd had done to the property had to be paid for and we were falling behind on our bills. Suddenly, $75,000 for three weeks' work began to look very attractive.

Kim asked me to do her make-up because she wanted me to be

there to give her confidence. But I did it quietly, in her trailer, without pay or credit, because of her old conviction that she should not be linked to a make-up man. Making that movie was the first and only time I ever saw her have trouble with her lines. She did take after take and she was really struggling. She was playing a serial killer and in one scene she had to play dead. She was actually pictured on the slab in a morgue in that scene and it was hard for her. It was also weird for me, because I was doing the make-up and I had to make her morbidly off-colour. Seeing her lying there looking so vulnerable gave me a chilling feeling.

One of the other actresses on *Killjoy* was Ann Dusenberry, who I'd worked with on Jaws II. I'd chased her a bit — unsuccessfully — so there was a bit of tension between Kim and her. Kim didn't enjoy making *Killjoy*; it was purely for the money. But it ended up winning The Mystery Writers of America's annual Edgar Award for best television mystery, and Bruce Broughton, who composed the music, was nominated for an Emmy for his score, so it wasn't a bad movie in the end.

While she was making *Killjoy*, someone sent us the script of *Cannery Row* and we both thought it was one of the best scripts we had ever read. Kim was up for the part but eventually it went to Debra Winger. Around the same time, Kim was very excited to get a call from Dustin Hoffman's people, asking her to have lunch with him. He was about to make *Tootsie* and there was a great, fun role for a woman for which he was said to be considering Kim. In the movie, Hoffman played an out-of-work actor who ended up having to pretend to be a woman so he could get a role as a motherly character on a TV soap show.

I drove her to the lunch at Century City, one of the major business districts on the west side of LA where many entertainment-related businesses have their offices, and waited for her. She came out of the restaurant and introduced me to Hoffman, and they were all smiles. But when she got into the car, she laughed, 'He's not interested in me for the role at all. He just wanted to watch me, to see how I eat, if I have any mannerisms that he might be able to use. It was all horse shit.' We learned later he went out with a lot of girls while he was preparing for that role, for the same reason. Years later a journalist, Matthew Gilbert, was to write in the *Boston Globe* newspaper that Kim had, 'A Georgia accent that's just this side of Dustin Hoffman in Tootsie.' I can't imagine where he perfected that accent!

Eventually, that role went to her old rival Jessica Lange, who had beaten Kim three times before, first of all when they were both up for the remake of *King Kong*, which became Jessica's first film. Kim and Jessica then competed against each other again for *The Postman Always Rings Twice* and *Frances*. Jessica went on to win the Best Supporting Actress Oscar for *Tootsie*, and was nominated as Best Actress for *The Postman Always Rings Twice*, so Kim and I often speculated about what would have happened if she had got either role.

Walter Matthau called me again. He seemed to be working non-stop and keeping me in work, too! I wasn't complaining, though. Money was still tight and besides, he was a good friend and good to work with. This time it was *I Ought To Be in Pictures*, with Ann-Margret. I started work on 17 July, 1981, not knowing that this would be my last official job for more than a decade.

Things finally began to look up for Kim. Charlton Heston was about to make an adventure film called *Mother Lode* with Nick Mancuso, and wanted Kim to be the leading lady. She was very excited about it. The only drawback as far as I was concerned was that it was being shot in Canada and was due to start while I was still working on *I Ought To Be in Pictures*. Kim told me I'd have to quit. I didn't want to do it but I knew she was right. That was the deal we'd had from the start and I knew she wouldn't be able to work if I stayed behind for even a few days. We'd never spent a night apart since I moved into Don Juan Place and she needed me to be with her.

I went into work and explained what had happened to Walter. I had never walked out of a job before in my whole 16-year career and I didn't want to appear unprofessional. He completely understood my position and told me to go for it. I found a replacement, Frank Griffin, whom I knew would be able to duplicate the looks I had already created, and headed north with Kim. Walter was very philosophical about the whole thing. He had always had a soft spot for Kim. So he looked at me and said, 'Go for it. If you've got to be with Daisy Mae, you've got to be with Daisy Mae. Besides, she's far better looking than I am. I wish you all the best.'

Chapter 6

Coughing, choking and spluttering, Kim came running through the smoke and flames with terror in her eyes, her face and hair blackened and glistening with sweat. Desperately, she tried to escape the burning mine before the inevitable explosion came. Then a familiar voice boomed out, 'Cut!'

Director and star Charlton Heston was not satisfied with the scene and needed his actors to do it again. Over and over, Kim and Nick Mancuso went through their paces, breathing the toxic chemicals that were being used to create the special effects to turn a converted warehouse on the outskirts of Vancouver into a rickety silver mine, supposedly in the Canadian outback. The mine scenes went on for days, and every night when Kim came back to the hotel from filming she was covered with black stuff. It stuck to her skin, caked up in her nose, got into her throat and made her cough and even rimmed her eyes and got into her ears. Then she started throwing up, something she hardly ever did, even though she was very delicate and had to watch what she ate. She couldn't work out what was wrong with her, and eventually we had to take her to hospital in Vancouver, where much of the film was shot.

With *Mother Lode*, we thought we had hit the big time. Kim was getting paid $175,000, the most she had ever earned, and we knew there was nowhere for her to go but up. She was the leading lady — though, admittedly, it was a very small cast and she was actually the only woman — and she had all the star trappings. She was thrilled to be working with such a legendary figure as Charlton Heston, because his name gave credence to any movie project. When we arrived in Vancouver, I checked out the hotel room and ordered cases of Evian water — Kim always drank Evian water — and special food for Kim, who was always very conscious of her diet. We had a second bedroom which I set up as an exercise room. Kim always travelled with videos of aerobic workout routines, and carried small dumb-bells for weight training so she could keep her gorgeous figure in shape. Since I had now officially given up work, she also insisted that her accountant organise it so that I went on salary as her manager, putting a percentage of her pay directly into my bank account. She wanted me to look after her at work as I did at home. I also did her make-up on this film, as I had for *Killjoy*, but in private, for no pay. Kim had never had anyone but me work on her since she started her film career and she only felt secure with me doing her looks. As always, it was a pleasure, because Kim is so beautiful and easy to work with.

In the make-up business, you allow two hours to prepare a star for his or her part, but Kim didn't care if I only took a few minutes because she knew I would always get it right. There are some stars who insist that you use the full two hours, even if they are ready long before that. Julie Andrews was always a stickler who demanded that you used every minute or she did not feel ready to go on.

In *Mother Lode*, once again Kim was playing an outdoor girl so I went for a natural look rather than glamour and it never took two hours to get her prepared to go on the set. Of course, this being the movies, even when she was put into dangerous situations she still looked more beautiful than anyone would if they were in real peril.

Physically, it was a hard shoot, with Kim being dunked in cold rivers and lakes as well as the gruelling scenes in the mine. But she was always very fit and athletic, and was happy to do the work because she wanted to make her mark in the feature film business.

Kim played Andrea, an adventurous young woman who headed for the Canadian Rockies when her mining engineer boyfriend went missing while searching for a mysterious and legendary gold-mine. Her travelling companion was Jean, played by Nick Mancuso, her boyfriend's partner, obsessed by the idea of striking it rich with a major gold find. Nick's character, Jean, sold all his possessions to buy a small seaplane and they flew north, lured on by a map with an isolated lake marked on it by the missing man. Their plan went wrong from the start, with Jean crashing the plane into the lake, forcing them to swim ashore.

It wasn't only their plan according to the script that went wrong, however. Before Kim and I arrived on the set, the second unit had been filming some of the special effects scenes, including landing the battered, leaking old float plane. The second unit director was Joe Canutt, an Indian and the son of legendary stuntman Yakima Canutt, an old friend of the Heston family who was Chuck's stunt double on Ben Hur. The plane flipped over on landing, completely by accident, and they couldn't right it again. So they decided to write that into the script. They could never have planned a crash like that on a film with a budget of just $6 million — it would have been far too expensive and risky. The storyline was changed so that Andrea and Jean had to dive down for all their equipment, and could not get away from the place because they could not salvage the plane. The crash scene was terrible to shoot. Kim and Nick were wearing wet suits under their clothes but the water was icy. It was high-altitude, glacial water and there's no way to stay warm in that. It was brutal.

Once Jean and Andrea struggled ashore, the story went, they met Heston's character, a wild old Scottish miner, a scruffy character with straggling hair and an unkempt beard, living in a lakeside shack. He promised to take them back to town the next day, and went out of his way to show them his mine, which he swore produced only a meagre amount of silver. Nick's character decided he was lying and was convinced there was gold in them thar' mountains. So he and Kim sneaked into the mine, which was promptly rocked by an explosion. To complicate matters, Heston actually played two characters — the miner and his insane, bagpipe-playing brother. Nick's character killed the mad brother, thinking he was the miner, and the miner kidnapped Kim. There were all sorts of melodramatic moments with Kim being pounced on in the dark and Heston's character taking vicious swings at her with an axe, and a lot of incredible, last-minute escapes. Kim did her own choreography and stunts for the axe scene. It was mapped out like a sword fight, with Kim having to know precisely where she was moving each second, because nobody wanted her hit in the head with an axe! Heston did part of the scene, but an old-time stuntman called Ted White, with whom I'd worked before, stood in for him in the rough parts, when he was falling over.

It was a hard shoot for Nick Mancuso, too. He wasn't as good in the water as Kim and actually complained he spent so much time with his teeth chattering in the icy lake he had to have the caps on his bottom teeth replaced at the end of the film. He moaned, 'I was almost killed three times. I got half-drowned, blown up and blown out.' And people think acting is a glamorous job.

Looking back, it was much more of a grown-up version of kids' Saturday morning adventures than a *Ben Hur* or *The Greatest Story Ever Told*. It was very much a family affair, with Heston's son, Fraser, the writer and producer, and Heston's wife, Lydia, doing the stills photography. Fraser's Canadian wife, Marilyn, was the publicist and assistant to the producer. Plus, of course, Kim and I were still like honeymooners, even though we were coming up to our first wedding anniversary. Nick Mancuso's wife was there, too. A lot of the film was shot on location outside Vancouver, in rural British Columbia for the beautiful outdoor shots, and the warehouse in the city of Vancouver itself was used for the mine scenes. All of this was done to take advantage of generous payments and tax concessions from the Canadian government in return for using a certain proportion of Canadian citizens in the cast and crew members. But, in the end, the Hestons went to private investors to cover the $6 million cost, so they would have more control over how it was released.

Despite the physical hardships, it was a happy shoot and everybody got on well together and socialised after work. Heston taught Kim how to handle a rifle and she became friendly with him and his family. He and Lydia were staying in a house on the outskirts of Vancouver while the rest of us were in a hotel in a suburb called Stanley Park. The location shooting was near Whistler, about an hour's drive away. Heston had a helicopter for the 20-minute flight in and out every day, and Kim could have hitched a ride with him. But there was only so much room in the chopper — not enough for me or Nick's wife — so all four of us used to drive up every day. One weekend, we had a terrific dinner with the Hestons. They'd been shooting a scene on a river with a bunch of Indians, led by actor John Marley, who were fishing for salmon. When the scene was finished, Heston packed up the salmon and took it home with him in the helicopter. He invited us over to try it, and barbecued it in pepper. It was very simple but very good.

Kim and I also became great friends with the producers, Marty Shafer and Andy Scheinman, who were boyhood pals of Fraser Heston and went to college with him. It was because of their friendship that Chuck Heston got involved in the first place. They were having problems raising the money to make the film so Heston came in to help them to give them some leverage. Then he decided to play the two brothers, and was eventually persuaded to direct. We hadn't been shooting very long when Andy Scheinman came to me and said, 'Kim's stealing the movie and Nick Mancuso's really mad, he's really mad. But Kim's an angel. She's really great.' It was the same old story! The script was altered again to give her a bigger part. They could see she had a lot going for her.

Heston was totally professional and looked out for Kim, especially when the shooting conditions were hard. He was very fond of her right from the start. He had never heard of her, but Marty Shafer had seen Hard Country and suggested her.

'We cast her without a test,' he recalled later. 'Aside from her stunning beauty there was, even then, a special presence the camera turns to.' He was also impressed by her professionalism, even at that early stage in her career. In his autobigoraphy, *In the Arena*, he acknowledged that Kim and Nick disliked each other so much they had no screen chemistry. But he praised her efforts at getting into the part.

'We had a scene where Kim wakens before dawn in her tent and finds Nick gone,' he wrote. 'Searching for him in the foggy woods, she encounters a shadowy figure and runs in terror ... into Nick. He comforts her in a warm embrace, nothing more.

'Kim simply couldn't/wouldn't do this. Desperate at losing my perfect, fog-wreathed forest light, I cleared the set.

'"OK, everyone back off ... I want to talk to Kim."

'They went.

'I took her hand and walked up and down the forest glade we were shooting in. "Look," I said, "I want you to help me get past your feeling about Nick. This scene is not about love, it is not about sex. It's about being scared. You did all that, very well. Now I need you to let him comfort you. Like this." I took her in my arms and held her. "Can you do that?"

' "Yes," she said. And she did. Through the rest of the shoot, she was a real trooper. She comes across wonderfully in the film. I like to think we gave her career some crucial early impetus.'

Naturally, everyone was concerned when Kim became so ill she had to go to hospital. We were all worried that the chemicals had had some dreadful effect on her. There are all sorts of rules about safety on film sets, especially in well-regulated countries like Canada, but there is always scope for accidents. On the other hand, Kim could have developed an unexpected allergy to something she was breathing or swallowing.

In the end, the answer was ridiculously simple — and at the same time heartbreakingly complicated. Kim was being sick for one of the most obvious reasons in the world — she was pregnant. We were stunned. We had talked about starting a family and decided it would be better to wait for a few years. Kim wasn't yet 30 and she was very healthy, so we did not foresee any difficulties with her getting pregnant if we put off having children until she had established her career. Talking to the doctors, we soon found out how our plans had gone astray. Kim was convinced that we didn't need to worry about birth control for the five days before and the five days after her period. It had always sounded a little crazy to me, and I thought we were probably taking a big chance, but there was no way I was ever going to turn down the chance of sex with Kim. So now we were about to be parents. But the doctors, who obviously knew what had prompted Kim to be checked out in the first place, were dubious. They talked about the chemicals, and the effects they could have had on the foetus growing inside Kim. Sadly, they told us that the baby had been exposed to many toxic substances. Kim lost the child, which left us both heartbroken.

Kim could not go on the pill because it made her skin break out in blotches and she didn't like using a diaphragm. Much of the time we relied on what Americans call the 'Santa Fe Train' — the one that always pulls out in time — but we had scary moments some months. However, she did not get pregnant again, even though we were taking risks, and she eventually asked me to have my sperm count checked. I think she was hoping it would be low, so she would not have to worry so much about birth control. I went to a clinic in Beverly Hills and Kim drove with me. We were not sure what to expect but we knew it had to be a fresh sample, so we parked in a car park and Kim helped me out with her hand. We had a plastic cup in the car and a few moments later we presented it at the clinic. I checked out OK in the end.

It was not long after shooting *Mother Lode* that we received some more terrible news. I was sitting up in bed at home in Don Juan Place on a Sunday morning watching the TV news with Kim still asleep beside me, when an item came on saying that Natalie Wood had drowned. Her body had been found floating in the harbour at Catalina Island, 20 miles off the Californian coast south of Los Angeles. It turned out that she, her husband Bob Wagner and her current leading man, Christopher Walken, had been staying on the Wagners' yacht, *Splendour*, and she had somehow drowned trying to take a dinghy ashore in the dark. I immediately shook Kim to wake her and tell her the sad news. It was a terrific shock for both of us. Kim had worked with Natalie on the television mini-series remake of *From Here to Eternity* and they'd become friends.

'Oh no,' Kim cried. 'Natalie told me, when we were walking down by Pearl Harbour on location in Hawaii, "I hate the ocean, I hate the water. I can't swim and I don't like to be around it." I can't believe this has happened.'

I knew Natalie, too, as it happened. I'd worked with her on a film called *The Last Married Couple in America*, with George Segal. I hadn't actually done her make-up but I knew her make-up man and they used to invite me into her dressing room towards the end of the day. She was always drinking margaritas towards the end of the evening. As soon as I heard the news, I called a friend of mine, a make-up man called Bob Jiras, who lived in Vermont and was a big friend of Natalie's. His nickname was BJ, and he'd also worked with Bob Wagner, whose nickname, of course, is RJ.

'Hi, BJ,' I said. 'You'll want to check this out, but I think Natalie's dead. It's running on the news.'

He was as shocked as we were. BJ was actually so close to Bob and Natalie that he stayed in a guest house at their place in Beverly Hills when he was in Los Angeles. Kim and I had been there for dinner once. He liked Kim. He had once confessed to me that one of his big sexual fantasies was making out with a cheerleader. So when I took a picture of Kim wearing her old cheerleader's sweater from Athens High School, I sent it to him for a laugh.

Breaking the news about Natalie to him took me back 19 years, to Marilyn Monroe's death. I was in the Navy Coast Guard reserve in those days, after doing a year of active service, and I was driving to the harbour at Wilmington, California, to go to sea on my annual tour of duty when the news came on the radio that she had been found dead. We didn't have mobile telephones in those days so I stopped the car at a phone box and called my father, who had been her make-up artist for years, and broke the news to him. By the time I came back from my tour of duty two weeks later, the funeral was over. My dad had been chosen to make her up for the last time, when she was laid out.

We had gone into *Mother Lode* with such high hopes, but the best things that came out of it were personal rather than professional. Marty and Andy, the producers, and I were all about the same age and became firm friends. We had a common interest in tennis, as did Heston, and once we got back to the real world of LA, Heston invited us to his house to play. Andy and I played him and Marty at doubles. They beat us, which pleased Heston, because he was so much older than the rest of us.

On another occasion, we went to a party at the Hestons' house and took our friends Ron and Linda Lang with us. Lydia Heston was having an exhibition of her pictures, including the photographs she had taken on *Mother Lode*. But the film was, frankly, a disappointment, and we were also trying to cope with our personal tragedy. When the Hestons took over the financing they also won the right to decide how the film would be released. Movies in the United States tend to be released all over the country at the same time, or in a very small way in New York, Los Angeles or, perhaps, San Francisco. Heston, however, chose Kansas City, Missouri, for his première.

'It's a good movie town, it has the demographics that we want for this kind of picture, it has a large population that spans many segments of society in a selected coverage area,' he explained at the time. 'How a picture does in the Kansas City market is a good barometer of how it will do in 99 per cent of the rest of the country.'

Before that small opening, however, Kim started looking around for more work. The *Playboy* piece had still not appeared, and in February we were flown to Chicago to do some additional shots at Hugh Hefner's place up there. Then, in March, she did the Revlon advertising which was destined to be released at the same time as her *Playboy* appearance. Although *Hard Country* had died and *Mother Lode* had not yet been released, Kim's name was becoming known and she was called for interviews. But she hated the stress of being inspected for work.

On one occasion, I drove her to Universal Studios for an interview. I told her I would wait in the car and she went inside. Twenty minutes later, she came running back to the car in a panic, looking white-faced and scared. 'I can't do it, I can't,' she sobbed, as she got back into the car. She had simply been spooked sitting and waiting, and fell so badly to pieces she couldn't go on. But, despite her worsening agoraphobia, she continued to go for interviews, because she needed the work.

One interview she didn't flunk was in August 1982. Sean Connery was planning his comeback as James Bond in the *Thunderball* remake *Never Say Never Again*. He had casting approval, and Kim was on his list to play Domino. We knew Bond girls had reputations for being bimbos by then, but if she got the part at least people would see her and know her name. *Never*

Say Never Again was guaranteed massive publicity regardless of how good or bad it was; most people still regarded Connery as the 'real' 007, but there were threats of lawsuits about his return to the Bond character flying around on both sides of the Atlantic, and the film was due out at the same time as a rival Bond movie, *Octopussy*, starring Roger Moore. The potential for worldwide publicity was endless. Millions of filmgoers were about to see Kim in action at last. She would be seen in magazines and on television around the world, and even if the film was no good, viewers and moviemakers could hardly fail to notice her beauty. We headed to London full of hope. We were also very nervous, but as things turned out, everything went right from the moment we boarded the plane. *Never Say Never Again* would have its share of problems, but once Kim got the part we knew that, whatever happened, she would be known.

Later that August, it was a bit of an anti-climax when we flew to Kansas City, in the middle of the American heartland, to promote *Mother Lode*, which was our first experience of an ordeal that would become all too familiar to Kim — the media junket. We were there for about a week and she and Charlton Heston did around 30 interviews with local papers, radio stations and television news shows, 30 interviews with journalists asking essentially the same questions. It was a double ordeal for Kim. She was so shy she hated doing it in the first place, even though she understood her obligation to promote and publicise the movie. And although she's a consummate actress, it was hard for her to sound fresh and enthusiastic talking about her experiences making the film for the umpteenth time.

After doing the rounds of suburban Missouri, *Mother Lode* opened in the more rarified atmosphere of the Deauville Film Festival. It then went into a slow, limited release through the Mid-west and South-west; and finally hit Los Angeles in February 1983. *Daily Variety*, the 'bible' of the film industry, called Kim 'a beauteous screen personality'. But the review added, 'With a perfect set-up for romance, there is none between Basinger and Mancuso, except for glances at the end.'

Susan King, writing in the now-defunct *Los Angeles Herald Examiner*, said, 'Nick Mancuso and Kim Basinger are attractive-*looking* actors but the characters they play are one-dimensional. There's never any relationship established between these two to push the story along.'

And *Los Angeles Times* reviewer Linda Gross wrote succinctly but scathingly, 'What Basinger is doing there is never made clear.'

By that time, however, we didn't particularly care. *Playboy* was on the stands and Kim was being talked about as a ravishing beauty. *Never Say Never Again* was almost finished, with Kim's luminous charm bringing Domino to life. And she was already getting ready to go into her next film, *The Man Who Loved Women*, with Burt Reynolds and Julie Andrews. 1983 was to be the year the world finally met Kim Basinger.

Chapter 7

Flying to London for the *Never Say Never Again* interview, we had a stroke of good luck that Kim also interpreted as a good omen for the future. There were only three of us in first class — Kim, me and an Indian businessman. It was our first transatlantic flight together and we were enjoying being pampered in those big seats in the nose-end of a British Airways Boeing 747. The service was great and they loaded us up with caviar and vintage Dom Perignon champagne. For once, Kim didn't insist on her favourite white wine, Pouilly Fuissé. Then the captain announced he was having a competition for the people in first class; they had to guess how many miles it was to the half-way mark between Los Angeles and London. The passenger who made the closest guess would collect £1,000, which was more than $2,000 in those days. Even if I hadn't done a maths degree at the University of California Los Angeles (UCLA), I would have quickly worked out that it was better to get 50 per cent of something than 100 per cent of nothing, so I introduced myself to the other guy and suggested we did a deal to split the money down the middle, regardless of who won. He refused. So Kim asked a flight attendant if she could see the cockpit. She spent a few minutes chatting to the pilots, and guess who won the contest? That businessman wouldn't have stood a chance even if his guess had been right on the button. Ever since that flight, British Airways has been my favourite airline.

After that, everything else seemed to go right. We had to go to the Grosvenor House Hotel to meet the producer, Jack Schwartzman, and Sean Connery, who had casting approval. Sean kept a suite in the Grosvenor House, a place we came to know very well. We were both very nervous at the prospect of meeting

Sean. He was truly an international superstar, even though at that time he was not so utterly revered as an actor as he is now. We knew a part in this film would be make or break for Kim, and that Kim was in with a very good chance of getting a part because she had been suggested by actress Talia Shire, sister of director Francis Ford Coppola and an old friend of mine, who was married to Jack Schwartzman. That at least gave us a bit of confidence.

I'd met Talia when I worked on the film *Old Boyfriends*, which also starred John Belushi. We got on well and she took me on to her next couple of pictures. She was married to a musician, David Shire, at the time, so it was a bit of a surprise when she turned up a couple of years later as the wife of the *Never Say Never Again* producer.

Kim and I were waiting in the hotel lobby to be called for the interview when Sean's wife, Micheline, walked through. We didn't recognise her, of course, and she had no idea who we were. Later, we learned she had rushed in to Sean's room and said, 'Come quickly — there's a girl standing outside in the lobby who would be absolutely perfect for Domino.' Sean was astonished to realise it was the girl he was interviewing anyway. It was obvious that all the tiles were falling into place for Kim to land the role.

Never Say Never Again was controversial right from the start. James Bond fans were delighted at the prospect of seeing Sean, even at 53, back as 007, because his replacement, Roger Moore, had never had the same screen presence. He was a more lightweight and light-hearted Bond, without the subtle air of menace Sean brought to the character in the first films. But Cubby Broccoli, the producer behind the Bond franchise, was furious at the idea and tried to get the project stopped. It was basically a remake of *Thunderball*, which was based on a story by Bond creator Ian Fleming, Jack Whittingham and Kevin McClory, who was one of the producers of *Thunderball*. The script was finished in 1960, but *Thunderball* was actually the fourth Bond movie, released in 1965. Fleming turned the story into a novel and when he did not credit him for his work in the novel, McClory sued him in a British court and won the rights to the storyline and characters, including Bond's boss M and M's secretary Miss Moneypenny.

Broccoli was working on his own Bond movie, *Octopussy*, and originally the two films were due to be released at the same time. Naturally, the money men were afraid that having two competing films would dilute the box-office take for both of them. But as far as we were concerned, the controversy was wonderful. It was bound to get both films talked about, and even if they lost money, it would not affect Kim's $175,000 pay packet.

Once Kim was cast, our lives suddenly changed. From being homebodies who enjoyed our suburban house and our animals, we became international jet-setters overnight. Although Kim had got the part and would be filming in London, she was committed to doing publicity for *Mother Lode* before she could start work. We flew home, then on to Kansas City where Kim did the rounds of journalists, then back to Woodland Hills to pack and say goodbye to the dogs for months. This was going to be a long shoot. Then it was back to London. We had been booked into a hotel somewhere in central London but it was such a dump there was no way Kim could stay there. It was so dreadful I've managed to forget the name. With some trepidation I explained the problem to Sean — I didn't want him to think Kim was letting her good fortune in winning the role turn her into a prima donna, something she absolutely was not in those days. I explained how sensitive she was to her surroundings, and how desperately she wanted to give the best performance she possibly could and he came up with a perfect solution.

'Why don't you move into my suite at the Grosvenor House?' he said. 'Micheline and I won't actually be using it so it would just be standing empty. Just sign for anything you want.' Of course, it wasn't actually Sean who was paying the bills; it was the studio picking up the tab. But it was Sean who arranged it for us. I couldn't believe this latest stroke of good luck. Not only was the Grosvenor House a wonderful hotel with a great location on Park Lane, opposite Hyde Park, but the suite was luxurious and big enough for Kim to set up her exercise area.

We were still strapped for cash. I hadn't earned a penny, apart from my cut of Kim's pay on *Mother Lode*, for nearly a year, and the money from *Playboy*, *Killjoy* and Revlon was just about gone. So the prospect of saving Kim's *per diems* — about $2,000 a week — and eating at the hotel for free was wonderful. On top of that, we also had the £1,000 we'd won on the plane for spending money if we wanted to splash out.

We worried in case it might be boring eating at the same place all the time, but we soon learned that the main restaurant, 76 Park Lane, was excellent. The staff quickly got to know us, and that we were staying in Sean's suite and that Kim was the new Bond girl. Every time we walked into the restaurant after the first few days, the pianist used to start playing the James Bond theme. Looking back later this was amusing, because John Barry's famous tune, which has been used to open every Bond movie made by Broccoli, was not actually to be heard in *Never Say Never Again*.

One evening, Claudette Colbert, who was appearing in a play in the West End of London, was dining there. Kim didn't know who she was but I was a fan and I was in awe of her. We were introduced to her and she was very old but very gracious.

The food was always first class, but there was one night I was forced to send my meal back to placate Kim. I'd ordered a salad and when it arrived I didn't recognise one of the ingredients. I asked the waiter and he said, 'That's hare, sir.' Kim heard him say this and gasped, 'Take it back, take it away.' She thought the man had said 'hair' and was disgusted. I couldn't really protest because she didn't like me eating meat at the best of times, and I'm sure she would not have approved of me tucking into a furry little bunny.

We had only been in London for a few days, however, when we flew off to France to shoot scenes in Monte Carlo, and then on to the Bahamas. Monte Carlo is a very James Bond sort of place and I couldn't resist going to the casino, but I found it very different from Las Vegas, where I was used to gambling. I was really surprised that the place closed up at about four in the morning rather than being open 24 hours a day.

We were staying at the Meridien Hotel in Nice, on the Promenade des Anglais, and we lived a quiet life. We wandered through little back streets behind our hotel where there were lots of intimate restaurants. I remember Kim had Dover sole for dinner nearly every night.

Once again, there were some days when she wasn't needed to work and we explored the Riviera and the inland regions. We went to Villefranche and took the same route on which Grace Kelly drove Cary Grant in *To Catch a Thief*, and the same road where years later, by which time she had married Prince Rainier and become Princess Grace — Monaco's First Lady — she would be killed. We also went to Grasse, the perfume capital of the world, and sat outside having lunch and smelling the flowers whose scent filled the air. One day we went to a nude beach and even though Kim can't sunbathe because of her incredibly fair skin, she did take her top off for a while.

Some of the scenes in France were shot on the *Nabila*, the luxury yacht owned by Saudi billionaire Adnan Khashoggi. It was the most lavish yacht you could imagine, with a heliport and its own operating theatre, as well as opulent state rooms and salons. Unfortunately, Kim was seasick. She went to a doctor and was given a special patch to put behind her ear and after that she was fine.

A perk of staying in luxury hotels I quickly got used to was access to health spas and gyms. I always had massages when they were available. At the Grosvenor House I would head to the massage room while Kim hit the gym, and then we'd both go swimming. We did the same in Nice. One day we went into the steam room together and were sitting there relaxing when in walked Kim's *Never Say Never Again* co-star Barbara Carrera, stark naked. She's a stunning-looking woman and I certainly enjoyed the view for a while before I decided to behave like a gentleman. I didn't want to annoy her — and I knew Kim would be furious if she caught me staring at another woman like that.

On another occasion, Kim had a mud bath. She was covered with this thick black ooze and you couldn't tell she was one of the most beautiful women in the world. Then this nerdy-looking attendant, with glasses that looked like the bottom of Coke bottles, picked up a hose and started squirting her with cold water. Just then, two other guys walked into the spa area and, of course, they stopped and stared at her. They saw me looking at her and thought I was just another voyeur, like them. They didn't know who she was, of course. To them, she was just a gorgeous, naked girl and they were enjoying watching this guy run the hose up and down her gleaming body. I found it strange that a man would be doing a job like that, but I guess the Europeans are more open about certain things than Americans.

One of the crucial scenes Kim had with Sean was in the part of the film set in Monte Carlo — though it was actually shot in London — involved them dancing a sensuous tango. Kim's character, Domino, was the girlfriend of Bond's arch-rival, the evil Largo, played by Klaus Maria Brandauer, and 007 was out to seduce her. Kim was determined to give a great, smouldering performance, so she learned how to tango and regularly went to a dance studio where we both worked out and she would practise her steps. Unfortunately, she overdid it. Right before the big scene she went and pulled a muscle in her leg. So, after all her hard work, when the moment came she was hobbling. She still managed to carry it off, though, and the tango scene between Kim and Sean is one of the most memorable moments of the movie.

Kim was unlucky as far as her health went during that shoot. Just over a week after she pulled the muscle, she contracted an eye infection, on the day after her birthday, and could not work for two days.

The shoot in Nassau, in the Bahamas, was great. Kim had to learn to scuba dive for this part. She'd never done it before but she was a great swimmer and learned quickly. She started off in a pool rather than the sea, and I went down with her because she felt confident with me there while she was learning. I had learned to scuba dive back home, when I used to hang out with a pal who owned a dive shop. Once the trainer and the stunt guy were sure she knew what she was doing, we got into a small plane and flew to Stanley Cay, another little island. Funnily enough, there was another island nearby called Bond Cay, which would have been a very apt place to shoot, but the diving there wasn't so good. They had a very good underwater cameraman who had had a lot of experience of this sort of work, including filming sharks. Kim did some more training to get used to the ocean, and they shot a lot of scenes in an underwater cave.

To get into the cave you had to dive under an arch, and you couldn't tell as you went in that there was going to be air at the other side. Once they got into the cave it was surprisingly light, because there was a hole in the roof letting opaque sunlight in. There was a tame barracuda living down there, and divers used to feed it. Kim was extremely competent and insisted on doing her own stunts.

However, she did have a stunt double for one water scene, set in North Africa but which was actually shot in Spain, in which she and Sean were supposed to jump off a tall tower into the sea on horseback. Kim was very worried about doing that scene because she was afraid that the horse would be hurt. They said the horse would be well rehearsed before the jump, but we weren't sure we believed that. We didn't think you'd get a horse to do that jump twice. In the end, though, I don't think he was injured. When the film came out in England, the Royal Society for the Prevention of Cruelty to Animals — better known as the RSPCA — called for the viewing public to boycott it because of this scene, claiming the horse was mistreated. Warner Brothers denied that any harm had come to the horse, but cut half a second from the British version so the audience did not actually see the horse hitting the water after a 40-foot fall.

While we were filming in the Bahamas, we flew out from

Nassau in the morning and back again at the end of the day's shoot. We met a really nice German couple who had a boat moored out at Stanley Cay. The film company hired them to help out in some way and we became very friendly. One day, when shooting finished early the crew flew back to Nassau and we stayed on for lunch. There was sort of a sexual aura, a little tension about the day, and we weren't sure what was going to happen. As it turned out, nothing did; we just had lunch and took a light plane back to Nassau in the late afternoon. The German man went fishing and speared a dorado with a harpoon gun. It tasted absolutely delicious and Kim tucked in with the rest of us, but I didn't dare tell her it had just been killed a few feet from her while her back was turned. She was very touchy about that sort of thing.

It was the same with her clothes. Barbara Carrera, who played Fatima Blush, had beautiful furs and leathers that Kim wouldn't want to wear. In those days, she didn't have the clout to refuse to wear specific clothes as she does today, but fur would not have made her happy. I think there was a bit of snakeskin or something on a costume which she wasn't aware of, so that didn't matter, but it would have bothered her if anyone had pointed it out.

Not all the food in the Bahamas was as good as that fish, though. Kim had a lot of trouble eating there. We didn't like the first hotel we stayed in so we moved to a suite at the Nassau Beach Hotel, which was much better.

We flew back to England and the Grosvenor House just before Thanksgiving came around. We didn't realise what the last Thursday in November means in England — absolutely nothing. For Americans, it's the most important holiday of the year and Kim wanted it to be special. She was homesick after being away from the animals for nearly two months. It was a big cultural shock to us and we thought about how friends at home would be enjoying the traditional feast of turkey and cranberry sauce with all the trimmings, probably under blue skies in California, while in London it was just another work day — and a dreary, grey day at that. So while Kim was at work, I put my new-found knowledge of the back streets of Mayfair and Shepherd's Market to good use. I'd noticed a little, traditional-looking bakery in my strolls, and went in and explained my predicament. They were absolutely charming and agreed to make individual pumpkin pies for us — and a turkey sandwich for me. Kim was always a strict vegetarian and normally I wasn't allowed to have meat at home, but she didn't mind making an exception for something as traditional as Thanksgiving. So we ate our makeshift Thanksgiving dinner sitting on the floor of our bedroom at the Grosvenor House. We were 6,000 miles from home but we found a way of getting back to America for the day. Funnily enough, we told our waiter in the restaurant about our snack, and the chef promptly rustled up pumpkin soup just for Kim. Everybody fell for her charm.

London was very exciting to us. We didn't have a car so we walked a lot. There were days when Kim wasn't working at all, so we explored the area around the hotel. Kim liked to go jogging and that was very easy because there was a tunnel under Park Lane that led straight into the park. We ran there, and discovered Speakers' Corner near Marble Arch, where amateur politicians and religious nuts stand on their soapboxes and hold court. She was fascinated by the idea of people just standing up and spouting off about anything they wanted.

Kim sometimes attracted stares, but that was because she was so stunning-looking, not because anyone knew who she was. Her anonymity would be gone forever once the film came out. We kept ourselves to ourselves, not because we wanted to be stand-offish, but because we didn't know anybody in London to run around with. We've never been into clubs and late nights — Kim had early-morning starts in any case — but we went to the theatre and the cinema a lot. We went to see American films, which was funny in a way because we never went to the movies much at home. I remember going to a screening of *Hard Country*, but after that she didn't even like watching her own films. The film companies would always send us videos but she didn't watch them.

Living in the hotel was quite an experience. There were a lot of Arabs staying there, and they seemed to cook all the time in their rooms. There were always alluring, spicy smells wafting through the air when we left our suite or got out of the elevator. I'm sure they weren't supposed to cook, but I guess they had enough money to be able to get away with it. Whenever we walked along the corridor, there were large bodyguards standing there. They got to know us pretty quickly because we were there for so long. But they wouldn't let anyone they didn't know wander around. We certainly felt pretty safe while we were staying there.

We had a running joke about the Arab women. Whenever we were in the lift and they got in wearing those black masks to hide their faces, Kim would say, 'It's the Lone Rangers!' I cracked up every time she said that, but, of course, it wouldn't have meant anything to the women, even if they could speak English. Kim wasn't saying it to be mean or racist in any way; it started as a natural reaction because she was so surprised at the sight of them. There was nobody that exotic in Athens, Georgia, when she was growing up, and even in Los Angeles we lived in a very conservative, white suburban area.

Although Mayfair was a long way from Woodland Hills and the Mexican restaurants we were used to hanging out in, we soon got used to the life. In those days, English pubs still had to close in the afternoon, but hotel bars could serve residents. On days when Kim was not working, we would always go down to the bar after it was closed to the general public because there was nobody else there — just the two of us and the barman. The first time we went in there Kim ordered a glass of Pouilly Fuissé, naturally, and I asked for a Carlsberg beer, or lager as it's called in England. The first taste was horrible. Both drinks were warm, compared to what we were used to. We complained, in a nice way — 'commented' would really be a better way to describe it — and the bartender explained that that was the way drinks were served in England. Kim asked for ice and we learned another thing about the drinking habits in England in those days — you got one, or if you were lucky, two cubes. Fortunately, everybody was always taken by Kim so the barman was happy to chill her wine sufficiently, and thanks to her they put a big washtub up on the bar, filled up with ice, to cool my beer. It became a regular part of our routine, heading down to the bar, enjoying our refreshing cold drinks and nibbling on titbits sitting at the bar. It was just after *ET* came out and the barman gave Kim an ET doll which she kept for years.

We also went shopping in our spare time. Selfridges was an easy walk away on Oxford Street, or we'd get a car and drive to Harrods. They were both enormous and seemed to sell everything. I remember buying Kim a gold Rolex watch at Selfridges. We didn't exchange a lot of gifts, so that stands out. Earlier in our relationship, when I'd won a bit of money on the horses, I bought us a matching pair of stainless steel Cartier watches. But now Kim was a Bond girl, I thought she should have a gold watch. Most of the time we bought presents for our housekeeper, Doris Gilmore. They were useful things — bathrobes, slippers, sweaters — stuff that would appease her because we were gone so long and she had so much responsibility taking care of the dogs. Kim did most of the choosing, but I went with her everywhere. She couldn't bear to go out by herself.

Kim was determined not to let Christmas become a repeat

performance of Thanksgiving. Even though it was obviously a major event in England and production of the movie closed down for several days, she did not want a second disappointment.

'We're going home,' she said. 'Call the housekeeper and ask her to get things ready.'

Doris went out and got a tree — a 10-footer — and put it up and decorated it all by herself. On 23 December we flew home, just to spend a few days together and to see the dogs again. Our suitcases were stuffed with presents but they weren't for us or our family and friends, they were all for Doris. We had also bought lots of Christmas ornaments in London — Christmas trees made of wood and silver, snow shakers, Christmas stockings, a stuffed Santa Claus and other trinkets. Doris was like a little kid when she saw all the presents Kim had bought her. She was so excited it made us feel happy too. On 27 December we were at Los Angeles International Airport, heading back to London, only this time our cases were empty. Kim had an incredible collection of matching baggage that she had picked up during her modelling days. On every piece of baggage she tied a piece of white cotton ribbon so we would immediately recognise our suitcases when they came up the chute in the airport arrivals area. It was a pretty good system, especially when you travel with 10 or even 20 bags, and I still use it to this day.

We stuck to one other American tradition when we were back in London — watching the Superbowl, the American football championship game which is played at the end of January, on television. Because of the time difference we sat up to the early hours for once, watching the Washington Redskins beat the Miami Dolphins 27–17, even though Kim was working the next day.

On our return to London, Kim was actually a little apprehensive about going back to work, because of something that had happened just before we left.

Kim had come back to the hotel and I could tell immediately something was wrong.

'What happened?' I asked.

She was very shaken and said, 'I went to say goodbye to Sean in his dressing room and wish him Merry Christmas and he grabbed me and started kissing me. I think he wanted to do more. I had to sort of wrestle away from him.' We were shocked because of Micheline, but I know that since then he has been accused of cheating on her with several women, so I suppose I shouldn't have been surprised. And I'd dated enough married women before I met Kim to know that a wedding ring doesn't mean a thing to some people if the opportunity is right.

However, she and Sean got on fine when they were working together again. He was very gracious, and told Kim he thought she had a great future. He even recommended her to TriStar for her role in *The Natural*, with Robert Redford. So she ended up working with three of the big screen's biggest sex symbols in one year — Sean Connery, Burt Reynolds and Robert Redford.

Kim and Sean also shared an amusing moment when they were walking down Piccadilly one day. They passed a man walking in the opposite direction and Sean did a double-take. So did the other man. It was Roger Moore, and he pointed at Sean and said, 'Sean, never say never again.' They may have been rival Bonds, but the two men were very friendly off-screen.

Never Say Never Again took so long to make that Sean ran into difficulties. I don't know what his situation is now, but back then he could only stay in Britain for a certain length of time without having income tax problems. Even though we did travel to France, Spain and, later, to the Bahamas to film, he was apparently cutting things fine. Because of that, there was one night when he was filming late into the evening and had a helicopter pick him up to make sure he was out of the country by midnight. There were all sorts of problems with the script and the production, and filming lasted far longer than anticipated. In fact, we thought we'd finished and Kim went back to the United States to film her next movie in Houston, Texas, when we were unexpectedly called back to the Bahamas and London in June 1983, ten months after Kim had started work on *Never Say Never Again*, to shoot some extra scenes.

By the time we returned to England, Kim had actually finished shooting her fourth film, a comedy called *The Man Who Loved Women*, which was directed by Blake Edwards and also starred Blake's wife Julie Andrews and Burt Reynolds. This time we were staying in a different hotel and didn't have our restaurant signing rights, which was a shame. We started trying different kinds of restaurants. I introduced Kim to Indian food on that trip. It was good for her because there are so many vegetarian choices, and she always liked spicy food. We ate a lot at Mexican restaurants at home, and she could eat food hotter than just about anyone I have ever known. We also experienced the fine British tradition of strawberries and cream and champagne in the most English of settings — The All England Tennis Club.

The Wimbledon tennis championships were in full swing and we decided to go and try the experience. We got Centre Court tickets for £60 each, thanks to the concierge at the hotel, because somebody else had returned them. We also got a car and driver to take us there. It was expensive for us, but Kim wanted to do it and I was happy to go along with her. We were the only Americans in our section when we got there. I think the British people around us, who were much more subdued, thought we were rowdy colonials. Roscoe Tanner was playing and we were cheering him on. Kim knew him because he was a friend of her brother, Mick, who played tennis in those days on what they called the satellite tour, a degree below the professional circuit. Tanner had even been to her house in Georgia. We didn't get to meet him that day, however.

There was an unexpected disaster in calling Kim back for more filming on *Never Say Never Again*. Instead of their bombshell Bond girl with golden hair flowing way below her waist, they had a new-look Domino with brown hair cut as short as a boy's! Kim's drastic change in appearance was called for by Blake who wanted her to have a completely different image for her role as the nymphomaniac wife of a Texan tycoon in *The Man Who Loved Women*. To repair the damage, the wig-makers got to work — to the tune of $10,000 — but the new underwater scenes were a nightmare because Kim needed a special waterproof wig and it kept floating off. In the end, however, they got the shots they needed. But being called back to work had a silver lining for us — literally. Kim was originally paid $175,000 and she was given an extra $75,000 for the re-shoot.

By the time we finally went home, we had accumulated 24 suitcases, all marked with white cotton tape. When we arrived at Los Angeles International Airport and reached Customs, the inspectors were making a lot of people open up their bags. I couldn't face the thought of having them go through all our luggage, with Kim having to hang around among crowds of people. I didn't have any contraband, or anything that we should have paid duty on, but it would have been very inconvenient, for us and for the two limousines waiting for us outside the arrivals hall. While we were standing in the queue I checked out all the customs officers and chose the youngest guy. I quickly opened up a bag with Kim's edition of *Playboy* in it and opened it on her pages. Then I made sure I opened up that bag first. I wasn't supposed to have a copy, of course; Kim didn't know I had sneaked one for myself. The officer looked at the pictures in surprise — then looked at Kim. He recognised her instantly. She autographed the magazine for him, and there was never any question of having to open up the other 23 cases.

In what was becoming an all-too-familiar pattern, *Never Say Never Again*, Kim's third film, became the third one to have its release date pushed back. In addition to problems with the script that meant shooting took longer than expected, Cubby Broccoli, backed by Ian Fleming's estate and United Artists, launched a legal battle to try to derail the project and keep the movie out of the cinema altogether. Fortunately, in June 1983, the London Appeal Court ruled that the film could go ahead, and it finally opened that October.

We didn't go to the première of *Never Say Never Again*, but I remember when it was opening, driving along Sunset Boulevard with Kim and there she was, on the biggest and most imposing billboard in Hollywood. It's always used to publicise the most important movie coming out, and it was amazing to see Kim and Barbara staring out from it, on either side of Sean. I got a picture of the giant poster with the life-size Kim looking tiny underneath it.

Once again, the reviewers were good to Kim, even though they weren't all wild about the movie. 'What clicks best in the film is the casting,' said *Daily Variety*. 'Basinger is luscious as the pivotal romantic and dramatic figure.' Arthur Knight in *The Hollywood Reporter* added, 'Basinger is at once sultry and naïve, a girl who could easily be sucked into the machinations of the evil Largo, yet ripe to the advance of an urbane Bond.' And in *Newsweek*, Jack Kroll wrote, 'Kim Basinger shows signs of being more than a Bond bimbo with her flashdance physicality and golden-eagle elegance.'

We were delighted by the praise and knew that Kim had finally, definitely, arrived.

Chapter 8

Making *The Man Who Loved Women* meant a radical change for Kim. People were talking about her ravishing *Playboy* pictures and there was a lot of early buzz about *Never Say Never Again*. Director Blake Edwards, who had wanted to work with Kim ever since he met her during the *S.O.B.* shoot, offered her the part of Louise, the nymphomaniac wife of a Texas millionaire, in the movie. At the time she was discussing the possibility of playing Debra Winger's best friend in *Terms of Endearment* as her next film project, but she immediately accepted Blake's offer because she loved him as much as he adored her.

Blake, the first *important* director to notice her, did not want to present his audience with just a beautiful blonde stereotype. So he tentatively asked, 'Would you consider changing your hair … cutting it?' She didn't even think twice before agreeing. But as things turned out, I think Blake got more than he had expected. We went off to Julie Andrews' favourite hair stylist, Michaeljohn, and he set to work. It was a Sunday and there was no one else in the salon except us and the stylist. Now, in the time we'd been together, her hair had never been cut, and I couldn't believe what happened. Throughout the time I'd known Kim, her hair had always been so long that it came down to below her waist, and I loved the look. But this afternoon she had it all cut off! I'm convinced Blake meant for her just to have a bit of a trim and a different style from her normal free-falling mass of blonde tresses. The stylist started cutting, and every time he asked her opinion she said keep going. It took six-and-a-half hours, but by the end she had next to no hair left — and then she had it dyed brown. That evening she left the salon with her hair only about an inch long.

When it was all over, the stylist phoned Blake to warn him what had happened, and he actually took it very well. I took pictures of all the stages and lengths her mane went through and always thought it would make a great picture spread, but at the end of our marriage Kim took all the photos and destroyed them so the world was robbed of the opportunity to witness the day her hair was shorn.

It was very brave of Kim to cut her hair, particularly as on the very first day of filming she had to perform her first-ever screen nude scene. First days are always difficult for actors and actresses and nude scenes, especially first nude scenes, are even more so. For Kim, it was doubly difficult because she was facing both without the protection of her hair to hide behind. In the final cut, the nude scene was left out, but it was still a hard thing for Kim to do.

She certainly had more guts than her co-star, balding Burt Reynolds, who would never be seen without one of his collection of wigs. Blake asked him, 'Burt, why don't you take off your toupee?' But Burt wouldn't do it. The funny thing is, Burt was always complaining that people didn't take him seriously as an actor. He wanted to be a Cary Grant for the 1980s. Blake suggested, 'Take off your hair like Sean Connery does and show people you're an actor.' Of course, the ironic thing is that Burt started to get real respect and launched a comeback after years in the doldrums when he dared to go bare.

And it was a strange and wonderful coincidence that when both Kim and Burt were on new professional highs after lulls in their once-stellar careers, they each won a 1998 Golden Globe Award for their supporting roles, Kim in *L.A. Confidential* and Burt in *Boogie Nights*. I was delighted for both of them.

Although that first day of shooting was very hard, having her hair cut helped boost Kim's self-confidence, which was always very shaky, to put it mildly. Once she realised she could no longer toss her mane and hide behind it if she felt nervous or self-conscious, she told me with some astonishment, 'I've always had long hair. Since I cut it off, I don't have my looks to fall back on. I've never felt so ugly in my life but I've never felt better. I feel so happy to be ugly. Isn't that weird? It's pushed me out of myself. I feel for the first time that I can be completely me.'

She also credited Blake with helping her a great deal. She had had problems with Irvin Kershner, the director of *Never Say Never Again*. Perhaps because working opposite such a big star as Sean

Connery, in what was clearly Sean's vehicle, meant she could not manipulate him into making her part more important as she had done in earlier films. She found Blake totally different from Kershner. At the end of the *Never Say Never Again* shoot, she admitted, 'I just prayed for that movie to be over. I vow I'll never go through anything like that again. Irvin Kershner and I didn't get along at all.' In contrast, at the end of *The Man Who Loved Women*, she said, 'Blake was wonderful. He brought out my best.'

Actually, although Blake didn't know it, while he was directing her he was bringing out a secret side of Kim's real life persona — her incredible appetite for sex, and bizarre and imaginative sex at that.

In the film, Burt, in the title role, plays a wealthy LA sculptor who cannot resist beautiful women. He is driven to distraction by his passionate affairs with women like Marilu Henner, Cynthia Sikes and Sela Ward, as well as Kim. Blake's own daughter, Jennifer, played a prostitute, the one woman Burt's character didn't bed. In her role as Louise, not only does Kim's lust match Burt's, she gets a special thrill from sex in public places and when there is a risk of discovery. She performs oral sex on David, Burt's character, as he is driving her Rolls Royce. And she gives a repeat performance at the races, when she leads him from her husband's private box to the box next door and quickly unzips his fly, while the legitimate residents of the box watch the horses thundering towards the finish line without ever knowing about the erotic scene going on behind them. They even enjoy illicit pleasures in a car as it goes through an automatic car-wash.

Kim threw herself into the part with gusto, winning praise from co-stars Burt and Blake's wife Julie Andrews, who played David's psychiatrist. They both predicted great things for her future. Burt said, 'She's stunningly beautiful. If she makes good professional choices, she will become a very big star.' And Julie added, 'Kim Basinger is going to emerge a star.' Kim was just as complimentary about Burt. She said, 'He's the most agreeable guy in the world, a good old boy, just as you'd think.'

Roger Ebert, one of America's top syndicated movie critics who reviews films for the influential *Chicago Sun-Times* newspaper and is co-presenter of Siskel & Ebert at the Movies, a widely watched television show reviewing new films, recalled that in *The Man Who Loved Women*, Kim 'didn't just go for the clichés; she threw herself into the part, draping herself across the star, Burt Reynolds, with such wanton abandon that the scene became hers, not his'.

But when I saw Kim on the screen in this movie, an English-language remake of a French film, while I could recognise her star quality, I could also see past the acting into the Kim Basinger only I knew. Well, I and one other person. When she told one interviewer, 'It was the most fun I've ever had in my life. Every scene I did was kinky,' I knew only too well just how much she had enjoyed it.

The Rolls Royce scene, naturally, reminded me of our exciting trip to Mammoth a couple of years earlier. But even before that wild drive, I knew that oh-so-shy Kim could also be madly uninhibited.

I have always been a very sexual person, willing to take my chance with a pretty girl. And I've never been shy about learning from past experiences. A few years before I met Kim, when I was making a film called *The Moneychangers*, with Kirk Douglas, I went out with a girl on the movie and took her home. She unlocked the door and we kissed goodnight. She'd already opened the door slightly, so I decided to take a chance. I put my hands on her breasts and pushed her back gently. The door swung open and I was in the house and in her bed.

That first night I walked Kim back to her motel room in Bakersfield when we were making *Hard Country*, the identical situation had presented itself. I kissed her hard and long and she responded with her tongue. So I moved my hands up her body to her breasts and she didn't resist when I pushed her inside the room. My mind was racing — I must admit, in a calculating way. I figured if a girl let me kiss her like that and touch her breasts without being offended, then there was no way this evening could be over. She went to the bathroom, and came back wearing a sort of leotard. I pulled it down to kiss her breasts, then all the way off to perform oral sex on her. She really got off on that. But by now it was 1.30 or 2.00 in the morning and she had to be back at work, looking good, at 6.30am. I decided not to push it any further and said goodnight. The next day there was a bit of tension between us, but it was sexual, not hostile. That night, she came down to my ground-floor room. I pulled her on to the bed, took her clothes off and we made love. It was fantastic. I thought, 'I'm really going to go for this. I'm going to take it as far as I can.' From then on, it was obvious to everyone around that we were very friendly on the set. Off the set we were hot and heavy. It was total lust.

After that first sexual encounter we were together every night on location. Kim was always very orgasmic, which was great for me. It made me feel like a hero. We were blissfully happy. We were always ready for sex. In the early days, I always watched football on television on Monday nights, which is a big deal in America. Kim said she liked that and I asked why. 'Because I know where you are,' she replied. Kim wasn't that interested in football and would be around the house doing stuff. But she'd always join me at half time — to have sex. During the break, most men get up from in front of the TV set to go to the toilet or pour themselves a beer, but Kim always had other things in mind. It became a regular weekly thing for us. The football game meant we had sex. I scored more often than the jocks did on the pitch!

Once I moved in with Kim, we never used the Jacuzzi, so we had it moved inside when we renovated the house, but we hardly ever went in it. We much preferred the big sauna we had put in, and had sex — literally hot sex — in there a lot.

I'm very visual and think in pictorial terms. With my other girlfriends, I'd always shot videos of us having sex — and shown them to the next girl to come along. Kim hated that. It was the old question, 'Why do you want to look at other girls, when you've got me?' She told me to get rid of them all and I promised I would. I hid them instead. Years later, I had them hidden in a secret compartment in a Porsche she'd given me as a present that was eventually stolen. I've often wondered if the thief ever found them; I hope he enjoyed them if he did.

Although Kim objected to my old picture shows, she didn't have any qualms about appearing in videos for me — and with me. I took pictures of her all the time, especially when she didn't have any clothes on. I watched her as she showered and washed her hair. I was relentless in documenting our intimate moments together photographically. When she was outside playing with the dogs, I'd follow her around with a video camera and do silly things like lift her skirt up and pull her pants down to play with her. She really got into it and did sensuous strip shows for me. She loved the still pictures I took of her and collected them into the 'goodies' albums she gave me. Later, when we were not together every single day, we started a tradition that whenever I was leaving her for a few days, I would take very raunchy, graphic shots of her to remind me of what I was missing. Those pictures were virtually nothing more than gynaecological examinations of her.

The other highlight of our first few months together was the day we had a threesome. Fantasies played a big part in our love-making and also we talked a lot about different experiences we had had. Kim told me she had once been to bed with a guy and another woman when she was in New York. I'd done three-and four-way sex a few times. Sometimes it was good, sometimes it wasn't. I knew she'd never let another woman into our bed, so I planted the idea of bringing in another man in her mind as we lay in bed one night. We had a big bedroom, about 30 feet long, and it was dark. We were making love and I told her, 'There's a guy just walked in and he's watching us. He's watching what we're doing.' A few nights later, I went through the same scenario and added, 'He's coming closer to the bed to watch us. He's holding your hands down on the bed.' Finally, after a few nights like this, I said, 'I'm backing off and he's taking my place. He's inside you, he's fucking you.' I knew that would turn her on because she'd already confessed one of her wilder fantasies to me — doing the guys in a fraternity at her High School. I'd pretend to be seven or eight different guys and she loved it. It was the same with the three-in-a-bed idea. Kim got off on the fantasy of it all and eventually said, 'OK, let's do it for real.'

It was a Sunday afternoon. It would have had to be a Sunday because that was the maid's day off and we always used it as an excuse for great sex — on the floor, in the back yard, in the pool. We loved to have sex all over the house. We had deep, shag carpets that were really comfortable for love-making. I think we had sex more often on the floor than we did in bed. We would sometimes take cocaine to give an extra rush to our sex lives, but Kim did not like smoking pot. Anyway, I knew just the guy to call to help me with our sex-scapade. He and I had done this before and I knew I could trust him. He was younger than me but older than Kim and he was no Clark Gable, so I couldn't see them running off together. Also, he was happily married so I knew he wasn't going to say anything. Right up until the time he arrived, I thought Kim might back out, but that would have been cool. I wasn't going to force her into anything she really didn't want to do. She had some of her usual Pouilly Fuissé white wine before he arrived and I think she took a hit of coke. This guy, Sandy, turned up and I introduced them. He didn't know who she was, of course, but he could obviously see she was beautiful. They started kissing and we all went into the bedroom. We stripped each other and I started performing Kim's favourite, oral sex. Then Sandy took over and they had sex. Then it was my turn. We kept swapping back and forth; everything one of us did, so did the other, and Kim came a lot. I talked a lot. I told Sandy, 'Isn't she beautiful? This is the girl I'm going to marry.' He was astounded that I'd want to share her. But for me, it was a power thing. That Kim would do this for my pleasure was a great feeling. Kim was moaning, 'This is great, this is great.' She loved every minute of it while it was happening.

He stayed for about two-and-a-half-hours and when he left, Kim and I made love again. It was really hot. Then we went out into the pool. She was topless and I pulled her bikini bottoms off. Suddenly she turned against me. 'Why did you make me do that?' she shouted at me. 'I didn't want to do it.' She was really upset and mad at me, even though I know she'd enjoyed it at the time.

In fact, she became so upset and angry that I decided to leave her to cool down for a bit and so I drove to the beach to think things over. I took out a note book and, to kill some time, I wrote down every intimate detail of the sexual encounter we had just experienced. After about three hours, I called her and she said she didn't want to see me. But I kept talking and she reluctantly agreed to meet me in a bar. We usually went to the Red Onion in Woodland Hills, where we'd had lunch the first day I ever saw her house, but we went somewhere different, El Torito, just down the street. We met at the bar and she told me, 'Tonight, your name is Bill and we've never met before.'

We had a few drinks and she began to relax. I started flirting with her as if I was trying to pick up a stranger and she flirted back. Eventually we left — but not to go home. We went to a motel and rented a room. When we first got together she told me I was her twelfth lover. That night, in a cheap, anonymous motel room, 'Bill' became her fourteenth. She let me back into her heart, and we swore we'd be together 'Longer than forever ...' Later, she told me she'd never been in a three-way situation before. It was just a fantasy.

We never had another threesome, but we used the memory to spice up our fantasy life. When we were making love, I'd say, 'Here's Sandy, he's coming back for more.' He never did, but we went through the routine of me pretending to be him for weeks. We often went to the beach and made out there — a lot of oral sex and sometimes full love-making.

One day, we were going to a private beach called El Matador and I said, 'Sandy's going to be there today.' Kim said, 'No, I don't want that. I don't want to go.' But she got in the car anyway. She was uneasy at the beach but she took her top off and wandered around. We started fooling about and I was eating her, and I looked up to see a guy watching us from the cliff, about 50 feet away. I told Kim it was Sandy and she said, 'I don't care, just fuck me.' The guy stayed until we finished. It wasn't Sandy, of course. I don't know who it was. It was just your typical voyeur-exhibitionist thing. He got lucky being in the right place at the right time.

That was far from the only time we had sex on the beach, the risk of being watched always gave it an extra edge. We made love on the make-up chair when I was working on *S.O.B.*, fooled around in cinemas and limos — anywhere we could. On Sundays, we often had marathon love-making sessions and afterwards Kim would be hungry. It was the maid's day off and Kim was not very domestic anyway. My standing joke was, 'Kim's only domestic quality is that she lives in a house!' So I used to pull on a pair of jeans and Kim put an overcoat over her naked body and we drove down to Ventura Boulevard to Ed and Evelyn Wynn's Village Restaurant and Delicatessen. I would park and leave Kim sitting outside while I went in and bought tuna sandwiches which she tore into ravenously on the way home.

Kim was really into taking risks. I know it sounds funny when you think of how outrageous we were in our love life, but sometimes we were uncomfortable having wild sex at home when the housekeeper was there, so we'd get into the car, drive down the road and — only a few hundred yards from our own home — we'd make out like school kids. Sometimes we'd go out to dinner and stop on the way to have oral sex, then come home and park outside our own house and make love.

I'd introduced Kim to cocaine, although she never used it as much as I did. I'd buy a quarter (eight grams) and it would last eight or nine days, but I'd use the vast majority of it. However, very often at the end of dinner, especially on a Friday or Saturday night when she didn't have to work the next day, she'd say, 'Ron, do you have a treat for me?' That was our private code word for cocaine. I'd give her some coke and she'd go to the bathroom for a hit. Then, when we left the restaurant, she'd be charged up sexually. We'd drive up and down Ventura Boulevard, the main street in Los Angeles' San Fernando Valley, taking hits. Then we would park in different places — outside a restaurant or in a dark street behind our house and have sex. I would go down on her and sometimes, not always, she'd jump on me. Sometimes we'd be full-blown nude in the car and people would walk by and not even notice. The thrill was in thinking what would happen if they did. At other times, we'd drive up and down the highway, the US equivalent of a motorway, in the nude. It was so bizarre to think about what would happen if we got stopped. If it was anyone else doing that the cops would just tell them to go home or book into a motel. But if it was Kim Basinger ... they'd call the papers.

Years after we split up, I read that she and Alec had been arrested for horse riding nude on the beach at Malibu. It reminded me of those crazy days cruising in the nude. When she was caught, Kim is alleged to have said to the cops, 'Well boys, I bet you haven't seen a pair of melons like these before.' Whether that particular incident ever really happened or is just urban myth, I don't know, but I certainly do know Kim continued to take risks when she was driving long after our time together. She once told an interviewer about being stuck in freeway traffic for hours in her precious 1954 Chevy pickup, which she had converted to an automatic gearbox because she never could drive a manual. 'I had on this see-through skirt and no panties,' she giggled.

Even when we were fully dressed, we managed to turn each other on while we were driving. I'd thrust my hand into her panties and fondle her until she purred with delight. She was completely oblivious to any truck drivers who might look down into our car from their cabs. I kept a record of some of our sexploits on a wall calendar, with notes like 'Great BJ' and SX, which was our code for sex in the daytime. I even marked on 26 June, 1982 that we had sex in the morning before going to Jenny Edwards' wedding.

Kim was not the only person who enjoyed the risk of being watched, as I discovered when we went to New York to make 9½ Weeks. We were living in the Parker Meridien Hotel and I spent many, many evenings in my room while Kim was working. I'd bought these high-powered binoculars and looked out of the windows into the high-rises opposite. There were so many people putting on shows, with the curtains open, obviously enjoying the knowledge that they could be spied on. There were straight couples, gay guys and lesbians, doing everything to each other, and they didn't care. So when Kim came home, I would backlight the room carefully and leave the drapes open while we made love. Nobody watching would be able to make out who we were; we were just another kinky couple. But I enjoyed imagining people watching the big show. I wonder how many people have got hot videotapes of Kim Basinger having sex and don't realise it!

I'm sure today Kim would say I pushed her into a lot of sexual situations. But after she made 91/2 Weeks, and she was asked about the sexual content of the film she actually said that our life together had been a liberating experience for her.

'I don't mean *just* sexual liberation,' she said once. 'I am very quiet, very shy to the world. And when somebody finally figures you out and shows you your inside — on *their* face — it can be quite scary, especially when they reveal your past and hidden fears. But when all of that is out, nothing can be more liberating, nothing can be more coveted than love in a relationship that has liberation. Then love takes on a whole other meaning than those things written on Hallmark cards. Once you've met someone who turns you inside out, it's another whole ball game. I'm a very lucky human being to have Ron. Absolutely.'

Not that Kim had anything against Hallmark cards; throughout our marriage she used to send me funny, loving cards whenever we were apart and even when we were together, and I still cherish them.

Actors always make a big deal about sex scenes being hard work and all about professionalism, not sex. It's true they are technically difficult, because they have to look right for the audience, even if that means not acting like you would at home in your own bed. But thanks to our sensational sex life, Kim allowed herself to enjoy them.

'In *9½ Weeks* and *The Natural*, I enjoyed the sexy part of being used for things,' she admitted to an interviewer. 'Enjoyed it immensely. Even at home I enjoy that. The sexy part has always been hard for me, although Ron's made it a lot easier. I like to be sexy for him, like *him* to be proud of me. I like him to be sexy.'

I believe I taught Kim to be more open about her sexuality. She was always a sensuous girl who bragged about learning oral sex in the fields around Braselton, the Georgia town she bought after we split, but I taught her to push things further. As she said, 'My idea of the greatest way to learn about sex is to explore. There are many more things to do than have intercourse. And they're so much more sensual and fun, so nasty and so powerful.'

Despite all our exploring and adventurous sex, we both always believed that one of the most sexual and sensual pastimes was kissing. Kim would say, 'A mouth is so attractive if it's clean and wonderful. Very few people in the world really know how to kiss and I'm not sure there are many people who really like it. That's the most important thing. You have to think it's as good as what's coming later. I like to be kissed with caution. And passion. Kissing is almost more fun than anything else. It's the sexiest part of the whole thing. It's where you can pay the most attention. It's also the chanciest thing you can do. It takes guts to kiss somebody and to be a good kisser.'

That summed up Kim precisely. Kim with her pouting lips was very oral, especially in our earlier days together. So it was funny that in *The Man Who Loved Women*, Kim was playing a woman who was orally active at every possible opportunity and took such pleasure in performing blow jobs anywhere, anytime and appeared to be so good at it.

One sign of Kim's growing stature by the time we flew to Houston — in Burt Reynolds' private jet — to make *The Man Who Loved Women*, was that we had acquired a bodyguard! Actually, he was more of a friend, a tennis pro called Pat Lynch whom I'd known for years. We met because I wanted to take up tennis again, but I knew Kim would hate being left at home if it was my idea to go off by myself to play. I suggested that she take tennis lessons, because she liked to keep fit. She agreed, and I booked her a lesson at a tennis centre near our house. She had one lesson, which she didn't enjoy much, but she said, 'Why don't you have lessons instead?' That was great. I went along and the teacher was Pat. He immediately knew I didn't need lessons and we just played — and became friends. Kim took to him and we all became very close and, once the movie was over and we were back home in California, we used to go out to dinner with him a lot. It was a help to know there was somebody else there if anyone tried to crowd Kim or get offensive; I could look after her knowing he'd deal with the situation. We were lucky enough not to be bothered too much by pushy fans, but having Pat around made life more relaxing for both Kim and me. He's a big guy and was a safety net for us in a way.

There were one or two instances when we'd be in a crowd and somebody would reach out to her, then one of us would grab their hand and say, 'Don't touch.' If there was a big crush around us, Kim would get a bit panicky and we'd stand between her and other people. It wasn't that she didn't appreciate fans, but she was naturally nervous in crowds and, besides, this was after the John Lennon shooting and everybody in the public eye was only too well aware that there are crazy people out there. Although she was not interested in having lessons, Kim could play tennis, thanks to her brother Mick. We sometimes played with Dudley Moore's old girlfriend Susan Anton, whom I'd made up on the film *Golden Girl*, and her husband, Jack Stein.

The shoot in Houston didn't take very long, because Kim's role wasn't that big — although she got the best reviews when it was released. Making the film itself was a breeze, because both Blake and Burt were easy to work with and fond of Kim, but there were a few bizarre and scary moments.

One day we were driving through Houston and saw a crowd standing outside a high-rise building, looking upwards. There was a man way up high on a ledge. Suddenly, he leapt off the building. We were all horrified, convinced we were watching a suicide. Then, when he was halfway down to earth, a parachute opened and he fluttered down to the ground. He was unhurt, but was arrested as soon as he landed. Kim was very shaken by that, because she really thought he was going to die.

On another occasion, we were shooting on a ranch outside the city. Southeast Texas is flat tornado country and we had to wrap early for the day and leave because there was a weather warning. Kim had seen what tornadoes could do, because Georgia was also prone to them. I hadn't a clue what to expect, because in Southern California you worry about fires and floods and earthquakes, not twisters. As we drove along the freeway heading back into town, high winds and rain started kicking in. The visibility was bad and the wind was pushing the car all over the road. Thank goodness for Burt. He had his own big, private customised bus which he always took on location with him instead of a regular trailer. So I was able to tuck our car in behind him so he could protect us from the worst of the weather. A few days later, there was another tornado, this time with a water spout as well.

While Kim was making *The Man Who Loved Women*, I noticed a funny-looking spot on my lip, where the colour was changing, and thought I'd better get it checked out by a skin specialist. I'd heard about a great dermatologist called Dr Laurence David back in Hermosa Beach, California, so when we got home I went to see him. He took one look at me and said it was cancerous and that I could eventually die if it wasn't removed. He'd just developed an experimental laser and tried it out on me. He even made an educational film of the treatment on my lip, though I've never watched it. It was bad enough smelling my own flesh burning. He warned me about the dangers of the sun, though it was a bit late for a blond Californian kid who'd spent half his life on the beach. He also checked Kim over, and instantly ordered her to make an appointment for a biopsy on her lip as well. She had two laser treatments and Dr David warned her that she would always be at risk, because she was so fair and she'd been burned as a kid.

The biopsy was agony for her. She said, 'I've had the worst menstrual cramps where my back went out but this, in my life, I'm talking about just so much pain.' But she liked him and trusted Dr David, and later helped raise money for his favourite cause, which was providing free medical care for children whose parents couldn't afford to pay. We were both on the board of his charity, the National Hemangioma Foundation, and years later Kim persuaded the makers of her film *Nadine* to hold the première as a fund-raiser.

I'd always insisted that she stay out of the sun as much as possible, because I knew what the sun could do to skin from a beauty and make-up point of view. I told her, 'Women should never go out in the sun anyway, and you're so fair skinned that makes it worse. If women lived their lives in a cave it would do them good.'

I made her sit in the shade when it was not absolutely necessary to be in the sunlight for a movie scene. And although years later — when she was making *The Marrying Man* with second husband Alec Baldwin in the California desert in 1990 — she was ridiculed for hiring a guy to hold a sunshade over her head between takes, I was the one who told her to use an umbrella in the first place. She took notice of me and wore big hats and dark glasses around the pool at home. But some damage had already been done. Near her home in Georgia there were lakes, and as a high school kid she and her friends used to go there in the summer to swim and sunbathe. People who don't have the ocean have to make do with lakes, which I'd hate — dirty old water. Anyway, Kim got so badly burned on her chest that it caused permanent scarring. She had these little spots like freckles all over her chest.

She had another little scar, too, on her leg, from a time when she was a teenager and went for a ride on the back of her brother Skip's motorcycle — something she wasn't supposed to do. She burned her left leg on the manifold and didn't dare tell her mother how it happened. And she got yet another scar making *9½ Weeks*.

With *The Man Who Loved Women*, for once in Kim's life she had actually made a film that came out when it was supposed to, less than five months after it was finished. It was released only two months after *Never Say Never Again* finally hit the screen. The critics generally hated it, but loved Kim. *Daily Variety* said the film would have been better if Blake had dropped the other women and let the whole film hinge on Burt's relationship with Kim. The paper wrote, 'Had not director Blake Edwards been fooling around with an "American extension" of Francois Truffaut's 1977 film of the same title, there probably was a better picture contained here in Reynolds' one really amusing sojourn into a bemused, adulterous affair with Kim Basinger. She's great as Houston millionaire Barry Corbin's kinky wife, given to stopwatch dalliances in dangerous places.'

Kevin Thomas, writing in the *Los Angeles Times*, said, 'Most notable among them (the women) is Kim Basinger, wife of a stereotypical Texas tycoon, as aggressive as she is rich. As in *Never Say Never Again*, Basinger projects class and intelligence along with sex appeal.' And the now defunct *Hollywood Dramalogue* wrote, 'Kim Basinger, a rootin' tootin' Houston oil woman with a libido to match her husband's millions, is an absolute hoot and a holler in the part.'

The Man Who Loved Women had established Kim as a truly talented actress in the minds of the critics. In my mind, watching her performance on screen just confirmed what I already knew because of our intimate personal life — Kim Basinger was *The Woman Who Loved Sex*.

Chapter 9

Kim was certainly on a roll in 1983. After starring opposite superstars Sean Connery and Burt Reynolds, her next film had her seducing one of the biggest heart-throbs in cinema history — Robert Redford. In *The Natural*, she played villainous Memo Paris, an evil angel bent on destroying Robert's character of Roy Hobbs, a mysterious, middle-aged baseball player who had appeared from nowhere but was the greatest player the game had ever seen. Once again Kim's new, short hairstyle caused consternation when she arrived to start work, just as it had when she went to do reshoots on *Never Say Never Again*. That problem was soon solved thanks to a wig specially made for her by famous wig maker Ziegfried H Geike. Zigi, as he was known to everyone in the entertainment business, was one of the top two wig makers in Los Angeles and he painstakingly solved the problem, sewing each strand of hair in to Kim's new wig by hand. It was a hell of a job.

Despite Sean Connery recommending her for the role in *The Natural*, she did not walk into it. They interviewed a lot of actresses and Kim read for it twice. She flew from London, at the end of the re-shoots for Never, straight to New York for two days of readings with Redford. However, director Barry Levinson decided she wasn't right for the role. One problem was that they were dubious about having three blonds in leading roles — Kim, Robert and Glenn Close, who played the 'good' girl in the life of Robert's character and the mother of a son he did not know he had fathered. But, suddenly, Barry changed his mind and Kim was in. Production had already been under way for two weeks when she was cast. It was exciting for Kim to be working with Robert, who had not made a film since he won his Oscar for directing *Ordinary People* three years earlier and had not appeared on screen since *Brubaker* in 1980.

Robert also missed some of the early shooting. *The Natural* got under way on 1 August, but on 20 August he had to fly to Colorado to comfort his daughter, Shauna, who was then 22, after her fiancé and college classmate, Sid Wells, was brutally gunned down. Police arrested his roommate, but had to let him go because of lack of evidence.

I had to leave for a while, too. Our housekeeper, Doris, took a holiday and I had to go home to take care of the dogs. A few days later, Doris called me, drunk, from her home in New York. Her drinking was to be a recurring problem until eventually we had to fire her.

For the best part of three months, we lived in Buffalo, New York, on the shore of Lake Erie. *The Natural* was a period piece that told a story which stretched over a 16-year period, from 1939 to the early 1950s. It was actually set in New York City, with a fictional team called the New York Knights, but Buffalo was the perfect location. It had an old baseball stadium, built in the 1930s, officially called War Memorial Stadium but always known as The Old Rockpile, where the Buffalo Bisons had played. Assistant producer Patrick Markey and Barry were said to have scoured the country to find it, and to have been delighted at the discovery that Buffalo also had a lot of unmodernised buildings with period architecture which they could use in the movie.

The story that did the rounds was that Markey had been told the stadium had been torn down a while ago, and only discovered it was still there right before production was due to start. But oddly enough, the last film to have been shot in Buffalo was *Best Friends*, in 1982, which starred Kim's last leading man, Burt Reynolds, and was based on the true life story of Barry, her current director, and his screenwriter wife Valerie Curtin. *Best Friends* was actually written by Barry and Valerie, so I was a bit suspicious of the tale of how Buffalo was found!

Kim and I set up house in a hotel suite, and I went through the routine of stocking the fridge with her essential Evian water and making sure she had a video machine for her exercise routines. By this time, I was acting as her manager, protecting her from the outside world. I also ended up doing Kim's make-up when the original make-up guy had to leave after shooting had started, but I didn't get paid or have my name in the credits. It was something I was happy to do for Kim, especially as *The Natural* needed that period look and I knew I had the skills to get the make-up absolutely right for her character and replicate the work done by the previous make-up artist.

We socialised with Robert Redford — whom Kim called 'Double R' — and we all had a great dinner one evening.

We went out to an Italian restaurant called Roseland, and Robert was worried about causing a stir when people recognised him. 'I don't want people to see me,' he said. 'I'll sit with my back to the room.' Robert insisted that, for security reasons, we enter the restaurant through the back door and go into the dining room from the kitchen, so that we wouldn't be noticed. But once we were all seated, we realised he was actually facing a huge mirror, and had the front door behind him, so whenever anybody came in, they could easily see he was there. I don't know if he did it on purpose or not, but he knew the restaurant well so he must have known where the mirror was situated. The other restaurant where we hung out was Oliver's, where we became friends with the owner, Henry Gorino, and his wife.

The Natural was based on author Bernard Malamud's first novel, published in 1952. He got the idea in part from the real-life shooting of a 1940s baseball star called Eddie Waitkus, who was shot with a .22 rifle in a hotel bedroom by a demented woman fan. Waitkus recovered from his injury and went on to play in all 154 games of the 1950 season and won the Comeback of the Year award. Malamud's tale was altered considerably to add a love story and play up the politics and intrigue of baseball, but at the end of the day, in America at least, it was still perceived to be a film about baseball and failed to attract the wide audience the movie makers had hoped for and expected because of Robert's popularity.

Many of the scenes were shot in the War Memorial Stadium and the events were supposed to unfold as games were going on. It would have cost an absolute fortune to employ all the extras who would have been needed to make the stadium appear full of baseball fans, so Barry's team came up with a very novel way of solving the problem. If anyone were to take a close look at those cheering fans in the background, they would notice something very unnatural about the spectators. Instead of hiring thousands of extras for most of the ballpark scenes, the producers employed C Taylor Kew, the president of a local packaging firm in Buffalo, to create more than 5,000 life-sized, cardboard cut-out figures. These were placed in the stands with about 150 actors to animate the scenes. The cut-outs cost $60,000 and saved a fortune — even on the beers and hot dogs with mustard the extras would have expected. It worked pretty well, but being so frugal did backfire the one night Barry wanted to fill the stadium with real extras.

Despite such cost-watching methods, the film went over budget and ran behind schedule because Barry became ill for a few days. Production was also severely hindered by poor weather conditions in upstate New York as shooting dragged on into the autumn. It was bitterly cold. The producers wanted to fill the stadium with live extras for the final night of shooting — but they did not want to pay them. They put the word out on the local WGR radio station that anyone who wanted to appear in a movie should show up at The Old Rockpile and that there would be loads of prizes and personal appearances by popular local disc jockeys during breaks in filming. TriStar had hoped to attract about 20,000 people but most of the locals were so offended by the company's meanness earlier in the shoot that only 1,800 showed up. It was the fledgeling film company's first movie and, unfortunately, shooting ended on a sour note thanks to the poor turnout.

Robert could actually hit a ball quite well. He had played baseball at Van Nuys High School, in the Los Angeles suburbs. A classmate on the same team, Don Drysdale, who went on to pitch professionally and is in the American Baseball Hall of Fame, recalled, 'He was a pretty good ball player.' Robert and some minor-league professional players, who had been employed to play team members in the movie, would warm up in The Old Rockpile by having batting practice and playing a bit before filming. So I joined in and played baseball with him and we had a lot of fun.

The film also did some shooting back in California and Kim continued to see Robert socially. He had a house on Old Malibu Road, near the beach, and she went there to have dinner with him. He was an important man in the movie industry, not someone to ignore if he takes an interest in you. She always came home by about nine or ten at night, but I couldn't help wondering if there was more to it. I thought he was a little enamoured with her. I never knew and I never confronted her, but I couldn't help remembering that she had talked about 'trying out' her leading men in the past and she was certainly very taken by him.

'He's a golden, golden man,' she gushed. 'I love every inch of that man, everything about him. He is marvellous, considerate, a complete professional, more quiet and subdued than Sean or Burt.' Anyway, if she was doing it with Robert that was cool by me, because she was certainly hot for me when she came home.

Some nightclub scenes were shot on the old luxury liner *The Queen Mary*, which is permanently moored in Long Beach, California, as a hotel. Rather than drive to the location every day, they gave us a state room and we stayed on board.

When it was released in May 1984, Kim and Robert went to the première, along with her old friend and booker from her modelling days, Sue Charney. Kim, who never liked looking at herself on the screen, did not enjoy the première, but she said it was a great thrill to see her name on the awning of the Ziegfeld Theatre, as she had predicted to her mother years earlier. Sadly, *The Natural* was a disappointment at the box office, despite having a great cast that also included Robert Duvall, Wilford Brimley, Richard Farnsworth and Barbara Hershey. There were so many Oscar winners and nominees in the cast that it should have found a much bigger audience. Robert had won for directing *Ordinary People* and had been nominated as best actor for The Sting; Duvall had been nominated three times in addition to winning the Best Actor award for his performance in *Tender Mercies*; Close had been nominated twice at that time, and Farnsworth once.

With so many highly-acclaimed acting talents in the film, it was great for Kim that once again she was singled out for praise by the critics. Cosmopolitan said, 'Kim Basinger is memorably hissable as a platinum blonde scheming to bench our hero by luring him into dangerously erotic dugouts.' *Los Angeles Herald-Examiner* film critic Peter Rainer wrote, 'Memo, the satanic temptress who represents the false grail pursuit, is a *film noir* vamp out of *Double Indemnity*.' And Andrew Kopkind wrote in *The Nation*, 'She's a natural too; at seduction, betrayal and misfortune.'

Although *The Natural* was not the smash the producers had hoped for, it did get some recognition for its actors. Glenn Close was nominated for a Best Supporting Actress Academy Award for her performance and Kim was also nominated for a Best Supporting Actress Golden Globe by the prestigious Hollywood Foreign Press Association.

Because of Kim's nomination, we made one of our very rare appearances at a Hollywood awards ceremony, the 1985 Golden Globes presentation. Usually, Kim shunned such occasions. She was very shy, had fought agoraphobia, and hated mixing with the Hollywood in-crowd. In retrospect, I also think she'd didn't like being seen with me at such occasions because I wasn't a famous actor or movie mogul. At the night-time party at the Beverly Hilton

Hotel, it seemed to me that all of Hollywood was there. The Golden Globes are always a much more relaxed event than the Oscars, but they carry a tremendous amount of power. Kim didn't win — she lost the coveted statuette to Dame Peggy Ashcroft in *A Passage to India*, who later beat Glenn for the Oscar — but it was an entertaining evening in its own way.

We sat at a table with James Woods, former Monty Python star-turned-director Terry Gilliam and *Rich Man, Poor Man* actress Kay Lenz. At another table was Robert Greenwald, who had directed Kim in her television series, Dog and Cat. The two had had an affair, but he had always told Kim she'd end up with a tall, blond all-American guy, not a short, dark chap like him. She introduced me to him and he immediately laughed, 'I told you so, Kim.' He was with a young blonde taller than him and he was almost saying to Kim, 'Look what I've got,' and it was as if she was responding, 'No, look what I've got.'

When we left the ceremony and were waiting for the limousine to pick us up, we were standing next to Brooke Shields and her mother, Teri, who was her manager in those days. Kim and Brooke had never met, but Brooke said, 'Oh, Kim, I think you're great, I love your work.' And Kim replied, 'Brooke, I love you, too.' It was a very Hollywood moment!

If the critics thought Kim's role opposite Robert Redford came naturally, her next part was widely regarded as totally warped. In *9½ Weeks*, one of the most controversial films of the decade, Kim played Elizabeth, a Manhattan art gallery director who willingly became the depraved sex slave of Mickey Rourke's manipulative money-man, John. It put a lot of strain on Kim because it was a difficult shoot in every way. But at least I never had the same worries about Mickey, who had starred in *Diner*, Barry Levinson's first film as a director, that I did about Robert; whatever Kim did with him on screen, she didn't get on with Mickey much so there was no chance of her cheating on me with him.

The negative attitude began when she first went to talk to British film director Adrian Lyne and Mickey about the role. The part was originally intended for Jacqueline Bisset and a number of other actresses, including Kathleen Turner, Isabella Rossellini and Teri Garr, were also being considered. We had read the script and we both hated it but for some uncanny reason we had both agreed that it was a film that would establish Kim in the minds of moviegoers and she should do it.

I remember the script arrived at our house around 6.30 in the evening. Kim always read the scripts first and then gave them to me to read. Then she'd ask me my opinion. It was gone 10 o'clock and Kim was sitting next to me on the side of our bed as I turned over the last page and sighed.

'Isn't it *horrible*?' she said.

I agreed, but added, 'I don't see how you can turn it down.'

'I know,' she replied. 'There's just something about it ... I hate it, but I know I've got to do it.' Kim even phoned her little sister, Ashley, to giggle about it.

Kim's agent persuaded her to meet Adrian and he eventually talked her into meeting Mickey. At that meeting she was asked to tape a scene as an audition. The scene was one of the hardest in the whole film, in which she was forced to act out a fantasy, pretending to be a prostitute, down on all fours picking up dollar bills in her teeth to turn Mickey on. The audition was held at a house where Adrian was staying, on Mulholland Drive, not far from where we lived. I drove her to the audition and waited outside in the car for her. She was gone for about an hour and was terribly upset when she came back to the car and said she'd had a rough time. She didn't want to talk about it at first and she was determined not to do the movie if she was offered the part.

'This was one of the worst days of my life,' she told me eventually. 'It wasn't a scene, but an experience. I was crawling around on the floor picking up money. Adrian said, "Do you have stockings on? Do you mind taking them off?" I got very defensive and said, "Fuck you, man, I'm not taking off anything. I don't go to test for a part and take off my stockings and roll around on the floor with people ... what the fuck is this?"' From her first introduction to this film she had found the whole thing emotionally draining and, even though it was acting, she didn't think she could live through a whole movie at that sort of passionate intensity. 'I just came apart, emotionally,' she wept. 'I cried and cried.'

But it turned out that Adrian and Mickey were thrilled by the way she had reacted, because that's how her character, Elizabeth, would have behaved. There are so many myths about *9½ Weeks* and everyone thinks Elizabeth is a passive woman who submits docilely to Mickey's character John. In fact, she is embracing her new sexual power and freedom. They were so delighted by Kim's test that they sent a bouquet of 24 red roses. Kim was not impressed by the roses, however. She phoned her agent and told him she absolutely refused to have anything to do with the film. But we heard that Adrian was going ahead with the rest of the casting on the assumption that she'd change her mind. For three or four weeks she couldn't sleep at night, waking up in terror at the thought of making the film and how she would react to it.

Eventually, it almost seemed like fate. She had lunch with Adrian, very reluctantly. He said, 'You know you have to do this movie, don't you?' She replied, 'I guess I am doing it.' I wasn't really surprised. Kim was frightened of how far she would be able to go on screen, how much of herself she would reveal and how far she would throw herself into the role, but she also saw it as a tremendous challenge and one that would expand her acting range. This wasn't a goofy comedy where the sex was played for laughs, and Mickey Rourke was no good ol' boy like Burt. I knew she had to do it and I knew she would do it well. And it meant her biggest payday yet, $400,000.

Before the movie started, we spent six weeks in New York, and at first Adrian was a sweetheart. Kim chose her clothes with him and a wardrobe girl down in Greenwich Village — lots of overcoats and men's suits — and did a lot of rehearsing, going through the whole story, even though she hated to rehearse.

Although we did not realise it at the time, there was already trouble brewing behind the scenes and 9½ Weeks almost never got made. The subject matter was always controversial, and Adrian spent two months in and out of meetings with executives at TriStar, the company making the film. They wanted him to soften up the story and finally, three days before shooting was due to begin, they abruptly backed out after a final row. Co-producer Antony Rufus Isaacs went to Producers' Sales Organisation, which was involved in selling the film in advance to overseas territories, and they agreed to back it. Later, after it was made, MGM/UA distributed it in the United States.

This was not the only film Adrian was to have problems getting released. More than a decade later he filmed a controversial remake of Vladimir Nabokov's novel Lolita, the story of an older man's sexual obsession with a 14-year-old girl, starring Jeremy Irons and newcomer Dominique Swain. The film, which cost $58 million to make, was finished in 1996 but was not released until two years later because distributors were worried about explicit sex scenes involving a young girl. The original Lolita, directed by Stanley Kubrick, was released in 1962 and starred James Mason and Sue Lyon.

Kim hated working with Mickey right from the start. He was nothing but trouble for her. After her test for the part, Adrian told the two of them he didn't want them to socialise at all. He wanted the tension on screen to carry on in real life, because he was afraid that if they became friendly it would affect the intensity of the film. The first time Kim laid eyes on Mickey after that meeting at the house on Mulholland Drive was in front of the cameras, when the two characters met in a Chinese market in New York. A lot of the film was shot in sequence, which is unusual for movies. It was very different from *The Natural*, where Barry Levinson often shot different elements of a single scene weeks apart.

Adrian had no need to worry about them becoming friends. Kim complained that kissing Mickey was like kissing an ashtray, and that was torture for her. She doesn't smoke and she's incredibly particular about hygiene. She used to walk round the house with a toothbrush in her mouth all the time, and used hydrogen peroxide to keep her teeth sparkling white. She knew her beauty was important for her career, but she wasn't just being vain; she was also concerned about good health. Mickey seemed to take the same instinctive dislike to her, and it got so bad that they refused to get in a lift together. To be fair to Mickey, he was fine around me, although I didn't have much to do with him. He once asked me, 'Don't you mind your wife doing a movie like this?' I told him that, as far as I was concerned, it was just work, that's what Kim did for a living. I didn't add that after she'd finished her hours on the set with him, pretending to have sex, she came back to me for the real thing, more often than not.

To be honest, I found the whole thing pretty exciting. Kim said later, when she was doing promotional work to push the movie, that making it had put pressure on our marriage and, indeed, on the relationships of lots of people involved. She claimed, 'My husband and I had a bad time during this movie. I think the strains of it — the realisation of the material being done — would have hurt any partner. I totally emotionally neglected him for a whole year. I just didn't have anything left to give and you can't do that in a relationship. If I had been Ron, I'd have left me. And he didn't. He supports me more than anyone I've known.'

I always supported Kim in everything she did and, as far as I was concerned, those sex scenes were not a problem for me. I never felt that Kim's character in the movie drove a wedge between us off the set. If anything, I thought it brought us closer together. I believed our relationship was still pretty strong in those days. Making the film exhausted and upset Kim, but not enough to turn her off sex with me.

What did bother me was that she had to go through so many trials and tribulations with Mickey, and once shooting got underway, Adrian was hardly easier. He told Kim he didn't want me on the set because he was afraid if she was naked and doing nasty scenes, I'd be jealous. She told him, 'Don't worry, Ron won't be anywhere near the set. I wouldn't want him there and, more importantly, he doesn't want to be.' Before long, she was having to fight both of them. If they'd had their way, it would have ended up being a triple X rating with the censors, and she wanted to make a movie that would be commercially successful.

When they were getting ready to film the scene where Kim is alone in the art gallery and masturbates, he said, 'Come on, Kim, let's make this real private. I'll clear everybody out of here and bring the camera in and you go ahead and do it and it will just be the two of us.' She said, 'No way. Get out of here. This is called *acting*, remember. That's what I'm here for — let's get on with it.'

Once, Kim and Mickey did get together off set, when they were doing some research. They went into a sleazy sex club and met a couple who were doing live sex on the stage, to ask them what it felt like knowing people were paying to watch them. Kim and Mickey even took this couple to dinner so they could get more intimate details about what it was like. I wanted to go with them, but Kim wouldn't let me. What she didn't know was that, often when she was working at night, which was a lot of the time, I used to wander down to 10th Avenue, where all the hookers and pimps hang out. I talked to whores but never paid them.

I also met a very different kind of prostitute one night, when I was leaving the hotel in the early hours of the morning. There was a gorgeous-looking, well-dressed woman leaving at the same time. I asked her where she was going at that time of the morning. She said, 'Nowhere.' I laughed and said, 'Come on, you've been working, haven't you?' and she laughed, too. She was one of the high-class hookers working for the so-called Mayflower Madam, Sydney Biddle Barrows, who ran the Cachet Escort Agency that was later exposed as a prostitution ring for the rich and famous.

Although Kim, as Elizabeth, was scared by being tied up, it was something she enjoyed from time to time as part of our sex play. I even had a pair of toy handcuffs that we used once, but they broke, so after that we used a scarf, as Mickey did in the movie. I preferred using a scarf anyway, because it used to come loose during our love-making and then Kim would hang on, so I knew she was enjoying it and was a willing partner.

After the film was over, she wore a miniature pair of handcuffs on a bracelet, as a lucky charm. I bought them for her as a memento. This little guy used to come on the set sometimes selling jewellery to the cast and crew. He had a captive audience, since making a movie involves such crazy hours that people don't have time for things like shopping. On one of the rare occasions I went to the set, I got talking to the jeweller and he showed me this trinket. I thought it was pretty neat so I bought it for her as a kind of joke.

Kim also enjoyed being spanked — though not hard — to add extra variety to our sex life. But even though I think we were pretty adventurous in bed and out of it, it was nothing like as extreme and emotionally exhausting as *9½ Weeks*. Sometimes she would lie awake at night worrying about a big scene she was going to have to shoot and then, when it was over, she'd come home and laugh, almost hysterically. She knew everything she was going through was making her stronger as an actress.

The film was shot all over New York, including Chinatown, Little Italy, the funfair at Coney Island, Bloomingdale's department store and the landmark Chelsea and Algonquin Hotels. I hardly went to the set at all. Kim had brought my sister, Sherry Snyder, along to act as her assistant and give her some female moral support against the onslaughts of Mickey and Adrian, so she went with her. But I joined them at lunchtime, in Kim's trailer or the apartment where most of the movie was filmed. Kim would switch off from the trials of filming and lose herself in her favourite television soap opera, *Loving*, and I brought deli sandwiches in for the three of us. New York is the greatest place on earth for deli restaurants.

I also used to pick her up from the set at night, however late it was. Kim's 'treat' was to go out for dinner, relax, talk and unwind. It was my job to make sure we had somewhere to go, even if it was 2.00am. We had two favourite Italian restaurants in mid-town. I'd call up Orsini's, who got to know us really well because we'd eat there three times a week. The owner would keep the chef on even though they were closed and he'd cook for us specially, allowing us to sit and eat into the early hours. Another place we used to go was Patsy's, which wasn't quite so formal but made great home-cooked, family-style Italian food. Sylvester Stallone was there all the time and he'd have his bodyguards hanging out in the kitchen, on the stairs and by the entrances. Patsy's had an upstairs where they used to seat all the celebrities. We never bothered with bodyguards. I was the bodyguard except for when Pat Lynch was around. However, I was aware how dangerous New York could be, so I started going around with a large knife tucked down the back of my trousers and hidden by my jacket.

One night, I'd taken my jacket off and the waiter came over very discreetly, tapped me on the shoulder and said, 'I think you've forgotten what's behind you, Ron.' He was very humble and polite. Suddenly I realised that my knife was on display for everyone to see, so I quickly put my jacket back on.

We also ate at Tre Scalini and Gian Marino. When Kim and I were first together, we ate a lot of Mexican food, but working in Buffalo and New York gave her such a taste for Italian food that years later, after we split she bought an Italian restaurant, Carmine's, in West Los Angeles, in partnership with *Taxi* star Tony Danza.

Kim didn't have many girlfriends, so I thought it was good for her to have some female companionship. She and Sherry also got together when she wasn't working. They used to go out together to the theatre. I arranged the tickets and the limo and met them afterwards for dinner. It was better for Kim's image if she did not appear in public clearly attached to a man, even though she happily talked about me in interviews. We were never a terribly public couple, especially in the United States. We were each other's best friends as well as lovers, and liked our own company. I had such a low profile that after Rolling Stone Ron Wood came on to the set one day — he was an old friend of Adrian's and he had a cameo in the film — *Playboy* magazine wrote, 'Ron Wood's *flame*, actress Kim Basinger, has found a small part for Woodie in *9½ Weeks*. Says Ron of acting, "It's just too much hard work. They keep making us do it over and over again. I need an easier life."'

That was hilarious. His part was so tiny he was only on screen for about a second. It was hardly a stretch. He was in a scene which was supposed to be a party and all he had to do was make small talk with the beautiful fashion model-types there. And as for him being Kim's *flame*, she laughed at him. She thought he was just this skinny little English person and she made fun of him to me. Besides, in those days we were not going out to dinner until nearly midnight at the earliest and then home to bed and she was working all day. There was no spare time for them to have an affair. They couldn't even have had a fling at lunchtime because I always turned up with the sandwiches.

Kim has talked about us having problems during the making of *9½ Weeks*, but in fact we had a lot of fun. On Sundays we used to take a limo and drive to upstate New York. Kim had the idea of moving there. Two hours out of New York and you're in beautiful countryside. We looked at houses and farms. We made a day of it, with a big picnic basket from the hotel or one of the delis we liked, and threw that in the back of the car with a bottle of Pouilly Fuissé.

We did actually find a farm that Kim loved. It was very old by American standards, more than 200 years, and had 18 acres and a stream. She was very keen on the idea and had plans for more animals, but I was horrified. I'm a Southern California boy through and through. I like year-round sunshine, living near the ocean and going to the beach, and I couldn't take the weather up there. So I said, 'Do you really want to do this? Think about it. You don't like it at home when the housekeeper gets in the way, but you know we have to have her because of the dogs. Do you think we could run this place without 17 or 18 people working here, running around and getting in your way. Do you think you'd like that?'

She thought for a moment and said, 'You're right, I guess I don't.'

We also looked at one of those Manhattan penthouses, but they wanted a million bucks for a tiny apartment. Even if it had been practical we couldn't have afforded it, thank goodness.

While there was a lot of faking in the film, it was actually physically hard on Kim. In the famous scene where Mickey feeds her, blindfolded, in front of the fridge, she really didn't know what he was going to put in her mouth. That scene, and the one where he rubs ice on her nipple and cold water trickles into her tummy button, have been imitated scores of times since then, so people don't think twice about them now. But this was the first time they had been done and they were very shocking and very erotic. In another scene, where they had sex in an alleyway under the railway after she dressed up as a man and they were chased by gay-bashers, Mickey was so rough she was left with a scar. She was very upset after that scene. Mickey ripped her shirt off, and she wasn't expecting it; it wasn't in the script.

'Why did he have to do that?' she complained afterwards, when she was back in her trailer. 'You know it was just to get my tits out. It was horrid being pushed up against the brick wall. There were rusty things going into my back, tearing my clothes.'

She cut her arm during that scene and still has the mark. In another scene, when John persuaded Elizabeth into a suicide pact and made her swallow pills which she thought were lethal but which are really just sugar, Kim looked too lovely for Adrian's liking. He wanted her to look like a woman in a state of total devastation. He took Mickey to one side and told him he had to break her down. Mickey went back and grabbed her arm, tightly, and wouldn't let go. Kim shouted at him and hit him — and he slapped her hard across the face. She began to cry hysterically and Adrian coolly said, 'Action.' He got the reaction and the scene he wanted.

There wasn't much love lost between Kim and Adrian almost from the start of filming. She felt that he and Mickey were working closely together. I kept a diary during the film and it is scrawled with comments like, 'Rourke asshole again', 'Mickey Rourke always a buttface', 'Kim slaps Adrian at work. Hates him. Cried twice', and 'Mickey prick.' She particularly hated some of the things Adrian said about her acting, because she thought he was putting her down when she had thrown herself body and soul into the part. She was so relieved when the main shoot was finally over that she did not even want to go to the wrap party.

'Kim is a bit like a child,' Adrian said. 'She's an innocent. She was that woman for 10 weeks. She didn't act her. In order for her to be angry, I would rage at her and she would rage back at me. There was a lot of yelling, with her calling me a motherfucker and vice-versa. Mickey also had to do it. He frightened her. And that was done purposely. The chemistry between Kim and Mickey was extraordinary. At the audition, I saw hostility and sexual energy between them. There was a lot of tension. A lot of the turbulence on screen was real. Without this kind of emotional engineering from the director, she would not have been able to fully realise the part. She's not an intellectual. She doesn't read books. She doesn't actually act — she reacts.'

Kim was furious at that assessment of her talents. But with all the controversy swirling about 9½ Weeks, and the seemingly interminable delays while it was re-cut and re-edited to avoid an X-rating in the United States, she was too much of a pro to criticise her director or her co-star.

When asked about Adrian's comments, she said pointedly, 'I don't identify with that description of me at all. To tell the truth, I deliberately didn't allow myself to see all the games being played to get the picture made. I thought that, for the character, I had to keep myself beaten down. If I ever stopped and questioned, if I no longer believed in Adrian, I would have been a mess.'

She even kept her cool talking about her relationship with Mickey during the shoot. 'We had no problem,' she insisted. 'I really didn't ever get to meet him, really get to know him.'

But in more unguarded moments, she admitted how difficult

Kim relaxes in her trailer between takes on *Blind Date*.

Top left and right: Kim and I at our wedding at the Chapel in the Canyon. We took Polaroid pictures of each other, holding the bridal 'bouquet' which was just one flower from our own garden.

Bottom: Kim skinny-dipping in the pool at our Woodland Hills home. Kim often swam 100 laps at a time to keep in shape.

Top left: Kim joined me in Hawaii for a romantic break while I was working on the movie *Buddy, Buddy* with Jack Lemmon and Walter Matthau in 1981. We were so in love. One day she took a stroll on the beach and wrote 'I love Ron' in sand on a log.

Top right: The first picture I ever took of Kim at her house, before we were married. We both liked it so much I had it blown up and put on the wall of my office at home.

Bottom: Kim relaxes in the nude in our bedroom in Woodland Hills. One of her favourite outfits was a smile, socks and clogs.

Chilling out in a pith helmet.

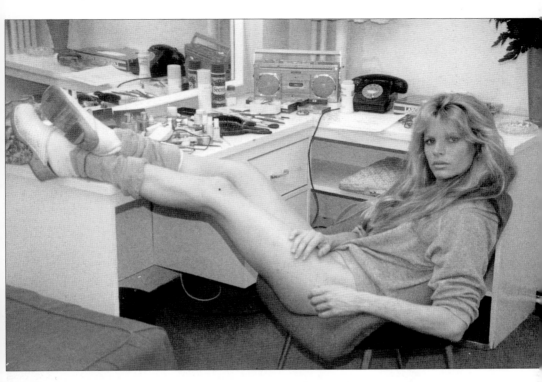

Top: Kim stretches out at the make-up mirror during a lunchtime break making *Never Say Never Again* at Elstree Studios, in 1982.

Bottom: Freezing after an ice-cold dip during filming of *Mother Lode* with Charlton Heston and Nick Mancuso near Whistler Mountain, Canada in 1981. Kim and Nick were 'escaping' from their crashed plane.

Top: Kim and I during happier times – on location for *9½ Weeks*.

Bottom: Filming a *No Mercy* action sequence with Richard Gere in the wilds of North Carolina. The first cracks were beginning to appear in our marriage.

Make-up man David Forrest, me, my sister Sherrill and Kim behind bars in Bourbon St Jail.

Top left: In Kim's trailer on the set of *Fool For Love* outside Santa Fe, New Mexico, in 1985. Although this was a short shoot – only seven weeks – all the filming was done at night in the freezing desert.

Top right: Kim and I cuddle up during a break from her famous *Playboy* shoot in the garden of our hotel on Kauai, Hawaii in 1981.

Bottom: Me, Kim's sister Ashley and her husband Joe partying at our Woodland Hills home in 1985, during one of their visits to see us.

A publicity shot from *9½ Weeks,* **1984.**

Top: Kim shows off the stunning beauty that made me fall for her.

Bottom: Kim and I snuggle up in a back street in France. I'm wearing our favourite jacket, which I bought in Nice in 1982. Kim wore it to the sets of her movies for years and we ended up squabbling over it during our divorce. I got it back in the end.

Top: Breakfast in Hawaii while on the *Playboy* shoot in 1981.

Bottom left: Kim lets it all hang out in a break from filming *The Natural* with Robert Redford in 1983. She is wearing a Marilyn Monroe-style platinum wig for her role as the seductive Memo Paris.

Bottom right: In Hawaii, Kim dons my official US volleyball Olympic team trial sweatshirt during the *Playboy* shoot in 1981.

Top: Kim gives the camera a sexy smile on the set of *No Mercy* in North Carolina in 1986.

Bottom left: Kim with Mickey Rourke filming *9 ½ Weeks* in New York in 1984 – an experience which left her totally drained.

Bottom right: A lighter moment for Kim and me in her dressing room on the set of *9 ½ Weeks.*

A moody portrait shot
of Kim that I took.

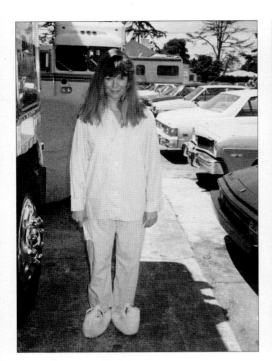

Top left: Kim outside her trailer during filming of *Blind Date* in 1986, wearing some very un-Hollywood slippers.

Top right: Kim and me with a neighbour's baby – the baby we never had.

Bottom: Kim with bodyguard Pat Lynch at Niagara Falls during a break from shooting *The Natural* in 1983.

Kim as Kitty Potter in *Prét à Porter*, **with Elsa Klench.**

Kim in her Oscar-winning role as prostitute Lynn Bracken in the smash hit movie *L.A Confidential.*

she had found the whole ordeal.

'It was the worst, the most depressing time I've ever spent in my whole life. I lived it for a full year. After that movie was over, I didn't want to see anyone I had ever seen on the set. If I ran into the guy who brought the *coffee*, I was going to kill him. And yet it was also like an exorcism.'

One long-lasting after-effect of *9½ Weeks* was Kim's identification with white slips for ever more. She did her strip scene, down to the slip, to Joe Cocker singing *You Can Leave Your Hat On*, and it was very erotic. In those days, you couldn't get away with scenes like Sharon Stone uncrossing her legs in *Basic Instinct*, so a slip like that was great because it covered her up but let you see her at the same time. For her next few movies, there was an obligatory scene in a white slip — her own white slip that she took from home, not one provided by wardrobe.

9½ Weeks followed the all-too-common pattern of Kim's films in being seriously delayed. In the end, by the time it was released, the movie she shot next, *Fool For Love*, was already in the cinemas. *9½ Weeks* looked as if it was going to get an X-rating, which would have meant no mainstream cinemas showing it in the United States, so Adrian had to cut it drastically for the American market. The scene that Kim had filmed for her audition where she crawled around on the floor picking up money with her teeth went, when a test audience hated it. In the European version, as Kim crawled over the floor Mickey lashed a belt on the floor, but did not actually touch her. The fake suicide pact scene also went in the US, as did one in which Kim held up a man in a lift at knifepoint, then sensuously kissed him. Again, American audiences found them too strong.

Kim was upset by that, after all the hard work they had all put into it. She complained, 'We all knew the film we were gonna make and we were all terrified, but we ended up making that film. Then the know-it-alls at MGM and PSO said the public wouldn't accept it. So they cut it all to pieces and made it look like a video. It's unfortunate, because I have the story at home. I have eight hours of this film.'

There was even trouble with the soundtrack. Geffen Records backed out of releasing it while it was still being edited, with the executive in charge of the project, John Kalodner, saying, 'I found the movie to be offensive to women and I just don't want to be associated with the picture. I don't care if the movie makes $100 million ... I've washed my hands of the whole thing. I think Adrian is very talented and I respect his work, but I just couldn't see having my name on this picture. Some people might find it titillating, but it made me nauseous.' Eventually, Capitol Records released the soundtrack.

When the film finally hit the cinemas, in February 1986, nearly two years after Kim started work on it, we braced ourselves for complaints from feminist and women's rights group. Much to our surprise, however, it was women who loved the movie. Women would walk up to Kim in the street and say, 'God, I loved that film. I know just what she was going through.'

The critics were less kind, though, as always, Kim came out better than the material she had to work with. *Daily Variety* wrote, '9½ *Weeks* is a steer, not the bull it wanted to be when it grew up, although there's plenty of the latter in it anyway.' But the reviewer added, 'Basinger is the film's one saving grace, as she manages to retain a certain dignity despite incessant attempts by Rourke and Lyne to despoil her.' *Box Office* wrote, 'Mickey Rourke doesn't stray too far beyond his usual crooked-smiled, whispery-voiced persona (which is especially effective in this current role), but Kim Basinger proves once again to be a serious actress with a dramatic range that equals any of her more "legitimate" peers. Unfortunately, the two have been left hanging in a story that is simply about two people who have only a marginally spectacular sex life together, hardly the basis for a feature film.'

Julie Salamon of the *Wall Street Journal* wrote, 'Kim Basinger, who plays Elizabeth, has the stuff for some crackle and pop. With her sensual, nervous mouth and slim voluptuousness, she looks like a shapely stick of TNT just waiting to explode. The problem is, Mickey Rourke is carrying the matches and he can't seem to get them lighted. So when Ms Basinger periodically writhes out of control, you get the feeling she's just ready to writhe, with or without Mr Rourke. In fact, the most erotic scene in the entire movie is autoerotic.'

And in the *Los Angeles Times*, film critic Sheila Benson wrote, 'Rourke wears only one expression, a mildly interested quizzicalness. Basinger is not only tremulous and touching, she manages a certain beautiful equilibrium, which under the circumstances is downright miraculous.'

Despite the negative reaction from mainstream America, European audiences, who saw a less censored version, loved it, and it was a smash hit both critically and commercially. Kim was invited to Europe to publicise it. She was also asked to attend the

Cannes Film Festival to promote *The Natural*, and looked set to become a bigger star in Europe than in the United States.

Kim herself was glad it was finally over. But she knew she had learned from the experience and said, 'I feel released, and feel that there isn't anything I can't go with and do as an actress.'

By this time, she was beginning to be a household name, not just known in the industry and vaguely recognised as a Bond girl. Fans would send notes to her table at dinner. My sweet, shy Kim was having to learn to build a shell around herself, to protect herself from the outside. She could no longer afford to be vulnerable and easy-going. One of the things I had always found attractive about Kim was that she was never a prima donna on the set, even though later in her career that became her reputation. Possibly the screaming fights she had on the set of *9½ Weeks*, raging at her director and co-star — even though they were egging her on — helped her develop that side of her character. I wanted her to be strong and able to stand up for herself, but always to be fair to the crew. And she always was. But I always made sure she got everything she was entitled to from the producers. I'd had 20 years in the business and I knew what stars were allowed. Years later, when I heard the bad reputation she got making *The Marrying Man*, I blamed it on Alec Baldwin, because I had never known her playing up on set. And she was never deliberately late. But if she was at war with the production team, I would have instinctively taken her side without knowing the circumstances. As far as I was concerned, she was always as professional as could be. I still believe it was her professionalism and commitment that made *9½ Weeks* the picture it became.

Chapter 10

Help me, Ron,' pleaded Kim on the telephone. 'I'm stuck here and I can't get out. I don't know what to do.'

'Where are you? What's happened?' I said, frightened by the panic in her voice.

'In the health food store,' she replied. 'I've got all this stuff in my shopping trolley but I can't leave. Everything's gone blurry and I can't breathe and I'm sweating.'

Ever since we'd been together, I had become more and more aware of how fragile Kim could be. Remarkably, for a former model-turned-actress, she had a pathological terror of appearing in public, which could appear irrational but which was certainly genuine.

'Okay,' I said, trying to project a feeling of calm and control down the line, 'I want you to leave everything you've bought — if we need it I'll go back for it later — and go to the car. Lock yourself in and drive straight home and call me when you get there.'

I was visiting a friend's house and it would have taken too long for me to go to her. It would be far quicker to get her straight home and wait for her call so I knew she was all right. I kept talking to her, giving her the same instruction over and over again. Throughout the ordeal she was suffering, I kept my voice calm so that she felt reassured and could not tell from my tone how worried I was about her.

Finally, she said, 'OK.'

Somehow, she got herself to the car and drove home at a crawl. Fortunately, the shop was only about two miles from our house, because she told me she panicked every time she saw another vehicle. We lived up the hill so even in traffic-crazy LA she would only have been confronted by a few vehicles on the twisty roads that lead up from Ventura Boulevard to Don Juan Place. When I got home she told me, 'I thought I was losing my mind. It was the worst feeling. I'd rather have died right there than lose my mind.'

Looking back on those earlier days from the knowledge we'd acquired by the end of the *9½ Weeks* shoot, it was remarkable to realise how far Kim had come. The mental and physical strain of making that film made Kim a stronger actress and a stronger person, better able to stand up for herself and her rights, and not allow herself to be pressured into things she didn't want to do. I was delighted at how far she had come since we had first met. In those days I had discovered that behind her beautiful face and body, Kim was a mass of insecurities. In front of the camera she had great presence — her motto was always that she lived between the director saying 'action' and 'cut' — but it seemed that without a director to guide her, she could not handle her life.

The first signs of this were subtle, when she asked me to collect her *per diems* and pay for all the dinners we had with the crew while we were working together on *Hard Country*, even though we had only just met. I soon realised she had no idea how to manage money, and the same held true for managing her life. Eventually, I mastered her signature and signed all her cheques for her. And in the early days I handled all her fan mail, signing glossy pictures in her trademark purple ink and adding her personal logo, a heart with a cross in it. I always went through the mail myself, though, and took out letters that looked as if they could be from potential trouble-makers or stalkers.

When we first got together and she asked me if I would give up my career for her sake when hers took off, that was partly so I could travel with her and stay with her when she was out of town. She was terrified of the dark and even kept a night light on in her own home until I moved in. She even used to check under her bed for 'monsters' before she could go to sleep. She always put on a fan in the bedroom at night, so she would not hear any noises outside. That drove me mad because I wanted to hear if anyone was breaking in. Eventually, I was able to persuade her to do without it. We also had a lot of security lights in the garden, that came on if their sensors had been activated by movement, but she was scared when they came on and she saw shadows. And with our family of wild cats living in the garden, as well as other local wildlife like squirrels, rats and opossums, there was plenty of movement to activate them. I could not understand how she could live with Chief How, the carved wooden Indian who had scared me so much the first night I spent at her house. She couldn't bear dolls or stuffed toys in her bedroom because she was afraid of them staring at her, and if she had clothes hanging in the bedroom she would wake up and imagine there was someone else in the room.

From the time I moved into the Woodland Hills house, we were always very much a stay-at-home couple. We lived well outside the Beverly Hills–Bel Air–Malibu axis where movie stars and other celebrities are supposed to make their homes, in a hilly, wooded community to the north side of the Santa Monica Mountains. Kim was happy to hang out at home with the dogs, and was never interested in the party scene or socialising with other actors once she was off the set. A few times in the early days we met her former *Dog and Cat* co-star, Lou Antonio, with whom I had also worked in the past. I quickly realised that Kim was a bit of a loner and she wanted me to more or less drop my friends. I stayed close to Ron and Linda Lang and she got to like them too, but that was about it.

In the beginning, it was hard to be cut off from my friends but I was happy to do whatever Kim wanted. Later, when we were mainly out of town for more than a year when Kim was making *Never Say Never Again*, *The Man Who Loved Women* and *The Natural*, it was easy not to let people know I was home again.

We did go out a lot to restaurants, which was great for me because I wasn't allowed to eat meat at home with Kim's knowledge. Ventura Boulevard, the main road running through the Valley, has scores of restaurants — Italian, French, Mexican, Chinese, Indian, American barbecue and burger joints — pretty much every cuisine you can think of. We had a few favourites where they let us enter through the back door after Kim started to become recognised. One of our regulars was a Mexican place right next to the health food store where Kim had been so scared, but we stopped going there after they had a rape and robbery. After that, I started carrying a gun when we went out at night.

Another favourite haunt was Barbata's, which is a steak house and bar just down the road from our house. It wasn't fancy but they knew us there so it was comfortable. It's kind of funny to think of Kim hanging out in a steak restaurant, but she could order fish or salads to make her happy. For three or four years in a row we went there for New Year's Eve rather than go to a party. One year, Kim was so tired she went to bed at 11.00pm and I saw in the new year by myself at Barbata's. When we went out with friends like Rick Provenzano or Pat Lynch, we would laugh and joke, and Kim would often laugh so much she was close to tears. Then I would turn to her and say, 'You're going to miss me when I'm gone.' She always replied, 'No I won't. You're always going to be with me.' That must have happened at least 50 times. That reinforced our slogan 'LTF...' Whenever we spoke our catchphrase out loud, we spelled it out, 'Longer than forever, dot dot dot.'

Generally, when we went out together I drove and when Kim had to go somewhere by herself she found it frightening. When we were first together and the shooting of *S.O.B.* moved from Malibu to Culver City and I had to leave her every day, she found it very difficult. She told me it was hard for her to force herself to get into the car by herself. I couldn't leave the set for too long, so I came up with a plan to get her out of the house. I suggested meeting for lunch every day, and got her to drive gradually further and further — nearer and nearer to me — until we had a regular 'date' at the Overland Cafe, just down the road from the studio. Kim was particularly terrified of the narrow canyon roads that snake south from the San Fernando Valley to the beaches at Malibu. Because of the rugged mountain terrain, when they built the roads the engineers blasted tunnels through the rock in some places. The roads leading to the tunnels are twisty, so when approaching them in the bright California sunshine they look like black holes because you can't see through to the other side. Kim could not drive herself through them because she was so frightened, and it was very frustrating. We spent nearly all our time together after we returned home from making *Mother Lode*, so I was able to take care of her and ferry her around. But when I wasn't around, she seemed to fall to pieces.

Then came the panic attack in the health food store.

When Kim came home she retreated to our bedroom, shaking. I tried to comfort her but she was so upset nothing I said seemed to get through. For weeks, she moped around the house, wearing her usual uniform of sloppy sweat suits and exercise shorts or dungarees. She could talk to the dogs happily enough, but as soon as I suggested going out somewhere she shrank into herself and said, 'No, *I can't.*'

Then I heard a radio programme about a man with the unlikely name of Dr Doctor — Dr Ronald Doctor, a specialist in this type of panic disorder. He had two offices in Los Angeles, one near UCLA in Westwood, and one less than a mile from our house on

Topanga Canyon. I made an appointment for Kim and kept my fingers crossed. He quickly diagnosed her as being agoraphobic. She was so relieved to know she was not alone, that millions of people faced the same demons and had learned to overcome them. He talked to her and explained that she could learn to overcome her fears in time. I was to be a part of the cure.

At his suggestion, I drove her to the mountain tunnels she dreaded so much, to be with her when she saw them. And I took photographs of them, for her to look at when she was back home. The idea was that as she gradually got used to looking at the images that frightened her so much, she would master her fears enough to face the real thing. It took a long time — more than a year — but it worked in the end.

Kim even struggled to turn her agoraphobia to her advantage, to use it to become a better actress.

'I've learned to understand that my anxiety attacks aren't going to kill me,' she said. 'They might help me as an actress. Under it all, anxiety is the spice of life.'

She still had bad moments during her treatment, however, like the time she fled a job interview — for *Eddie Macon's Run*, which was eventually made with Kirk Douglas and John Goodman — at Universal Studios when they kept her waiting for 20 minutes, and we both knew she would never be completely cured. But once she knew what she was fighting, she drew on it to give her strength. Eventually, that would lead to her having the strength not to need me to lean on. In the meantime, she turned down live television chat shows in favour of programmes taped in advance, so if something went wrong they could re-shoot. And as she became better known, she was invited to be a presenter at the Academy Awards, but always refused because the thought of being on a live, worldwide television broadcast terrified her.

Agoraphobia was not Kim's only health problem in those early days. She was diagnosed with TMJ syndrome, a painful jaw complaint which is often brought on by chronic muscle tension caused by stress or anxiety, and had to wear a mouth guard for a while. In later years, she became so obsessed by having perfect teeth she used to fly to New York to visit her favourite dentist there, a guy she had gone to in her modelling days. It seemed to me we were forever spending $3,000 each to fly to New York for the sake of Kim's beauty,

We were also terrified at one point that she had breast cancer because she had fibrous lumps in her breasts. She went to the doctor for a regular check-up and he said she had to have an operation right away. We panicked and sought a second opinion. Eventually, we found Dr Paul Kaufman, in Beverly Hills. He ordered a mammogram and did a thorough examination and said there was nothing to worry about. When he gave us the good news, he said, 'If they were any better I would get arrested for checking them out.' And she used to visit Dr Laurence David to have spider veins removed.

Our family and the few friends we saw knew little of Kim's struggles, because she was fine with me there to reassure her and, after all, she is an actress. As well as our wild and imaginative sex life, we did the usual things a couple in love do. I took her to meet my dad fairly soon after we got together and they hit it off. I knew he'd love her, because she reminded him of Marilyn Monroe. We went to see him on his boat, a 38-foot California sailing boat, which he kept at a marina in Playa del Rey. There was talk of a movie about Marilyn's life and we discussed the possibility of Kim doing it. Not only did she look like Marilyn, she had the same kind of breathless innocence. Nothing ever came of the film in the end.

We didn't see my dad a lot, because there had been strain between the two of us ever since he and my mother divorced. He had remarried, a woman called Margie Pletcher who had been Marilyn's costumer. I got along well enough with her, but I always took my mother's side. However, every once in a while we would all get together with my sister, Sherry, and go to a Mexican restaurant for dinner. Ironically, my mother, Beverly, often used to join us. She and my dad had managed to remain friends after the divorce.

I went with Kim to Athens, Georgia, to meet her family, but not until after we were married. She broke the news of our wedding to them by phone. There was never any big, formal announcement, because of her image. She said, 'You know, the studios don't really want me to be married.' I don't know if anyone had actually said that to her or if it was her own idea, but that's why I kept such a low profile while we were married. I got on fine with her family, even though I'm not a big family man. On that first trip, Kim got me to drive her to all her childhood hang-outs. We went and parked above the school football field, beside a bridge and along a river bank, and made out in the car. They were the places she learned about teenage sex. And, of course, she took me to the famous fields where she said she had first experienced oral sex. Whether they really were her classrooms I don't know, but if they were, she learned her lessons well. We talked about what she had done as a teenager and what she would have liked to do, and with my imagination we re-enacted her young loves. Of course, we made love in her bed, the bed she slept in as a little girl, which I found kind of weird. We developed a habit of stopping over in Georgia when we travelled. We flew in on the way back from the *Never Say Never Again* shoot in Spain, right at the end, and again when she finished *The Man Who Loved Women*. And we took a detour to see her folks on the way to New Orleans for the start of *No Mercy*. Her father, Don, and mother, Ann, who had split up years before, came out to California to see us on different visits. Just days after Kim and I split up, I was very touched to get a note from Don, saying how sorry he was about the break-up and asking me to keep in touch.

Kim's sisters, Barbara and Ashley, were very close, but her brothers had left Athens. We went on a trip to see Mick, who was married and lived in Florida. He was the tennis player and we knocked a few balls back and forth and hung out on the beach. Kim's other brother Skip was a motorcycle racer who then joined the navy. He used to visit us when he was posted to Port Hueneme, in Ventura County, north of Los Angeles, before he was posted to a long stint in Antarctica.

Ashley was a regular visitor to Woodland Hills, with or without her husband Joe, and she turned up unexpectedly in New York when Kim was making *9½ Weeks*, which was a welcome diversion for Kim.

As soon as Kim and I became friends during the making of *Hard Country*, we started developing little signals between each other. We used her nickname, Chelsea, if I wanted to speak to her without drawing attention to the fact that she was Kim Basinger. We had a hand signal — crossing the two forefingers on each hand — that meant, 'Everything's OK, I'm here'. We'd use it if she was having a hard time on the set, or if she was caught in a crowd. She also made that sign whenever she passed or saw a cross that stands by the San Diego Freeway in the Sepulveda Pass, one of the mountain roads leading from the Los Angeles basin to the San Fernando Valley. Although she had been brought up as a Methodist, sang in the choir, and treasured the miniature bible her father gave her when she left home for New York, Kim was by no means religious in a traditional fashion.

But she was very spiritual, in her own peculiar way. She believed she was an alien who would live forever in some form and go to another planet. And in me she saw a go-between to the mystic world she believed in.

It all started because on *Hard Country* I was very good at anticipating what she wanted. It was a gambit I always used when I was working, to get the actresses to like me. Kim really thought I had some kind of psychic power. And when she asked me if I would love her forever and I came up with 'Longer Than Forever', she loved the expression so much it convinced her of my assumed powers. At first, she was impressed by what were really just lucky guesses. And, of course, as I got to know her better, it was easier to anticipate what she wanted.

It sounds crazy, but in her mind I wasn't Ron Snyder or Ron Christian or Ron Britton; I was Charlie in the Upstairs Room or I was communicating with Charlie. Of course, we never told any of our friends about this; they'd have thought we were both certifiable. I tried to play it down, because she wanted me to be a sort of Christ figure for her, and I was scared of the day when she would ask me to perform a miracle and I would not be able to do it. That scared me, because she was so insecure and becoming so dependent on me that I was afraid that when she realised I was just a mere mortal after all, it could do her some psychological damage. I wanted to help her become more stable and self-confident. When I gave her a prediction or some advice, she'd say, 'Have you been talking to Charlie?' or 'Did Charlie tell you that?'

But there was one occasion when I deliberately manufactured a 'miracle'. I was at home in Woodland Hills, which is north of Los Angeles and Kim was filming in Anaheim in Orange County, way to the south. It was the afternoon and she telephoned me in a panic.

'I can't go on,' she said, and again I could hear the all-consuming fear in her voice. 'I can't do anything without you here.'

At that time of day, it would have been at least a two-hour drive for me, probably three, and I knew Kim was too professional to want to hold up the shoot.

'There's no way I can get to you in time,' I told her. 'You can do it. Go into make-up and relax and start shooting without me.'

'I don't think I can do that,' she said, and I knew she was really terrified.

So I said, 'Tell you what ... you've got to trust me. Go into make-up, now, and I'll be there.'

As soon as I put the phone down on her I called the local

airport, Van Nuys, which is just a few miles from Woodland Hills. It doesn't have any commercial passenger flights but it's the busiest airport for small planes in the United States.

'Have you got a helicopter I can hire? And how much will it cost?'

I think it was $500 an hour, but I didn't care. Then I called Kim's driver who was with her on the set and told him to pick me up at Fullerton Airport, near Disneyland, in half an hour. That was only a few minutes from the set. I told him not to say anything to Kim. I raced to Van Nuys and climbed into the helicopter and off we went. On the way, flying through downtown Los Angeles, there was a big fire in a high-rise building. The pilot wanted to fly closer so we could have a look at it, but I said, 'No, get to Fullerton as quickly as you can.' So, 35 minutes after Kim had called, knowing that I was such a long drive away, I was there. The door of the make-up trailer was open and I walked casually past without looking in or saying anything. She thought she saw me but she knew it couldn't be me. But that gave her the confidence to come out of the trailer and then I let her know I was really there. That was during the filming of *My Stepmother is an Alien*, aptly enough.

Charlie in the Upstairs Room was not Kim's only unusual belief. She has often said that people who don't love animals have no souls, but she was also convinced dogs are aliens, who know more than we can understand. She bought me a lot of shirts as presents during the time we were together and always got two identical ones. 'That's so the shirts won't be lonely,' she said. 'And they'll always have a friend.'

It was the same with our Christmas trees. We never went shopping early but waited until late in the Christmas rush. Kim explained why.

'All the good trees will have been chosen, and just ones nobody else wants will be left, the ones with broken branches or gaps in the foliage. We can save one of those trees and give it a good home.'

She had such a big heart, none bigger. We always put the tree on the roof of our house, with a gold star Kim had kept from her school days on the top, and I would fix lights to hit the tree and the star. We had a ten-foot decorated tree inside, as well. She also enjoyed decorating the house for Hallowe'en, with cobwebs on the windows, a headless body hanging from the pine tree in the front garden, and scary music playing. Only kids who knew Kim came trick or treating, and she gave them way too many sweets.

There was something childlike about her that was so endearing. At Christmas, we always went to an area of Woodland Hills called Candy Cane Lane. It's actually three or four blocks of big, ranch-style houses where the residents put up the most elaborate decorations you have ever seen, with elaborate light shows, life-size nativity scenes, flying reindeer and elves. Thousands of people flock there every year, mainly to show it off to children. But Kim always wanted to go as well, and videotaped the scene like a tourist.

One year, at Christmas Eve, she saw a Mexican woman, a maid, waiting for a bus at the end of our lane. Kim said, 'Give her some money.' So I stopped the car, got out and walked up to her and she was very nervous at this big guy approaching her late at night. She didn't speak much English and I don't speak much Spanish, but I somehow made her understand and gave her a $100 bill for Christmas. We also collected clothes to give away to charities, and toys that she gave to an organisation called Toys for Tots, which gives presents to underprivileged kids.

Kim had other obsessions, too. She was concerned about her own health and hygiene and she was very conscious of what went into her body. She taught me two tricks that I still use to this day. Whenever she bought soft drinks in cans, she washed them before she opened them, to clean off any dust and dirt that might have settled on them while they were on the shelf. And she always washed fruits and vegetables, not just under the tap but soaking them in a bleach solution. You should see what comes off them! All the colouring and dyes and pesticides wash off. They do have a bit of a chlorine smell, but I guess they are more pure.

When I first met Kim, she was taking guitar lessons from Bud de Shields, who was a famous folk singer in California when I was a kid. He was half of Bud and Travis, who were the forerunners of groups like Peter, Paul and Mary. She had always loved music and had a beautiful voice, and had written hundreds of songs and poems. When she was not working, she spent hours sitting at a white baby grand piano I gave her, composing songs that we recorded in the studio at the back of the house.

The baby grand was the second major present I ever bought Kim. Like the mirror that hung over our bed, I bought it after a big win on the horses. Her favourite song that she had written was called 'Birthmark', about how being born beautiful can, in its own way, be a blemish or a curse. It started:

Just because she's blonde with her big blue eyes,
She can't really help it; she was born with that disguise.
But try to tell the woman that, and try to tell the guys,
How many tears have fallen from those big blue eyes.

Kim used to record her songs in the studio in our back house, and then post the cassettes to herself, registered mail, to copyright them. I still have some of the unopened envelopes. Some of the songs are called 'Chasing the 'Feelings', 'Under the Street Light', 'Brown Skin Boys', 'Cause the Nights Can Be So Long', 'Revival in the Sun', 'Crystal Indian' and 'Crash Landings'.

She always dreamed of recording an album and singing on film. Her dream came true with the soundtrack of *The Marrying Man*, which many people compared favourably to Michelle Pfeiffer's singing in *The Fabulous Baker Boys*.

After *Mother Lode* it looked as if Kim's career was going nowhere, and her self-imposed seclusion did not help. We talked about her future and the sort of films she should do. She got depressed. I told her, 'Don't worry. You're going to make a million dollars. I know it.' I said she should wear glasses in the movies because I always think pretty girls look sexy in specs. She never did until we split, and then for her next role, Vicki Vale in *Batman*, she wore glasses, and now she often wears them in real life. We dreamed of doing a remake of *Bell, Book and Candle*, which was a Kim Novak movie, or *The Man Who Knew Too Much*, which had Doris Day singing 'Que Sera, Sera'. We never did get those projects off the ground, but Kim was convinced she was on the brink of breaking through. She just needed an extra push.

Her lawyer, Barry Hirsch, who is an entertainment specialist, knew there was a lot of talk about Kim and thought it was time to 'package' her differently and try to get her into bigger pictures. She was still with her original agent, Martin Gage, and she was grateful for what he had done, getting her a start in television, but she needed someone with great power. After talking to a number of people she joined the prestigious Creative Artists Agency, headed by top Hollywood power player Michael Ovitz, with Rick Nicita as her new agent. Martin was furious and blamed me totally for losing his client and accused her of being disloyal.

'When Ron came into the picture I knew I was out,' he stormed. 'She needed someone to be there 24 hours a day and I couldn't do that.'

That was when people started calling me a Svengali who was

out to control Kim and her career. But it wasn't like that; it was Kim's decision. She burst into tears after she severed her connections with Martin but she knew she had to do it and she was quite ruthlessly determined to advance her career. Ironically, a few years later when Kim wanted to fire one of her advisers, I told her she should be loyal to the people who had stood by her through the hard times and she agreed. Then, when things started going wrong between us, he turned on me pretty badly. I can't blame him, though. She had all the money!

As Kim started to get better parts in more important films, I stressed to her that it was important that she should be treated right. I had been in Hollywood a lot longer than her and didn't want producers or directors to walk all over her. She took notice as I insisted on having things changed if they were not good enough for her — the plane seats on the way to Hawaii, our first hotel in London. She was a great actress and a professional and I wanted her always to get the respect she deserved. So I was delighted when, during the making of 9½ Weeks, she stood up to Adrian Lyne and Mickey Rourke, and when she tore into her next director, Fool for Love's Robert Altman, when he wrongly accused her of being late on the set. I was not trying to boost her ego or turn her into a prima donna. Far from it; if she asked my opinion, I always told her the truth, even if it was not something she wanted to hear. If she asked me how she was in a scene or in a movie, I would be honest and say, 'God, you were great' or 'Well, you were just there'. She treasured my truthfulness at first but, perhaps predictably, as she became a bigger, and bigger star, she always wanted to hear 'yes' and hated it when I said 'no'. She turned from wanting my counsel to wanting to be surrounded by people who never criticised her or said anything she didn't want to hear. Suddenly, Charlie had lost his place in the Upstairs Room and was just a mere mortal, an imperfect husband.

Chapter 11

After the months of high tension Kim had endured in New York working on *9½ Weeks*, she needed to unwind. Her next movie project was also about unconventional sex, a big screen adaptation of actor-turned-playwright Sam Shepard's critically-acclaimed stage play *Fool for Love*. But this time there was no pressure on Kim to strip naked in the high-brow tale of tragic human relationships and incest between a man and his half-sister. The most sensuous scene in the film called for Kim to bathe her bare legs in a sink in a rundown motel room, while wearing the white slip which by then was quickly becoming her trademark.

Sam played Eddie, a mischievous rodeo cowboy on a mission to win back his lover. He obviously wrote the part for himself because he is a fanatical horseman and plays polo, and they used Sam's own horses in the picture. Kim was chosen to play the object of his affections, his half-sister, May. Sam's real-life live-in lover — and Kim's old rival — Jessica Lange was pregnant, so she wasn't considered for the part. It was poetic justice as Kim had lost out on so many parts to her in the past. Controversial movie-maker Robert Altman, whose credits included *M*A*S*H*, *Popeye* and *Come Back to the Five and Dime, Jimmy Dean, Jimmy Dean*, directed the film, which was shot on location in the New Mexico high desert outside Santa Fe.

Altman had never heard of Kim when Sam telephoned to say she might be right for the part. Sam told him he knew little about her either, but that she could have the right look for May and he'd be happy to work with her if Altman liked her. As it turned out, Altman took to her a great deal. They met in a hotel so he could interview her for the part. She got there first. He walked into the room and just said, 'Hi.' She said the same. Then he said, 'Now, listen, I don't know you at all. What have you done? Have you done anything?'

Kim told him, 'Well, I don't know you at all, and I don't know anything you've ever done either.' Kim might have seen something of his on a late-night movie on television, but she hadn't a clue; she hadn't even seen *M*A*S*H*. Their mutual honesty got them off on a good footing.

To get a short break and spend some time alone together, instead of flying from Los Angeles, which would have taken less than two hours, we decided to drive the 900-mile journey. We intended to be leisurely about the trip, taking our time and stopping overnight in out-of-the-way places when we felt tired. As always, I was to do the driving because Kim could not drive a vehicle with a gear lever. Kim had given her brother Skip the black Corvette she had got from the studio as an inducement to make *From Here to Eternity*, and in return he had *sold* us a big old green Ford van he owned. That was the way it was with Kim; she'd give someone something and in return end up buying something from them. We gave the van, which we nicknamed the Green Bean, to my sister Sherry Snyder, who bred and showed long-haired dachshunds, because she needed a large vehicle to transport the dogs in their big travelling kennels to competitions. We borrowed the Green Bean back from Sherry and packed it up with Kim's exercise equipment and her sound system. Kim had a heavy-duty workout programme that involved using cassettes by Jane Fonda, and an even more strenuous routine called 'The Firm'. We also packed a cooler full of her favourite Pouilly Fuissé wine and sandwiches that Doris, the housekeeper, had made for us.

We liked to take road trips and whenever we travelled it was always the same; the number of clothes Kim took could have been packed into a thimble but the exercise equipment and other junk filled whichever vehicle we were using. She never cared much about clothes and most of the time would take baggy sweat shirts, exercise trousers and old trainers to wear on our trips. However, it was essential that we packed the pillows from Kim's bed at home. She would never sleep on strange pillows in hotel rooms.

We hadn't even driven out of the LA city limits by the time we had eaten all the sandwiches, so we had to pull over at a supermarket and buy extra supplies in case we got hungry before we reached another town. Once you get outside LA, it can be quite a while before you reach another community large enough to support a decent food market and Kim was always very particular about what she ate. After our shopping expedition, we set off again.

It was the first week of May 1985 and the weather was fabulous. Kim, who was wearing a loose blouse, short, flimsy skirt and no underwear, rolled down the windows and spread her long legs, one resting on the dashboard and the other with her foot draped out of the van. She sure gave any truck driver in a high vehicle who peered into the van a view to remember. I'm surprised I didn't see a few of them swerve off the road.

After a couple of hours we reached Barstow, a small desert community in the middle of nowhere, the sort of place where you expect to see tumbleweeds rolling down the street. Even though we'd eaten Doris' sandwiches, we were ravenously hungry and, besides, we wanted a break so we pulled into a truck-stop for a meal. Whenever we travelled, I'd have to stop every hour no matter where we were because Kim would always want to pee. I guess it was all that Evian water she drank.

While eating, Kim was soaking in the atmosphere of Hicksville USA. Suddenly she said, 'That's it. I've got it. Listen to the way that woman is talking over there.' Kim had been eavesdropping on another customer's conversation. 'That's the way May would speak,' she said confidently. We'd only left home a few hours and already Kim had found her character, and that was the accent she used in the movie.

We drove late into the night, Kim dozing with her head resting on my shoulder. As I began to get tired, I nudged her and we looked at the map to find the nearest place to stay. My body always let me know when I'd reached the point where I'd need to stop in about an hour. About 40 minutes' drive from our designated destination, Kim reached into the back and opened up the wine and we rolled slowly into town sipping on Pouilly Fuissé, which was kind of fun and decadent. Unlike the times when we were on location filming and staying at the finest hotels and eating in the best restaurants, on these road trips we took we got to stay in very plain motels, we ate in down-home diners and saw how ordinary people lived. However, the trips could turn into a bit of a nightmare because we always wanted to eat late at night when we arrived in these small places, but they usually closed up early.

Our idea was always to drive into the night, then rest as long as we wanted before getting up and setting off again. So we never really got an early start. When we got into a town, I'd find us a diner, but outside the big cities these kinds of cafés serve basic foods such as hamburgers and steaks, because that's what folk want with their beer. There's not much demand for goat's cheese salads, tossed spinach leaves and the kind of fancy stuff Kim wanted to accompany her cold white wine. The motels were pretty basic as well, although they were never as seedy and dilapidated as the one which was the setting for *Fool for Love*.

It took us two days to get to Santa Fe, an artistic community full of adobe-style homes, art galleries and trendy restaurants. It's just over an hour's drive from Albuquerque and has become a popular retreat for celebrities. Sam Shepard and Jessica Lange have a home there, as do Val Kilmer, Gene Hackman, Julia Roberts, Lauren Hutton and Carol Burnett among others. As a result of so many high earners living at least part of the time in such a relatively out-of-the-way place, the town has a disproportionally high number of fancy places to eat.

We were there for eight weeks and although filming was mainly at night on a location way out in the desert, we still got to sample all the in-places such as the Lone Wolf Restaurant, where we used to go to with Sam and Jessica, even though she and Kim didn't really hit it off. American football star-turned-sports commentator Don Meredith, whom Kim knew from her days in New York, and disgraced Watergate conspirator HR 'Bob' Haldeman used to hang out there. We'd also go to the Santa Café, a restaurant where they had paper tablecloths with crayons as centrepieces so you could doodle while you were waiting for your meal. Once, Sam drew a horse and it wasn't at all bad, much better than the animal I drew.

Although there was a sort of rivalry between Kim and Jessica, Kim still got on well enough with Sam. She said, 'He's strong, silent, vulnerable. He has a great presence, but he's a sweet man. Some parts of him are very volatile but he's got a great sense of humour and he laughs — a big laugh. I like that about him.'

My sister Sherry joined us in Santa Fe to work as Kim's assistant. Kim used to call her 'Sherry Amour' after the Stevie Wonder song, 'My Cherie Amour'. She'd ask, 'Where's Sherry Amour today?' Kim always needed someone around to do chores for her and she didn't want me on the set all the time. However, sometimes I'd drive out to see her and I'd hang out with her co-star, Harry Dean Stanton — who played the Old Man, a shadowy, sinister character who turns out to be May's and Eddie's father — and the late country singer Roger Miller, the guy who had hits with 'King of the Road', 'England Swings' and 'Little Green Apples'.

Roger, who had a reputation for his appetite for drugs and partying, knew Harry. He had a 20-acre spread near Santa Fe and liked to come over to the set and watch them work. In the early 1980s, he'd decided to turn down most of the work which would keep him away from his third wife, Mary, and their two young adopted children. As a result, I think he missed the glamour of showbusiness and being on the set kept him in touch with it. Often while the cast were filming, Roger — who claimed publicly to have turned his back on his wild past and drugs — and I would sit around smoking a joint and chatting. I was very sad when, in 1992, he died of throat cancer at the age of 56.

The movie was shot with the characters wearing summer clothes but the New Mexico desert at night is bitterly cold and it poured with rain during the time we were on location. To make matters worse, the set also had a moth infestation. Afterwards, Kim would recall, 'Millions of bugs, like *The Birds*, would come down. We'd have to turn out the lights for two hours.' Kim hated being on location, not just in Santa Fe, but anywhere. She preferred being at home with the animals. When we were away, she used to put up photographs of the dogs all over the walls of her trailer or dressing room.

She got on well with Altman right from the start and went on to work with him again after we'd split up. She said, 'He was truly a delight to work with on *Fool for Love*, because he's so confident. There are directors and *directors*, and then there are filmmakers and *filmmakers* who know about film, who've been around the block, made asses of themselves, been wonderful, praised, done everything and yet can do it all over again, every day, and find it fascinating. That's Altman. Also, he trusts people. He knows and he trusts.'

She had gained strength after *9½ Weeks* and was not in the mood to take any rubbish from anyone, including him. Due to a timing confusion by the crew, on one occasion, he wrongly thought Kim had kept the cast and crew waiting. As she walked on to the set he made a comment like, 'Oh, Basinger's here now, so we can all begin.' She went for him. 'Don't you ever accuse me of being late,' she shouted, 'because I am a professional. I am here and on time, and you've gotta get *your* act together!'

Afterwards, Altman said, 'I thought she was going to knock me through the wall. She didn't talk to me for two days. I finally went and apologised to her.'

What Altman didn't realise was that Kim, who adored him, had gone back to her trailer and cried her eyes out, she was so upset at the incident.

Unlike most locations, the trailers on *Fool for Love* were dumps. The movie very nearly didn't get made because they could not raise any money until Cannon Films came along and provided $6 million in funding. This meant Altman was on a tight budget. The film is set in this awful motel and behind it is a squalid trailer park. To save money, the set trailers doubled up as the actual trailers for the cast. This wasn't usual practice but everyone in the cast wanted to make this film because it was so deep and dramatic, and they all agreed to this inconvenience to help get the movie made. Kim even took a pay cut, to $208,000, less than half of her $500,000 for *9½ Weeks*. Until this time, her pay had always gone up from movie to movie, but she was willing to work for less because it was such a prestigious project and Sam and Altman were both legends.

Kim showed the most strength, not by standing up to Altman, but on one night when Jessica turned up to watch a particularly tense scene between Kim and Sam. Sam started sort of showing off on the set, making kind of an ass of himself. It was a big, sexy scene that Kim had to play with Sam, and he brought Jessica in and sat her down in front of the set. Altman went to Kim and offered to clear the set. He told her, 'I don't want you to do this scene with Jessica sitting there. It's not fair to you.' However, Kim just gritted her teeth and told him, 'I'll do it.' She was furious about the situation and Altman knew it, but she went ahead and did the scene anyway.

When Kim got back to our hotel she told me about the incident. 'Here we were, hugging and kissing, and all of a sudden there's this *girlfriend* standing there.'

For years after, Altman remembered, 'Kim was great. It was a really courageous, strong, good move for her to do. She certainly was professional.' Whenever Kim was reminded of that night, she would scowl and say, 'It was sad because Sam and I got along very well. There were just some outside forces that shouldn't have been there. I was a little shaken to say the least. But I said, "Boy, this has nothing to do with me whatsoever. Now get out there and just … fuck 'em." '

Despite Sam's lack of tact on that occasion, he still remained friendly towards Kim and, in fact, she felt he was hitting on her. 'He's coming on again,' she'd tell me.

I'd heard it so many times. I could imagine it was true because she was such a good-looking woman, but I also knew that Kim wanted her leading men — and her directors — to be enamoured of her. If they hadn't been smitten she would have been worried and probably conjured it up in her mind that they were coming on to her anyway. She wanted them to, and she'd have felt insecure if they hadn't.

Kim told me, 'After *9½ Weeks*, I don't think there is another part in this whole world that I couldn't play. Not anything. I don't want to make it sound like *Fool for Love* was easy, but it was a welcome change.'

However, she became furious with producer Menahem Golan, who, along with Yoram Globus, ran the Cannon Group. In an interview about her, Golan said, 'Just looking at her makes me want to screw her.' Then he gushed, 'She is Marilyn Monroe, Brigitte Bardot and Judy Holliday in one girl, with the talent of Julie Christie.' But all the compliments in the world didn't matter; the damage was done. Kim was hurt and outraged by him being so crude. He sent her 72 roses in a bid to appease her, but it didn't make an iota of difference.

Fool for Love, the first of Sam's plays to be turned into a movie, was met with mixed reviews by the critics. The psychological drama was so intense and arty that it never found a wide movie audience. Nevertheless, when the film was released, Kim was adored by the critics. After the première, we all went down to Sardi's, the famous New York restaurant where traditionally actors and directors go to await the arrival of the first editions of the next day's newspapers at around midnight.

When they arrived, overall the reviews were mixed but the critics loved Kim and that's all that mattered to us. Writing in the *New York Times*, Vincent Canby said, 'Miss Basinger, who was pursued by Robert Redford in The Natural and was the cheerful nymphomaniac in Blake Edward's remake of *The Man Who Loved Women*, is stunning as the besieged, foul-mouthed May, who looks like a kewpie doll that's been dropped once too often. She's not broken, but chipped.' The review in *Box Office* magazine read, 'Basinger is pure silk in a dusty kind of way.' And Sheila Benson of the *Los Angeles Times* described Kim as 'ferociously wonderful'.

At the time *Fool for Love* was released, Altman invited us to a dinner party at his home in New York state. It was just us, the Altmans and actress Rebecca de Mornay and her partner. It was long before she became involved with Canadian singer Leonard Cohen. I thought she was one of the most spectacularly beautiful women I'd set eyes on. I'd like to have taken her home but no such luck. Rebecca was cast by director Roger Vadim to star in the 1988 remake of his classic hit *And God Created Woman*, in the role originally portrayed by Brigitte Bardot. Vadim had considered Kim for the part but in the end he preferred Rebecca's look.

We enjoyed our road trip to Santa Fe so much, just the two of us and the open road, that when she made Nadine the next year we borrowed the Green Bean from Sherry again and drove to Austin, Texas, for the location shooting.

But we should have learned from our Santa Fe experience that, for us coming was always easier than going back. Our return trip from Santa Fe in mid-summer found us driving towards Las Vegas in temperatures of 107 degrees without air-conditioning. We were sweltering. However, that was nothing compared to the journey back from Austin when *Nadine* wrapped. I had to fly home a few days early before the movie ended because Doris had to go into hospital. Kim certainly wasn't up to driving the old manual clunker home. So I hired Pat Lynch to fly out to Austin, pick up the van and drive home. Unfortunately, unlike after *Fool for Love*, this time it was winter and the snows had arrived. As he drove over a bridge in a rural outback, the van skidded and it plunged over the parapet before coming to a stop in a snow drift. Luckily, neither Pat nor the van was harmed, but he had to get it pulled out and righted. He was shaken but eventually both Pat and the Green Bean made it home relatively unscathed.

Although Kim didn't like to be away from home and the dogs, during our time together we got to see a lot of the world and had quite a few adventures on our travels, not just the experience of dusty American highways.

I'll never forget the sight of Kim Basinger, whose body was lusted after by men around the globe, sitting next to a group of nuns on a train sharing Pouilly Fuissé with them and sandwiches that she'd made. I think they would have been in confession for a week if they'd realised the young woman they were talking to had stripped naked for *Playboy* and had enjoyed on-screen depraved sex with Mickey Rourke. We'd been in Deauville, on the north-west coast of France, to attend the film festival where *The Natural* was being shown.

At the end of the festival, we decided to have a few days rest and relaxation in Paris. We thought it would be a great lark to take the train, but we didn't know if you could get food on French trains, so we went to a local store and bought bread and cheese and other good stuff. Kim, who is not the most domestic person in the world, didn't want to get messy making the sandwiches so she went into the bathroom, got in the tub and squatted down cutting the bread and slicing the cheese and tomatoes and the other ingredients we'd bought. Not long after, we found ourselves in a train carriage seated opposite the nuns in their habits. When we came to unwrap our meal, we felt so guilty that they would have to watch us eat that Kim offered them some. As usual, we'd gone completely over the top and made far more than we needed anyway. The nuns were delighted to accept our hospitality and gleefully bit into the food. When we offered them the wine they accepted just as eagerly, which surprised us a bit.

This was the first of many visits we made to the City of Lights together and we loved it right from the start. We came to know the city almost as well as we did London, and Kim was destined to work there when she made *Prêt à Porter*, again for Robert Altman.

We did all the usual tourist things, walking along the banks of the Seine, strolling down the Champs-Elysées and visiting the somewhat kitsch artists' quarter at the top of the hill in Montmartre. And, of course, the Eiffel Tower, one of the best-known tourist attractions in the world. The height made Kim nervous, however. When we revisited it with a group of friends during a publicity tour for *Nadine,* she became very anxious when we reached the first level. Kim's hairdresser, my old pal Rick Provenzano, was there, armed with my video camera, and I still have the video of her saying, 'This is for you, Daddy,' and bursting into song, just as her father told her to do when she was scared, singing 'East side, west side, all around the town …' There was always this refreshing, joyous youthfulness about her. In those days, Kim always was a real, genuine person and not a movie star.

She wasn't the only one who could become nervous when we travelled. We had several close calls on airplanes but none closer than when we took a weekend break in Bucks County, Pennsylvania. We wanted to go searching for antiques and kick back in the country. Rick Provenzano is from Princeton, New Jersey, which is just over the state line from Bucks County, and he was visiting his folks so we all agreed to meet up and hire a small four-seater light aircraft to fly us back to Washington, DC, where we were to pick up a scheduled flight. Kim and I had been staying in a really nice bed-and-breakfast hotel. In the United States, B & Bs are not someone's home, where they are making a bit of extra pocket money by renting out the spare bedroom. They are really fancy, small boutique hotels with a lot of character and old-world charm and the one we stayed in was no exception.

When the break was over, Rick joined us and we set off back to do business. It was a very windy day and as we reached the small airport at Doylestown, we realised it was going to be a rough ride — but we didn't know *how* rough. We hadn't been in the air that long before the plane started pitching and being tossed around all over the place. Kim grabbed my arm tightly and I could see the fear in her face. We were sure we were going down. The pilot was having a terrible time trying to keep the plane, which was being thrown around like a small leaf, in the air. We were all praying and looking at each other, saying, 'This could be it.' I kept wishing we'd never got on the flight. I thought to myself, 'Who cares if we'd missed the next plane?' Thankfully, we lived to tell the tale, but after that I'd never let us get on a small plane again in bad weather conditions. And if ever there was a problem and a commercial flight was delayed for technical reasons, I always insisted we got off and took a later flight.

On one occasion, we were at Atlanta airport and the plane we were due to catch had engine trouble and was delayed for more than an hour. We understood there was some kind of electrical problem and possibly an engine fire. The passengers had just got on the plane when they apologised but said we'd have to disembark and wait. We were hoping they'd put us on a different plane but after about an hour they said the problem had been fixed and we could return to our seats. That didn't sound like a good idea, so we told them to unload our luggage. We re-scheduled for the following day and retreated to the airport hotel. We rented a classic black-and-white *film noir, Caged*, for which Eleanor Parker was nominated for a Best Actress Oscar in 1950, ordered loads of food and wine and played nasty all afternoon. Making love to Kim and taking it easy was far more attractive to me than being seated on a plane that we thought might fall out of the sky.

Not every flying experience was a bad one. Once, we were visiting Kim's folks in Athens and Kim bumped into singer Kenny Rogers' then wife Marianne. Kenny and his wife were also from Georgia. The girls got talking and they discovered that we were all due to travel back to Los Angeles on the same day. 'Why don't you fly back with us?' suggested Marianne and Kim gratefully accepted. We met at Athens airport and flew in a small plane to Atlanta where we boarded Kenny's fantastic aircraft. It had a private bedroom and luxury living quarters. The girls sat on one side of the plane and talked like machine-guns the whole journey. Kenny and I sat on the other side and played backgammon. When we were over Oklahoma, Kenny became hungry so he had the plane land so we could stock it up with peanut butter sandwiches and while we were there we refuelled. During the flight, Kenny, who is a fanatical and extremely good photographer, showed Kim the book of portraits he had just had published. He asked her to pose for his second book but unfortunately their schedules never coincided. Kenny used former *Charlie's Angel* star Jaclyn Smith, who had been a Breck model like Kim, in the book, in a pose wearing leathers on a motorbike. That was the pose he had wanted Kim to sit for. When we landed at Los Angeles International Airport, we taxied to the special section of the tarmac where private planes park for the passengers to disembark. Kenny and his wife had a limousine to collect them. As we were saying our goodbyes, I said to Kenny, 'I don't know what to say.' He replied, 'Just say "Thank you." ' That's exactly what I did and he was extremely happy. He was one of the nicest and kindest men I've met in the business.

Whenever we had a few free days and we were away from home, I'd say, 'Let's go somewhere.' We took a short break in Nassau after doing publicity for *The Man Who Loved Women* in Florida. We went to Japan to promote *No Mercy*, the first film Kim made with Richard Gere, and at the end we decided to take off for a few days. We went to Hong Kong and stayed at the luxurious Regent Hotel right on the harbour. We bought antiques and had them shipped home. During the same Far East trip, we went to Bali, which was great because we both love swimming. It was a place I'd always wanted to visit. But it is very hot and the sun is strong because it's right on the equator, so Kim had to keep in the shade and could only go swimming in the early morning or late afternoon. One day she got into a kayak, which she'd never done before, and she was a natural. She went paddling along as if she'd being doing it all her life. We were larking around and I got on to a windsurfer. Rick was with us, as usual, with the video camera going, and Kim made a mock news show about me, as if I was a champion windsurfer and she was a television commentator. I fell off the windsurfer and she said, 'That's the nastiest boy I've ever known.' We were so relaxed and having such a good time.

The good times stopped when we got back to Jakarta airport, however. At passport control they said my passport was invalid because it was about to run out. They took me into the sort of room where they do strip searches and my heart sank. You never know what's going to happen in a foreign country, even though these guys knew who Kim was. So I slipped $500 into my passport and gave it back to the inspector and said, 'I'm sure you've made a mistake; please look again.' I knew I was taking a chance because I didn't know what sort of bribery laws they have in Indonesia, but it worked, thank goodness.

On another occasion, my knees shook in an airport when we had to change planes in New York. I thought I was going to end up in jail — but not for the same reason the airport security people were after me. We were flying with PanAm and were waiting for our connection at JFK airport. As we waited in the first-class lounge, an announcement came over the intercom system, 'Will Mr Ron Britton please come to the podium?'

I had a small bit of cocaine hidden in my sock and I was really worried. As I walked up to the counter, I was sweating and thinking, 'How did they know? It's only a small amount, enough to keep us going for a couple of days. They can't know. What do they want? Geeze, what if they find it? They must know.' All these crazy thoughts were going through my mind. Then I thought, 'Oh God, if they do find it and I'm travelling with Kim Basinger, it's going to be all over the newspapers.' When I reached the desk I braced myself and said, 'Can I help you? I'm Ron Britton.' They had X-rayed our bags and I'd forgotten that I'd packed a handgun in one of the cases.

The authorities in New York take a pretty dim view of people carrying guns on to planes and they wanted to know what I was up to. They made me open up all the luggage and show them the gun. Luckily, I'd done everything right. I'd placed the unloaded firearm in one case and the ammunition in another bag, which is allowed as long as the luggage is going in the hold. I explained that I was with Kim and said we'd had some problems with crazy fans and I was carrying the gun for protection. I kept talking, telling them how difficult it is for a big movie star, especially a beautiful woman, in this day and age and that there are a lot of crazy people out there who get their kicks stalking people. They were pretty cool about it and became less concerned once they understood the situation. I always carried publicity shots of Kim, so I called her over, introduced her and got her to sign the pictures for them all. In the end, I became quite relaxed even though I was standing there chatting to the cops with some coke hidden in my sock.

That wasn't the only chance I took to make sure I'd always got some drugs with me while away from home. I knew it was dangerous to travel with cocaine or dope so I bought some books and cut a square compartment out of the centres — just like you see in spy movies — and arranged for friends to buy me whatever I needed. Then I'd arrange to have one of the books wrapped up and couriered to wherever we were staying. I'd go down to the concierge station and collect my package. If ever I felt nervous or thought there was something strange, I'd either not collect the envelope or I would not open it and say, 'I don't know anything about this parcel, send it back.' I don't know if I was just lucky or crafty, but thankfully I was never caught.

Looking back on it, I certainly took some chances. We once arrived in Madrid in Spain on a promotional tour. We were travelling with our friend Linda Lang, who took over from Sherry as Kim's assistant in the later years we were together. I got talking to the guy who had been hired to do the public relations for us and drive us around. He told me that he had previously been with a famous rock 'n' roll band who were being chauffeured around town and if there was anything I required he'd be happy to get it for me or show me where to go. I knew the band was heavily into drugs, so I said, 'Anything?' and he assured me he meant anything. He took us all to an expensive-looking high-rise apartment building in a ritzy suburb on the outskirts of town. I left the girls sitting in the car and went in.

'I'm just going to get something,' I told them. 'Wait there, it'll be fine.' They whined 'Ron' incredulously. Sure enough, I came back with the cocaine I wanted, but I now realise if anything had gone wrong it would have been me who was the dope.

Kim realised that drugs were becoming a problem for me. One day, she left a Hallmark card on my pillow. It had a sketch of a duck and a bunny on the front with the words, 'God made us just the way we are!' Inside it read, 'It's nice to know he has a sense of humour!' But the more important message came from Kim's heart. She wrote, 'I love you, darling — Please get rid of this stuff — We don't need it or want it in our lives.' She put in a desperate plea for me to send the drugs back to my supplier or give them to a friend to get rid of for me. 'It will make us strong and happy and together,' she said. She signed it, 'Always, Always, Always LTF …', followed by her usual heart with a cross in the middle. Although Kim enjoyed her occasional 'treats', she also knew how bad drugs are for you. She often begged me to give them up and sometimes

I made a big show of throwing coke down the drain. But I usually substituted baking soda and she was none the wiser. I'm sure Kim was able to stop doing cocaine easily when she was out of my influence.

She once admitted in an interview with *Cosmopolitan*, 'When I tried cocaine, I found that it made people sleep during the day. Every time I took it I said, "This is a joke." It's a debilitating drug. I hated it that it made me feel so worn out. A lot of people use cocaine every day. I'll tell you what cocaine did for me. It made me very smart in one way. It made me know that you could never use it and get by. Believe me, I'm no Mother Teresa. I've done a lot of wildass things in my life. It's just that I can be wild without drugs or alcohol. And so can anybody. Cocaine doesn't break your inhibitions like you think it does. I don't think there's anybody alive who can really handle drugs. I thank God, I really do, with all my heart.'

Kim used greetings cards for every occasion. If she was happy with me she'd give me a card with a scrawled message — her handwriting was almost illegible. If she missed me on the rare occasions we were apart, she'd send a card. If she was mad at me, she'd tell me so in a card. I received hundreds and hundreds of cards from her, some funny, some heart-wrenching and some infuriating.

Once, when I was going on a brief trip, she gave me a card that read, 'What is green, has two legs and isn't going on your trip with you?' Inside was, 'Me'. She wrote, 'I love and adore you, darling!!!!! and more. Be careful — wear your seat belt.' She signed it 'LTF' and wrote 'Dot. Dot. Dot.' Another time, I opened a card to be confronted by a picture of a heart-shaped emerald in an open gift box. Inside, the message read, 'It's all yours.' She wrote next to her usual sign of a heart with a cross inside, 'I promised Forever and Longer Than, Me.'

These messages proved to me that in real life Kim truly was a *Fool for Love*.

Chapter 12

Kim's first million-dollar payday had finally arrived, and once again she was being paired on the screen with one of Hollywood's most desirable hunks. This time it was Richard Gere, playing a Chicago cop out to avenge the murder of his partner, reluctantly helped by Kim's character, an illiterate wild child from the swamps of Louisiana who was actually the sex slave of a New Orleans mobster. *No Mercy* had been originally intended for Nick Nolte a few years earlier, but director Richard Pearce wanted Richard and Kim.

The film started work in New Orleans for a few days, before moving on to Chicago, where we moved into the Ambassador West, which is a great hotel. The cast were due to have six weeks of rehearsals. Kim always hated rehearsing so that did not make her happy. She went off with the two Richards, and she didn't warm to Richard Gere at all.

We had sex every afternoon for those first few weeks. She would come back to the room and jump on my bones, which was cool for me. She was so tightly wound up with her antipathy to Richard that she had to find a way to relieve the tension and I was glad to help.

Still, I worried that their relationship might become so acrimonious it could affect the picture. They were both big names by now and the last thing Kim needed was people poking round the set writing gossip columns about trouble between the two of them if their private animosity became too public. About three weeks into rehearsals we were going out for dinner together and walked through the Ambassador Room, which is a very famous lounge bar in the hotel. Richard Gere is a great, great pianist, and he was sitting at the piano playing away. Kim's a pianist, too, so I said, 'Go on, go and talk to him, tell him how much you like his playing. It might help patch things up between you.' But she didn't want to do it. Five or six weeks went by and she still couldn't take to him.

We went home for Christmas 1985 and filming moved to Wilmington, North Carolina in the new year. I hadn't really met Richard even by this time, but he took us out to dinner one night soon after we arrived there and I realised how right Kim was about him. The people in Wilmington weren't very hip, but they were extremely friendly and delighted to have such stars hanging out in a local restaurant. Richard ordered a Montrachet wine, a top-quality white Burgundy, and the waitress pronounced it wrongly. Richard gave her a really hard time about it. He went on and on and wouldn't let go of it. The waitress was upset and I don't blame her. There wasn't much call for expensive French wines in rural North Carolina in the late 1980s so I was amazed that the restaurant even had it on the wine list. It could have been worse, though, if Kim had insisted on her favourite white Burgundy, Pouilly Fuissé, because that's even harder to pronounce.

We were living on an island in a big rented beach house, right on the ocean. It was off-season, winter, so it was great to walk along the beach by ourselves. The weather was warm and we found sheltered spots to have sex, just like we did at home in California. Kim didn't want me on the set and I didn't want to be there, so I had to amuse myself during the day. This was before I had taken up golf, unfortunately, because there are some good courses out there.

While we were in Wilmington, the Challenger Space Shuttle blew up shortly after take-off, killing Christa McCauliffe, the first teacher in space, and six other astronauts. Kim was very upset by that. Cape Kennedy was less than 300 miles south of Wilmington, as the crow flies, and the explosion would certainly have been visible to anyone who happened to be looking in the right direction at the right time of the morning. I remember we went along the coast wondering if anything from the shuttle had washed up on the shore. We were always looking but, of course, there wasn't anything.

About three months after rehearsals had started, Kim changed her attitude towards Richard. All of a sudden, it seemed that every other night she would have to work late with him, doing the rehearsals she hated so much, going over lines and talking about the film. She would come home at 10.00 or 11.00pm, which is late when you're working on a movie and have to be up first thing in the morning looking good. The rest of the time we had dinner together as normal and I certainly had no complaints about our sex life. For some reason, I thought about what she'd told me in our early days together, about 'trying out' her leading men. 'After all, I can always lay the actors,' she had told me.

About the third night Kim announced she had to work late with Richard, I became very uneasy and unsettled. I didn't know what to do with myself and decided to go and get some food to bring home. I drove to Chez François, the restaurant where we ate most of the time, and there they were in the car park, making out in his car. I could clearly see them kissing and cuddling. I could tell they were kissing really deeply. To me, that sort of kissing is much more intimate than plain genital sex. It's the most intimate thing there is. Kim always says that, but I was the one who put the idea into her head. I went home, wondering what to do and what to say, and waited for Kim.

Throughout our years together, I had pushed her into the company of her co-stars and she had always come back to me. It was a thrill for me to know that she'd been in the arms of a Burt Reynolds or a Sean Connery but had come home to make love with me. Whatever my fears about Robert Redford, I had never had any proof or ever looked for it. Now I had seen the evidence with my own eyes that Kim was not all mine. When Kim came home and I asked what she had been doing, she said, 'Oh, we had to do some work on a scene.'

'I'm not going to set you up to be caught out lying to me,' I replied. 'That would be too easy. I know what you've been doing. I pulled in behind Richard's car and saw you making out. I'm not trying to pull anything on you. I just want to let you know that I know. I saw you guys. You can't deny it.'

She went crazy, of course. 'How could you do that?' she shouted. 'How dare you follow us?'

'That's beside the point,' I yelled back. 'I did it. Don't lie to me.' The ironic thing is that I hadn't gone to the restaurant with any idea of trapping them. It was just the obvious place to go. It was pure luck — bad luck.

The next night she was with me, but then on alternate nights she stayed out with Richard until 10.00pm. I did some hard thinking about the future. I wanted to be with Kim and had always thought she wanted me. But now I wasn't sure. I started taking cocaine every few days and we rowed all the time. 'How could you do this, how could you cheat on me?' I yelled at her. She never admitted to having sex with him but, to me, hugging and kissing was enough for it to be cheating, especially the way I had seen them kiss. Finally, I stormed, 'Why don't you just move in with him and have done with it? I'm going back to California.'

Kim was very upset and said, 'No, it's not like that, don't leave me. Please stay here.'

So I stayed until the end of the movie, but I always said, 'Just tell me if you want me to leave.'

She said, 'No, we're never going to split. Besides, nobody would ever believe you would leave me.'

I said, 'I don't care how you put it. You can tell people you threw me out.'

But she never asked me to leave.

And when we were together, we still had great sex. I really didn't want to leave. I didn't know what to do. It was particularly hard for me because although I had taken an instant dislike to Richard, I was worried that Kim liked him so little in the first place and had encouraged her to get to know him better. I never really got to know him, but as far as I'm concerned, I could find few redeeming features.

'Of all the people in the world, why did it have to be him?' I demanded.

But Kim had no answer. I realised why Kim had changed from not talking to Richard. He was having problems with one of the producers, D Constantine Conte, having arguments on the set. Kim would always back one of her co-stars against the production executives and I was proud of her for doing so. She and Richard became comrades. And I wasn't surprised that Richard took a fancy to her. But I was devastated that she went for it because she always told me she would always come back to me. I never wasted any time wondering why he, a man who could surely have had any woman in the world he wanted, should have gone for Kim when he knew she was married and I was there with her.

In fact, I had been unfaithful to Kim before she ever was to me. About three months after we were married, I went to see my old girlfriend, Chris Filice. I'd always felt a bit guilty about the way I had walked out on her and abandoned her for Kim. So we met up and went to bed. I don't think I told her I was married. I saw her again after that. To add to my sins, shortly before Kim started work on *No Mercy* I met up with an old love called Shane. I'd known her years ago, when she was a kid studying at the University of Southern California and I was playing volleyball on the beach, and we were together for two or three years. Then, about ten years later, after she was married, we had a brief fling. Around the time Kim and I were due to go to Chicago to join Richard, I spotted Shane by chance in Beverly Hills and followed her into an estate agent's office to say hello and suggest getting together for a chat about old times. She was divorced by then and I soon realised she was interested in more than talking, and so was I. Although I was madly in love with Kim, I did not know if being married to a woman who was becoming a bigger and bigger star was going to last for ever. I had a gnawing sense of insecurity that even though I'd given up work for her sake, to ensure that she would not be associated with a mere film crew member, she was beginning to be acutely aware that she was 'above the line' as they say in the movies, and that I was 'below the line'. So I decided to take a chance.

Shane was working for the estate agent where I had found her. In California, it is very common for estate agents selling houses to have 'open house' at the weekend. That means the owners go out for the day and the agent sits in the house or flat with a sign outside inviting prospective buyers to look around. It was perfect for us, because I used to visit her at her open houses and take advantage of all the bedrooms!

Kim and I were both unhappy when we returned home. Fortunately, she was very busy, so there was a lot going on to keep our minds off Wilmington and stop us rowing about it. Almost as soon as *No Mercy* wrapped, she was cast opposite Bruce Willis in *Blind Date* and in the title role in *Nadine* with Jeff Bridges. *9½ Weeks* had finally opened after all the cuts and changes and Kim was very much in demand. Work was stacking up and I hoped with so much to keep us busy and new people to work with, we would be able to put the past behind us and rebuild the love and trust we had shared for six years.

Then, at the end of April, I went out to our mailbox to collect the post. There was a letter addressed to Kim and written on the back of the envelope, was 'Gere' and his New York address. My heart fell. I gave it to her but she didn't say a word. Her sister Ashley was visiting so I did not want to upset her by having a showdown. And she was about to start work on *Blind Date* and did not need any aggravation. After that letter arrived, Richard phoned her at home a couple of times. I don't know what they said; I could not bear to be in the room while she was talking to him. I didn't realise it at the time, but *No Mercy* was the killer. It was the beginning of the end of our marriage. We still had some good times in front of us, but they would always be overshadowed by the knowledge that we were living a lie. I would often bring it up and throw it in Kim's face, especially when I was stoned. I don't know what would have happened if I hadn't done that. Once we got things smoothed over I thought I'd be able to live with it, but I couldn't. The seeds of doubt had been sown and after that it seemed there was always something gnawing away at me inside.

To add to our troubles, as *Blind Date* came to an end, our housekeeper, Doris, was causing us problems. Kim had poached her away from her old New York boyfriend, Tim Saunders, soon after she moved into Don Juan Place. Doris was from Harlem in New York and did not know anybody in California, so she was understandably lonely. She had a lot of responsibility taking care of the animals while we were away, and unfortunately she started hitting the bottle. She'd been an alcoholic who had sought help from Alcoholics Anonymous and we thought she'd recovered from her addiction. Sadly, we were wrong and her problem was quickly becoming worse. The more we were away, the more she'd turn to drink and then we'd get calls from her at all hours saying she couldn't cope, or there were problems with the dogs, or there was some other drama. We packed her off for a break in the hope of resolving the problem at least for a while.

Then Kim received a call from the *No Mercy* production people, saying she was needed back in Wilmington for two weeks of re-shoots. Because of the situation with Doris I could not go with her, and that was a worry for me. Kim knew I was upset and came up with a solution. 'I'll call my daddy and get him to drive up to the set to be with me,' she said. She thought I'd feel happier if he were there to chaperon her and I'd feel that she wouldn't fool around with Richard if her father was with her. Don drove up there from Georgia with Kim's sister, Ashley. They were with her every day, and she phoned me every night to reassure me that whatever had happened did not mean anything. I wanted to believe it so I told myself I *did* believe it, and we went on as we had done before. But I could not help wondering why she did not invite my sister, Sherry, who had worked as her assistant on the main shoot. As things turned out, that was the last time Sherry ever worked with her.

While Kim was away, she showered me with notes. One of

them read, 'It's just all been so unreal. I feel so much emotion sometimes. I don't know where to channel it because some things I guess just can't be talked about ... Take care of yourself. I miss a lot of things. LTF ...' In another she said, 'Darling, I love you more than anything, any world, any time, any place. Please be strong and know I'm with you ... Can't wait till I get home and then this will all be behind us. I adore you, miss you, will call often. Sleep well, forget everything and rest but think about me. LTF ...' Still another went, 'I just wish you were here so much. I'm sick of this ... I miss you so much.'

On one, with the quotation 'What a tangled web we weave' on the front, she wrote, 'when we practise to deceive' and added, 'I love you, darling. Thanks for everything you've done the past week for Doris, puppies, me & all. It will all be the best it could ever be from now on, meaning new things have got to and will happen.' One of them which she signed 'L.T.F... Chelsea', read, 'I adore you always, even during the other times which will lessen and lessen and become non-existent.'

I don't know what happened between her and Richard that time around, but I know there were rows on the set, and at one point Kim locked herself in her room and refused to come out. A publicist said she had stomach flu. But while Kim was penning notes to me, she was also writing to Richard. Later, I found a fragment of a note which she had apparently written to him for his 38th birthday on 31 August, 1986. I don't know if it was a first draft, or if she never sent it. Part of it read, 'I hope this isn't too late ... I wanted it to get to you before tomorrow.'

When Doris returned and the re-shooting ended, I flew out to join Kim and we drove to Georgia to visit her family. When we got home there was still tension between us.

No Mercy was not even a good film, and whatever Kim and Richard were doing together during those evenings in Wilmington, there was scarcely a spark between them on the screen. As cop Eddie Jillette, Richard poses as a contract killer to make inroads into New Orleans' underworld society, snatches Kim's character, Michel Duval — the only witness to his partner's murder — away from her mobster lover and heads to the Louisiana bayou with her handcuffed to him. Naturally along the way they become friends and then lovers, finally teaming up to see off the bad guys. The critics and viewing public both hated it, and it grossed less than $10 million in the USA.

'True to its title, *No Mercy* doesn't show any,' critic Jerry Roberts wrote in the *Santa Monica Evening Outlook*. 'No Mercy is one of those hard-edged, gritty, down-and-dirty, no-nonsense, vengeance-orientated, street-smart bleeders of runny hokum that isn't thickened anywhere along the way by common sense.'

Peter Rainer in the *Los Angeles Herald-Examiner* wrote, 'No Mercy deserves little. It's yet another cop-avenges-his-partner's murder movie, with a script that doesn't even pass muster as a B-picture star vehicle. Richard Gere and Kim Basinger aren't B-stars either. They're what passes for megawatt starpower these days. The lack of allurement in the case and in the script makes this venture dismal indeed. It's a real power-outage of a movie.'

David Edelstein in the *Village Voice* said bluntly, 'In No Mercy a couple of cold fish (Richard Gere and Kim Basinger) pretend to be HOT STUFF, so they screw half-dressed against a wall, lit by a shard of neon. Gere and Basinger look like they couldn't warm up to each other if they were cremated together. I've seen more sizzle at Madame Tussaud's.' Duane Byrge in the *Hollywood Reporter* had faint praise for Kim, at least, saying, 'Basinger's alluring in her sheer, wetted-down role. Always dripping — from tromping through swamps, showering or trudging through the rain — it's the kind of part that posters are made from.' Julie Salamon, on the other hand, hated the wetness. She wrote in the *Wall Street Journal*, 'The problem with all this high-tempo motion is that none of it really makes any sense. Mr Pearce also hasn't resisted the temptation to keep dousing Ms Basinger in water; wetness is becoming the trademark of this actress, who is forever sweating or having ice-cubes rubbed on her body.'

Kim knew it was a terrible movie and blamed the failure partly on all the rehearsing and agonising over the film, which resulted in so many changes being made that it lost its original direction. 'I like to read a script once before I make up my mind about it,' she said. 'Then close to the start of production I'll read it again. That's it. This whole business of making movies is over-analysed. That's why a lot of flops are made, because they're analysed to death in production. That's what happened to No Mercy. There was something in that screenplay. I was going to play a wonderful Cajun woman, interesting, spiritual, crazy. That character was free, if I really could have played her the way she was written. She was cut off from freedom, not so much because of the guy she was with but because she was illiterate. She didn't have the confidence to strike out on her own since she couldn't read or write. But then we had two-and-a-half-weeks of meetings in a Chicago hotel and the whole project was analysed to pieces. By the start of the film, I knew we were in trouble. By the end of a week, I knew we were dead. We were dust. Everybody's talent got lost. Hell, I did it for the money, totally. *No Mercy* was a nightmare because it was very unorganised. Everyone had his own idea of the film, his own dream. The director had an idea, the writer had an idea, Richard had an idea, I had an idea.'

However much she hated the film, she always made it clear her dislike did not extend to her co-star, despite her initial animosity towards him. Talking about the days she spent handcuffed to Richard up to her waist in muddy water, she laughed, 'I treasure that time more than most. A great, strange time with Richard. I laughed more with him than on any movie. I love him dearly. A very sensitive soul and a little bit on the misunderstood side. He's very, very funny.'

To the outside world, we were still the same Kim and Ron, but our relationship was slowly changing. I still loved my beautiful Kim. She was getting more beautiful as she got older and our sex-life was still great. The girl who had written me dozens of notes saying things like 'I love and adore you, darling ... LTF and always always Dot Dot Dot' started telling me, 'I *love* you, Ron, but I'm not *in* love with you.'

We did not discuss the letter I had seen from Richard Gere, but I did see a letter she wrote back to him. Richard is a devout Buddhist, a staunch follower of the exiled Tibetan leader the Dalai Lama, and he persuaded Kim to send money to support his cause. She didn't tell me, but I looked after the money and when the cancelled cheque was returned with our bank statement, I saw it and we had a row. Not because of the cause or the money — it was her money, after all — but because of the connection to Richard and *No Mercy*. Finally I could not bear speculating over Richard any longer. I was alone in the house one night, while Kim was staying in a hotel during the shooting of *My Stepmother Is an Alien*. I had been drinking and doing coke and I started searching for the letter he had sent her.

I found it tucked away in a drawer in our second house in the back garden — and there was a second note, postmarked a couple of days after the first. I could not resist reading them and I even videotaped them to have as a permanent record. I was so upset at what I read that on the video you can hear me cursing Kim and Richard.

The first letter, dated 27 April 1986, was four pages long, handwritten on the kind of lined yellow paper American lawyers use to make notes. Richard was pouring out his heart with love for Kim and begging her to let him know if his feelings were returned.

In the making of just one movie, Kim had managed to break two hearts. Even though Kim appeared to have rejected him once the film's main shoot had finished, and had organised her chaperons for the re-shoot, I still felt betrayed. I never liked Richard from the moment I met him and I never will, but I understand the pain he was suffering and can even empathise with him. After Kim and I finally split up, I heard she went back to Richard briefly. Surprisingly, Richard's hurt never turned to anger, which so often happens. He has always remained highly complimentary about Kim and even worked with her again on *Final Analysis*, but by that time Kim was so totally smitten by Alec Baldwin that nothing could have prised them apart.

To this day, Richard has continued to behave like a true officer and a gentleman towards Kim. In a 1996 interview he said, 'She is probably the most beautiful woman ever put on the planet and she's so talented. If she didn't look like that, probably people would notice the work more.' He rated Kim ahead of his stunning ex-wife Cindy Crawford, as well as gorgeous co-stars Diane Keaton, Debra Winger, Lauren Hutton and Julia Roberts. Kim truly was the prettiest woman in Richard's mind, but she showed no mercy to his heart.

Chapter 13

After all the strain of *No Mercy*, Blake Edwards' invitation to Kim to star in his upcoming comedy *Blind Date* opposite Bruce Willis, an actor who had never made a movie and was best known as second fiddle to Cybill Shepherd in the hit television detective show *Moonlighting*, seemed to offer light relief. The film was originally meant to be a vehicle for Sean Penn and Madonna, shortly after they married in 1985. Then it was to be Madonna and Bruce Willis, until a month before filming started. But Madonna had scheduling problems because she was finishing an album which conflicted with Bruce's availability. He had to complete the film during his summer break from *Moonlighting*.

Kim's casting was announced on 9 April 1986, and the film started shooting less than a month later on 5 May. Kim was playing Nadia Gates, a girl unable to hold her alcohol who ends up going on what turns out to be a disastrous blind date with Bruce's character Walter Davis. It was based on a real life blind date that the movie's scriptwriter, Dale Launer, had once experienced.

Kim got on remarkably well with Bruce and found him to be 'gentlemanly in an old-fashioned way, very much a woman's man — he gives them respect, and he gets it from them'. And, obviously, she always enjoyed working with Blake. She said, 'Fear runs like wildfire through the movie industry and he's not afraid. He'll trust you; he'll try anything.'

It was a mutual admiration society. Bruce managed to snub his *Moonlighting* co-star, another former Breck girl, by singing Kim's praises in an interview with *Prevue* magazine. When asked directly if Kim was easier to work with than Cybill, Bruce replied, 'Yeah, she was, and maybe that's because she's in movies, not TV.

Cybill's been around a long time, so maybe her fuse is shorter — I don't blame her.'

Blake also liked working with Kim. He said, 'She's a very complicated person. There's this child-woman thing she has, that Marilyn Monroe had — you see that childish vulnerability, but then she can suddenly throw it into a different gear, and there's a woman, a surprising woman. She can get defensive and tough if she has to, but there's a real fragility there.'

We were briefly on location in Monterey, just south of San Francisco. We flew up there in a private plane owned by Blake, who is known as Blackie by his friends. However, most of the shooting was done in the studio at Culver City and around West LA. We became friendly with Billy Vera, who was the lead singer of his band, Billy Vera and the Beaters, who were in the film. They had a hit at the time and we used to hang out with them when they performed at a small club called My Place in Santa Monica, which is a community by the beach in Los Angeles. Billy played there every Friday night so we'd turn up to watch his gig and as soon as we were seated, he'd stop and turn to the audience and say, 'Ladies and gentlemen, I'd like to introduce the fabulous movie star Kim Basinger. Please give her a hand.' It was sweet of him but it always embarrassed Kim.

Bruce had a driver called Dave Wright, with whom I used to play football years before. Dave was a mountain of a man — 6ft 6in tall and weighing 20st 10lb. He used to own a bar called D-Wrongs, which he ran in his spare time but he made most of his money as a professional bodyguard. After all our rows since *No Mercy*, I was not going to the studio every day with Kim, and I asked Dave to keep an eye on her and make sure she was OK. He called her 'little sister' and used to say, 'Come here, little sister.' He knew I was worried about her — he didn't know why I was so concerned, but then he didn't know I'd nearly lost her to Richard Gere — and he made sure no one, and I do mean *no one*, went near her.

We gradually seemed to be getting back on an even keel. Even though I was unhappy, I didn't want to lose Kim or be out of the marriage, and we both appeared to be making an effort. People would always ask why we got married and Kim used to reply, 'What's your dream worth if it's not worth failing for.' I never understood what the hell she was getting at but in her mind it was deep and meaningful, and it gave me the hope that we could patch things up for good. I don't know whether Kim felt guilty or was trying to win me round but she bought me a surprise gift — the best Porsche that had just come onto the market. For as long as I could remember I had always driven Porsches. But they were little Porsches and this was a turbo. One night we took the wardrobe girl and Kim's hairdresser out to dinner to one of the restaurants we used to go to regularly, Monty's on Ventura Boulevard. Even though it was a steak house Kim liked it and she could order her usual fish and salad. I was meeting them all there. I pulled in and as was always my custom I gave the parking valet $10 up front. I discovered long ago that if you tip the guy in the beginning and you're in a good-looking car, he'll always park it right outside the restaurant, in a good place for getting away quickly. He'll make sure he looks after you so you'll look after him again when you are leaving. Besides, if the car is in full view at the front it is far less likely to get damaged or stolen. At least, that's the theory. I handed him the keys and dashed in to meet Kim. I'd only been sitting in the restaurant for a couple of minutes when he came in looking very worried and asked out loud, 'Where is the customer who owns the Porsche?' I thought he was going to burst into tears when he explained that as I pulled into the car park, I had been followed by another car and as soon as I was through the door one of the men in the second vehicle had got out, pulled a gun on the valet and stolen my Porsche. Using my mobile phone I called the police and when I described my car they told me that a ring of car thieves was working the San Fernando Valley, specialising in taking Porsches. What Kim did not know was that my prized collection of home video tapes of me with old girlfriends was hidden in a compartment inside the car.

But worse than losing my car and the sex tapes was the fact that my house keys were attached to my car keys and had also gone. The detectives who came to the restaurant told me that probably everything would be OK but that there was a chance the gang might try to hit our house, because they knew anyone who owned a Porsche had to be rich. In California you have to keep a copy of your vehicle registration documents in the car, and they include your address. One of the uniformed cops was especially nice and said that he was on duty overnight and would patrol past our home every hour or so to make sure everything was cool. Still I was not happy and I feared for our safety, so I checked Kim into the Marriott Hotel in Woodland Hills, which was only a couple of miles from our home, and then I went up and stayed up all night on guard duty, armed with my arsenal of guns and knives. The next morning I hired a private detective service to supply round-the-clock security for the weekend until I could get a firm in to change the locks.

I did come close to death that weekend but it wasn't because of any guys with guns trying to break in. And the guard outside our door didn't come to my rescue because he didn't know I was in danger. It was Kim who saved me. She returned to the house after I'd arranged the guard service. I was in the kitchen making a tuna sandwich when, for the first time in my life, I started to choke. I was really choking and turning blue as my throat was blocked and I was unable to get any air into my lungs. Kim saw this and started pounding on my chest. She didn't know the Heimlich manoeuvre and after a few seconds she ran to the door to call the guard but her beating me had dislodged the piece of food that was stuck and I started breathing again. I was very lucky and we were both lucky, that, thankfully, we didn't have any visitors wearing face masks and brandishing guns.

The cops told me that one day I'd probably get my Porsche back. They were right. Some months later, I got a call to say it had been found — well, what was left of it at least. They'd found the shell. The engine, tyres and everything inside including the seats were gone, and the body was burned out. The cops never mentioned anything about videotapes so I guess they went as well.

As Kim matured she became even more beautiful. Her body only got better and more solid, toned and muscular. She was so worried about staying in shape that she increased her workout routine. We had had a gym built into the guest house at the back of the property when we did our first renovations and went in there to exercise. Kim mainly did aerobics and lifted free weights. As time went on she became ever more obsessive about taking her aerobic tapes whenever we were on location so she could maintain her exercise regime.

Kim was so determined to stay in the best shape possible that she hired a personal trainer, an Australian bodybuilder called Phil Walsh, who had been recommended to us as a fitness expert. After a few weeks of working with him, I noticed that Kim, who was usually so sloppily dressed that you would think she was a bag lady, was starting to wear these really sexy exercise outfits. I was feeling pretty prickly and vulnerable after Gere and I jealously mentioned that she appeared to be more concerned about her looks around this muscular, young guy than she was the rest of the time when she was with me. She was always admiring his body and flirting with him. Strange to say, it came as no surprise that after we broke up, I discovered they were dating.

Kim and I had been in New York, where she was preparing for her role in *Blind Date*, when the telephone rang and it was Robert Benton, the Oscar-winning writer-director of *Kramer vs Kramer* and *Places in the Heart*, wanting to talk to her. He had been told all about her by his good friend Robert Altman, and thought she might be right for the title role in the comedy thriller he was writing. Altman, who had directed Kim in *Fool for Love*, had raved on about her so much and insisted that Benton, who is always known simply by his surname in the industry, should get in touch with her.

Kim had been experimenting with hair colouring for her part as Nadia. She had had a brown, horrible-looking rinse put in. She liked it, however, and told me, 'I am in my Maria syndrome.' She always had the ambition of playing Maria in *West Side Story* and here she was in New York with dark hair. So now, out of the blue, she'd had this call from a director she'd never met, but who had probably seen her in films as a vision of blonde loveliness, and she was going to meet him with an unfamiliar hair colouring.

In the morning, she got into the shower and suddenly she screamed, 'I know I am not this dirty,' pointing to all this brown stuff swirling around her feet. The new colour was washing out. She got out of the tub and looked in the mirror. As she stood there her hair was changing to a reddish colour. Kim was not sure what her hair would look like when it dried, so she decided to leave it wet. She rushed round to Benton's office, which was only a block away from the hotel where we were staying, panicking because she felt insecure with damp, stringy, reddish-brown hair.

She need not have worried. The moment she walked into the room, he knew she was right for the role of Nadine Hightower, a manicurist in a 1950s Texas beauty salon, who gets involved in a wacky tale of love, marriage and murder with her down-on-his-luck, estranged husband Vernon, after she poses for some *artistic* pictures taken by a small-town photographer claiming to be a friend of Mr Hugh Hefner of *Playboy* magazine. When she came back to our hotel, she told me with delight, 'He didn't even mention my hair, so I instantly fell in love with him.'

Benton admitted that casting Kim was a 'yes-at-first-sight' situation. He said, 'I swear, when Kim walked in the door for that first meeting, she was Nadine. The only other time in my life I've had that experience was when I was looking for Joanna Kramer in *Kramer vs Kramer*, and Meryl Streep walked in the door.' He added, 'Usually, when I start writing I have an idea who I want for the part. Not this time. Halfway through the script I began to get nervous. Then Kim walked in, and by the time she walked out I knew I had my Nadine. My only worry was that she'd get pregnant and give up acting because I didn't have a second choice.'

Kim was equally enthusiastic about the meeting with Benton. She had not read the script and really knew nothing about the film but she felt that meeting him was one of those rare instances where creative minds meet and instantly mesh. As she left the meeting, she told him, 'I would walk over high water to work with you.'

Benton later recalled that he considered Kim to be a cross between legendary actress Carole Lombard and notorious bank robber Bonnie Parker, whose story he'd detailed in the 1967 classic gangster movie *Bonnie and Clyde*, which he co-wrote with David Newman. He said, 'What makes the part of Nadine work is that she is able to reveal the kind of vulnerability that is essential, yet she is the most perfect-looking creature you've ever seen. When you go into the make-up trailer at the crack of dawn, you know what kind of shape someone's in.' Kim believed that the reason they hit it off immediately was that Benton was from Texas and she was from Georgia, so they shared a Southern link.

We decided to embark on another of our road trips rather than fly to the location in Austin, Texas, so we borrowed the Green Bean from my sister again and set off on the 1,400-mile journey. We seemed to be putting our troubles behind us as we drove across country for three days, drinking our wine as we pulled into small towns and enjoying playing at being plain old Joe Anybody.

The movie was a light-hearted comedy thriller, also starring Jeff Bridges as Nadine's husband, Rip Torn as the bad guy and Gwen Verdon as the mother figure who is Nadine's boss and confidante.

Kim really liked the character. She said, 'I think Nadine has something that is very difficult to play, in a strange way. You know how you see someone and admire someone on the street — something they do and are not aware of, something dear, admirable and pleasant. She is very unaware of how much she lives out loud. Nadine doesn't go to shrinks. She could be one. She is a character who will not take "no" for an answer in life. I can see this woman as an old lady, later in life, saying, "I did it all". I love her freedom. She's sort of fearless in life. Maybe it's out of ignorance. I call her real trashy class.'

The film had a team who knew each other and worked well together. It was produced by Arlene Donovan, a former literary agent at ICM who sold *Kramer vs Kramer* to producer Stanley Jaffe. She had been at Benton's first meeting with Kim and was equally enthusiastic about having her star opposite Jeff. The director of photography was Nestor Almendros, a Spanish-born cinematographer who had worked on Benton's other movies, *Kramer vs Kramer* and *Places in the Heart*. To round things off, Benton had worked with Jeff Bridges when he made his directorial debut movie *Bad Company*, a post-American Civil War drama released in 1972.

For Kim, the entire 11-week production went as smoothly as the initial meeting. She and Jeff hit it off right away. 'Jeff is one of the most agreeable and hardest-working actors I've ever met. When you love your character, the story and your co-workers — and have a director like Benton — the only variable, really, is the weather.'

Everyone could tell that Kim and Jeff worked well together. The cinematographer complimented them because he felt they had good timing.

We quickly settled into life in Austin. We rented a wonderful, old house way out in the country where wild deer roamed freely and the brave ones would even come up almost to our door. As usual, we found our favourite restaurants. We discovered that one we were particularly fond of was run by Sherry Lazurus and her chef husband Alan. They were displaced Californians who originally came from Palo Alto so we had to have things in common. They almost became our surrogate family in Texas, so we had them over to spend Thanksgiving Day with us while we were there.

Kim talked about Nadine being fearless, and the script called for her to be just as bold. There was one scene, actually filmed in San Antonio, Texas, where Nadine and Vernon make a daring escape from two bad guys who are chasing them. They had to make their way across a ladder used as a bridge from the top of one huge old house to another. It was really tense, yet, at the same time, funny and fast-paced. Kim and Jeff were rushing here, there and everywhere and their co-ordination was just great. The abandoned houses were real enough and, in fact, they had been slated for demolition. The set designer cleaned up the interiors with wallpaper and paint. But these houses were only two storeys high and the script required them to be three. So the set designer got builders to add the façade of a third storey and then used paint to age it to match the real houses.

Tommy Prate, the grip, built scaffolding between the two houses, so even though Kim was actually crawling along the rickety ladder, more than 30 feet in the air, there was a mattress very close under her, just out of the frame. There was a platform on scaffolding big enough for a camera dolly and the whole crew to work on it, more than two storeys off the ground. But there was one camera angle when it was shot from the ground so that the audience got the full effect of how high up Kim was. The platform could not be there for that scene so they used a stunt girl, because it was too dangerous for Kim. They couldn't afford to lose their star by getting her hurt or worse.

We also had our financial concerns while on location in San Antonio. One day, Kim's business manager Mitchell Freedman came to see us to discuss some outstanding financial matters from before our marriage. We were all sitting in our hotel suite when, all of a sudden, Freedman turned to me and said, 'You know, Ron, I'd feel a lot more comfortable if you'd leave the room.' I was taken aback. Here we were, man and wife, and this guy was trying to kick me out of my own hotel room.

'Really,' I said. I could feel the tension in the air and rather than push the point, I thought it was simpler and cleaner to just leave the room. I said, 'I'll see you later.'

We'd never had any financial secrets and I had always looked after the money for both of us. That was the first indication — even with all the heartbreak and upset we'd been through over Gere — that maybe we wouldn't be together 'Longer Than Forever ...' after all.

I knew that our flame of passion for each other was nowhere near as strong as it had been, but I didn't realise how close to dying out it was. Emotionally, we were struggling but we were putting on pretences and trying to fool ourselves and each other.

I had to return to Los Angeles for a few days to sort out some problems. We were staying in Austin and Kim wanted to have sex before I left. What she didn't know was that I'd arranged to see Shane on my way home to Woodland Hills. So after we'd fooled around for a while, I faked an orgasm. I knew that in a few hours I'd be in bed with Shane and I was insecure about my ability to perform twice in a short time and I wanted to satisfy Shane more than I needed to satisfy Kim. That's the kind of insecurity that only a man of 50 or more who was using drugs can understand. I thought to myself, 'Hell, in about two hours I'll be back in the saddle again,' and I wanted to ensure that I could perform, which isn't always the case when you've done drugs.

There were two weeks of rehearsals before filming began. Jeff loved to rehearse, he'd be happy to run through a scene 150 times before doing it for real, but Kim always detested it. She made a joke of it to Benton. At the end of filming, she asked him, 'Did rehearsals help you? They didn't help me at all.' Her motto has always been that she lives for between 'action' and 'cut'. That's the way it was with her; she'd read a script, get on the set and want the cameras to start rolling. She believed that she would use up all her talent and emotion during rehearsals and have nothing left for the actual scene, especially if it was a scene where she had most of the dialogue. Kim always felt she did her best acting on the spot. She said, 'You either sink or swim. I like that fear. That fear leads me into who it is I'm playing. I like to do a scene once, maybe twice, and that will be my best work.' Despite Kim and Jeff being as different as chalk and cheese, she loved him and he became one of her favourite actors.

While in Texas we met John Connelly, who had been Governor of Texas and was shot when he rode in the same car as President John F Kennedy when he was assassinated in 1963. He seemed like a nice guy, not the kind of guy who deserved to be shot.

After filming was over, Kim said, 'Though I've had the opportunity to work with some incredibly talented film makers, I've never had a connection with a director like I did with Benton. It's as though he and I sat around and talked with this ghost called Nadine.' For the first time in her career, Kim could see Nadine becoming a franchise. She said, 'I can see Nadine movies happening to the end of my life; Nadine Goes to Paris, Nadine Faces Death, Nadine for President.'

We socialised with Benton quite a lot. He invited us to his house in up-state New York and once, because of him, we went to an amazing party, which was held in Yoko Ono's house. Yoko had invited more than 2,000 people. The famous Grease producer Alan Carr was there, as was Bob Fosse, who'd directed Cabaret and Sweet Charity, and several other celebrities, but everyone wanted to meet Kim. I hired a small plane to get us from New York to Benton's place. We had sex in the air and again in a room at Yoko's, except no one knew what we were doing. We stayed up there for a few days and went antique shopping with Benton.

Nadine had a benefit screening at the Directors Guild in Los Angeles to raise money for the National Hemangioma Foundation, a group that works to further research and help people who have disfiguring birthmarks like the one then Russian leader Mikhail Gorbachev had on his head. It was run by Dr Lawrence David, who had removed cancers from both Kim and me and we were on the charity's board. Kim hosted the event and Dr David was the guest of honour. Everyone attending the event wanted to talk to Dr David about the laser treatments he had developed and was pioneering to remove these birthmarks. Among the celebrities there were Patrick Swayze, Barry Bostwick, David Niven Jr, Teri Garr, Perry King, Alexandra Paul and Corbin Bernsen. Kim pushed hard for the première to raise funds for Dr David's charity. She told me that when she was growing up in Athens she knew a woman with a severe facial birthmark and never realised it was treatable until she met our Hermosa Beach-based specialist.

We were invited to tour Europe to help promote *Nadine*. While in Italy, we visited the famous Trevi Fountain in Rome and, just like so many tourists have done, we both threw in coins and made wishes. I wished that we would always stay together and be prosperous. Kim asked me what I'd wished so I told her, but she never would tell me what her request was.

My fondest memory of our Roman Holiday, however, took place in the bathroom at our hotel. We were staying in this hotel with long corridors and dark wood and it felt like we were the only people there. It was 3.00 or 4.00am and I was stoned — I'd been doing drugs — and we were heavily into lust. We started fooling around in the bathroom and quickly one thing led to another, and before long Kim was sitting astride of the sink and we were banging away as if our lives depended upon it. It was just as we were coming that we went flat onto the floor. Kim and I carried on until we were done, but we were laughing so hard because the sink had broken away from the wall under the weight and fierceness of our enthusiasm. Water was pouring out from where the taps had been. After we'd finished, I composed myself and telephoned reception.

'Hello,' I said. 'I can't imagine what's happened but our bedroom is full of water. We've just woken up and it appears the sink has fallen off the wall.' Within minutes, our room was full of maintenance men. They couldn't understand what had happened, the sink was smashed to pieces as if an elephant had sat on it. They mopped things up and as soon as they left, I collapsed on to the bed in agony — my thumb was throbbing. I thought I'd sprained it in the fall. It wasn't until I got home to the United States that I discovered I had actually broken it. I had an X-ray and ended up with my right hand in a cast for weeks.

It was not only a sink and my thumb that were broken on that trip. We were staying in Paris at the Royal Monceau, a really fancy, old hotel full of antiques, just off the Champs-Elysées, when Benton wanted to see Kim alone in his room. I was down in the restaurant with Kim's hairdresser Rick Provenzano and Linda Lang, who had taken over as Kim's assistant. It was great for Linda, because she had never been to Europe before; in fact, she'd never been outside California, and she loved the experience. I was called to come up to Benton's room, and when I got there the antique coffee table was broken. They told me they had been talking and Benton had sat down on the table, which had broken because it was so old.

While we were in Madrid, Benton celebrated his 54th birthday. We organised an impromptu party for him at a restaurant and even got them to bake him a cake. Everybody was laughing and joking and Kim started singing 'Happy Birthday', mimicking the breathless way Marilyn did it for President John F Kennedy at his famous birthday bash which is often shown on television. Kim got that little girl voice just right and I was reminded once again of the tremendous similarities between these two women who were both international superstars; my father had worked with one and I'd known them both, but I had the pleasure of making Kim my wife. We all laughed and ate and drank, and had a great time at that party so far from home.

Having Linda replace Sherry worked out well for Kim and me, as it happened. Our long-running problems with Doris came to a head and we knew we had to get rid of her. It was an unpleasant job, but I phoned Sherry and asked her to go there and fire her, and move in to look after the dogs and the house. As soon as we got home, I set about finding a replacement. I'd never had any experience of hiring that type of employee so I went to a domestic agency. I interviewed a few people and would have loved to have hired a willowy Swedish blonde, but Kim wouldn't have it. Then I realised that the best person I had talked to while I was looking for a replacement for Doris was the woman running the agency. She was a Brazilian woman called Fatima. We made her the proverbial offer she couldn't refuse and she moved in with us. She stayed with Kim for years after I left and introduced her to her Brazilian holy man.

Kim often got calls from magazines asking her to do photo layouts but she always insisted those days were behind her. However, there was one project she could not resist — a photo shoot for *Vogue* on safari in Kenya.

It was her sister Ashley's 29th birthday at the time, so we took her and her husband Joe Brewer, who ran Papa Joe's bar back in Athens, Georgia, along with us. It was an amazing experience, very exciting and very different from our normal existence. We stayed in Nairobi, at the old Norfolk Hotel. It was terribly romantic and we had a huge mosquito net over our bed, so we didn't waste much time before getting underneath it and fooling around. We were driven all over the place to have exotic pictures taken of Kim for the spread. We went out to a ranch where Kim made friends with a jaguar called Dooms. She stroked him and he was tamer than our feral cats back home. He actually purred and nuzzled up to her! She also put on a special leather gauntlet and held a trained peregrine falcon. She was not so keen on him, however; he was very beautiful but he scared her.

We went out into the bush at Ambaseli at the foot of Mount Kilimanjaro, and slept in tents. Admittedly, they were luxurious tents but they still had their primitive side. We had to sleep under nets to protect us from the mosquitoes and Kim had to be careful putting her bare feet on the floor in case she trod on a scorpion. At the back there was a zippered canvas flap which you lifted up and there was the toilet — a hole in the ground with a shovel next to it. There was also a shower back there, which was simply a hole in the top of the tent. Centipedes were crawling up the inside walls. There was a huge staff, and when you wanted a shower they brought a bucket of warm water and sloshed it into the hole, over you. Kim washed her hair every day and she needed two buckets, at least. I don't know if the guys pouring it could see anything, but they spent a lot of time up there with their water buckets. They all liked Kim; they called her 'Mem-Sahib'.

The staff did all our washing, except for women's underwear. They had some kind of religious objection to that, so the girls had to rinse out their own things. There were Masai tribesmen living there and Kim danced with them and in front of them, and they started singing to her with a staccato beat to match her dancing. I drank scotch and the local Tusker beer with the tribesmen and bought a spear and a walking stick whittled out of a root from them. Masai warriors have to kill a lion when they are 12 or 14 years old, as a kind of initiation rite, and my spear had been used to kill one. I didn't tell Kim that, though.

The only drawback to being on safari is the food. Kim was vegetarian and could not eat it. It was brought in from the city and it would go off after two or three days. It was kept in a special tent but baboons used to come into the camp and steal it. On the last day, a herd of elephants even wandered in looking for food and were generally being nosey. The servants put nets over the food but it was no good; there were flies in the porridge and ants in the sugar at breakfast time. In addition to that, the servants used to wash the dishes in dirty water. Every so often we had to drive to a hotel on the edge of the reserve to get her some decent food. But, even though we had come armed with Lomotil tablets to ward off bad stomachs, we still got diarrhoea.

We also took pictures — Kim posed in the nude — at the house which *Out of Africa* author Karen Blixen owned and where Meryl Streep and Robert Redford shot the Oscar-winning movie of the same name.

When we went back to the Norfolk Hotel, there was a big surprise for me. There, in the hotel's famous Long Bar, was Shane. She had remarried and was on holiday with her new husband and it was bizarre meeting her so many thousands of miles from home. Neither of us had any idea the other was going to be there.

Then, all too soon, it was time to return home via London and the Concorde to Washington. Steve Martin was on the plane and he and Kim chatted for a while. It was strange to go from a place where life has been unchanged for centuries for many people to the space-age environment of a supersonic jet.

Kim's next role, in the comedy *My Stepmother Is an Alien*, was also a space-age project. In her most unusual role up to that point, she played Chief Extragalactic Probist, a woman from outer space who arrives on earth knowing nothing about sex and, pretending to be an earthling named Celeste, marries an eccentric scientist in an attempt to save her own planet from destruction.

Before it finally started filming in early 1988, with actor-turned-director Richard Benjamin at the helm, the script had been in development for six years and had been with three studios, had three titles, at least eight writers had worked on it and it had been re-written more than 15 times. What was once a nightmare tale about an alien plotting the earth's destruction was transformed into a contemporary romantic comedy. Kim replaced Shelley Long, one of a string of actresses who had dropped out of the project, opposite Dan Aykroyd playing the bumbling boffin. My actress wife, who had played so many sexy roles in *Never Say Never Again, The Man Who Loved Women, The Natural, 9½ Weeks, Fool for Love, Blind Date* and *Nadine* and was so sexually adventurous, was now playing a woman with zero sexual experience. She said, 'I loved not being expected to know about sex.' Kim had been beaten up in *9½ Weeks,* boozed up in *Blind Date* and now she was being beamed up — or rather down.

In the hope of capitalising on the success of films of a similar genre, like *ET* and *War Games*, the movie was rewritten from being about a teenage boy and his mean and vicious but beautiful stepmother to the story of a teenage girl whose widowed, scientist father weds a kind-hearted, stunning spacewoman. The stepmother's appearance and character had changed with every actress who was considered to play her; she was less attractive and funnier when Bette Midler was the front runner; sweeter when it was supposed to be Julie Andrews; but sexier again when Raquel Welch was due to go before the camera in the role. Other actresses who were considered included Joan Rivers and Cybill Shepherd.

Benjamin was yet another director who discovered that Kim hated rehearsing. He said, 'She doesn't like to rehearse a lot, and she doesn't like to talk about it; she likes to get up on her feet and do it. There's no actor-at-work or worrying thing.' What did worry him was the fake nails Kim wore for her character. He said, 'The most horrifying call we would ever get was from her driver, saying that on the way in, a nail broke.' He should have worried about what the critics were going to think of his film.

When it was finally released that winter, Kim earned praise, as usual, from Duane Byrge of the *Hollywood Reporter*, who wrote, 'Not only should the film's co-star Kim Basinger become a household name after *Stepmother*, but the entertainment community should arrive at some sort of consensus on how to pronounce her name.' The *Los Angeles Times'* Kevin Thomas said, '*My Stepmother Is an Alien* is a wild and wacky romantic comedy, rowdy and brash yet surprisingly tender. Dan Aykroyd and Kim Basinger match up like Laurel and Hardy. Big, bulky Aykroyd is the perfect comic foil for the sexy, madcap Basinger.' But overall the movie was critically slammed and it bombed at the box office. *Daily Variety* summed up what most critics felt, '*My Stepmother Is an Alien* is a failed attempt to mix many of the film genres associated with the alien idea into a sprightly romp.'

We had started to renovate the house in Don Juan Place again, this time with a view to selling it and moving to a bigger property. The movie was filmed in and around Los Angeles but Kim told me that living at home would be too distracting for her because of all the noise, dust and disruption. She couldn't cope with being around the maid and the dogs and the builders, so during the week she took up residence back at the Woodland Hills Marriott Hotel. Her driver collected her in the mornings and drove her to the set. I turned up when filming was over for the day, took her out to dinner and then we returned to the hotel. I would leave her there so she could rest and read the script for the following day, and I would go home. Occasionally, we'd still have sex but that did not mean we were not becoming estranged, although I did not take that on board at the time. I should have known that our love story was heading for a sad end but I had not figured out that the rewrite of our screenplay was almost finished. I was terribly lonely and used to stay up all night taking cocaine and falling deeper and deeper into depression. Kim knew I was in bad shape and wrote to me on the hotel's stationary, 'Ronald, you'll feel so much better if you get 3 or 4 hours of sleep.' She told me she loved me and asked me to call her later. As always she signed it 'LTF ...' but it was during that depression that I found the letters from Richard Gere. From reading them it seemed she had backed out of whatever relationship they had had for my sake, but it was too late to save us.

Sometimes I went to the set of *Stepmother* because I knew most of the crew, but I would just sit in the trailer by myself. It was pretty boring and I don't think Kim wanted me around anyway. A cold chill was creeping into the air between us.

Our personal relationship was in turmoil, although I had not realised just how far things had deteriorated between us. While I was at home overseeing the builders, Kim was dropping heavy hints that I was soon to be history. Veteran entertainment writer Jim Jerome sat down to talk to her for *Self Magazine* to promote the soon-to-be released *Stepmother*. She talked about falling for one of her leading men.

'I don't easily fall in love,' she said. 'I am not easily attracted to anyone. I'm not up for grabs. But I have been in love with someone that I've worked with and I'll always love him. We all do things we want.'

She went on to tell Jerome, 'I don't know where I belong. Life is one big never-ending transition, isn't it?' Quickly realising she was disguising a point, he asked, 'Surely that doesn't include your marriage?' She whipped two fingers across her lips and said, 'Don't know. Can't say. Zip. Look, relationships change all the time.' Referring to me, she added, 'But he's a good friend of mine now and has a great sense of humour. I can't talk about my marriage right now. Maybe in a month or two, but that's a whole 'nother time frame.' A writer I'd never even met knew I was being dumped before I did. His article appeared that November in 1988, only days after I learned the awful truth.

Chapter 14

Sean Young's misfortune in falling off a horse and breaking her arm was a massive stroke of luck for Kim. Dark-haired Sean, who had previously appeared in *Blade Runner*, *Young Doctors in Love* and *Wall Street*, had her unlucky break just a week before the filming of *Batman* was due to start. Kim, who years earlier had turned down the role that Sean played in *Blade Runner* because she felt it lacked emotion, was called in as a replacement to play Vicki Vale in what was already one of the most hyped films of the 1980s before work had even begun. She couldn't go wrong with this film. It had Jack Nicholson and Michael Keaton, but above all it was *Batman*. We flew in September 1988 to London, where it was being shot, and moved into the luxurious St James' Club. I did my usual chores of making sure everything was perfect for Kim and that her private exercise room was set up in the suite. We met Jon Peters, once the hairdresser boyfriend of Barbra Streisand, now a top Hollywood mogul and producer of *Batman*.

Filming had not started but Kim was doing rehearsals, and we went out to dinner with Jon when they finished work. At the weekend, while we were there he hired a couple of limos and we went out into the countryside, to visit a farm. He was very friendly towards me and he and I never had any cross words. So I was astonished when a story started doing the rounds later that one night at dinner I was 'verbally abusing' Kim so much that he grabbed me by the throat!

We had to fly to London at short notice and after about two weeks Kim asked me to fly home to check that everything was OK and that the animals were well. I was used to hopping on planes for this sort of visit and did not think anything of it. In any case,

Kim had to fly to New York a couple of days later for a screening of her latest film, *My Stepmother Is an Alien*, and to do some publicity pictures for it. I was to fly East to meet her there, then we would go back to London together to finish *Batman*.

On our last night together in London, we went out to dinner, came home and I did a little cocaine before making love. Afterwards, I left Kim and went to sleep in the second bedroom because I wanted to stretch out. At about six o'clock the next morning, I was woken up by Kim crawling into bed with me. She sat astride me and started making urgent, passionate love. I was delighted to have such a romantic send-off, but I was supposed to be on a plane at 10.00am so we couldn't linger. When we were dressed, we went into the front room of the suite and all of a sudden she grabbed me and started kissing me really deeply.

'We'll always be together,' she said unexpectedly.

'I shouldn't be leaving you,' I replied.

Then the car came and took me to Heathrow. I jetted out of chilly London and, because of the eight-hour time difference, I was back in Woodland Hills under the balmy Californian sunshine that afternoon.

The phone call came the day after I got home.

'I want a separation, a trial separation,' said Kim. I was dumbstruck. I couldn't believe it. Only a month earlier, Kim had given me a quirky gift – a print-out of a heart scan and ECG she had had during a routine medical at the Brotman Medical Centre. On the brown envelope she had written, 'Heart for Ron only'. To add to the irony, she had checked in as K Britton. I sat around the house thinking, agonising over what I should do. Even though I'd been unhappy for a long time, I felt that I had to make one last attempt to smooth things over and at least attempt to keep us together. Really, I wanted to stay with her, I thought, so I decided to fly to New York anyway. I called for a limousine to take me to the airport to get the next flight so I could be waiting for her when she arrived at John F Kennedy Airport. I spotted her in the luggage lobby waiting for her bags to arrive and I shouted out, 'Hi, Chelsea. What's up?' I didn't want to call her by her name because that would bring attention to her and people might bother her or there could have been paparazzi hanging around. I always used her nickname in public. We embraced and kissed and she was crying. Her hairdresser Rick Provenzano was with her. She said she had to go to her hotel. She seemed very, very nervous and upset and I comforted her. She told me we'd get together later.

I had a limo waiting for me and so did she. The hotel where she was staying was fully booked so I'd taken a room at another hotel further downtown as I didn't know whether she'd want me to share her suite. She told me she'd send Rick to get me later. But when he arrived he suggested we should take a walk in the park.

'She can't face this now,' he said. 'She doesn't want to confront you now so will you please go home?'

I agreed, but I knew where she was going to be shooting her public relations stills and I decided to stop there on the way back to the airport, to say goodbye. I didn't even stay in Manhattan overnight. As I walked on to the shoot, I could see she was shocked to see me. I said, 'Hey, Chelsea, what's the deal? I've just come to say goodbye.' She was polite and pleasant and hugged me goodbye. She told me we needed time to think about our future. She gave me a quick kiss and as I was leaving, she flashed me our sign, the two fingers across each other. I knew it was over, but at least I had given it a try. I flew back home to Woodland Hills to consider my position. What I didn't know at the time was that Jon Peters had booked the suite above hers. When I learned that he was there, I called her and she insisted that she didn't know he was going to do that, but I never truly believed her. Shortly afterwards, top gossip columnist Liz Smith broke the news that Kim and Jon were together. They hadn't wasted much time after she got rid of me. Smith also pointed out the irony that Kim had swapped a make-up man for a hairdresser.

Then Kim's attorney, who was actually our joint lawyer in those days, called a few days after I returned from New York to say she was going to file for divorce. I was shocked but, in a bizarre way, happy. It sounds incredible, but in many ways it was a relief because we had been living a lie. If Kim had not walked out on me, I would never have left her. I was seeing other women but I would have kept it going if Kim had wanted it, even if she was sleeping with other men. But I had not been truly happy since she made *No Mercy* and even before that I'd been fooling around. She was the one going out to work but always coming home for me. But for the past few years we'd been drifting apart. I couldn't go to a movie set and order her to come home. If she didn't want to come to me willingly it wasn't working for me.

Thinking back on it, it's funny to imagine that I'd spent all those years with one of the most beautiful women in the world — a woman most men would have died for — and yet I wasn't happy and I'd sought comfort in the arms of other, in most men's minds, less attractive women. It dawned on me that, for years, we hadn't been living a married life the way most people think of a marriage.

Kim's lawyer advised me to get a top-notch attorney; I went to a friend and tennis partner, Forrest D Concannon — Con to his friends. Con and his partner Irving Hartman took on Kim's hot-shot legal team and I think they did a good job for me. In fact, they looked after me so well that in my opinion they made her fancy team of legal eagles eat their words.

I had first met Con in the early 1980s, through Pat Lynch, his best friend. Kim and I met them in a sushi restaurant in the Valley, with two other people — business executive David Cronenbald and this big black guy — Al Cowlings. Cowlings, usually known as AC, was to have his own 15 minutes of fame in 1994, when he drove his best friend, former football great OJ Simpson, on his notorious low-speed car chase after Simpson's wife Nicole and her friend Ron Goldman had been brutally murdered. AC, who became one of my tennis partners, did not normally drink, but this night he had had two Japanese beers and they affected him so much that he couldn't remember names. He called me Roy, Con Paul, because he had another friend called Paul Kahn, and Kim, for some reason, became Robin.

At first, Kim and I were comparatively friendly after the split. She even asked me to break the news to her family. I thought that was a bizarre request but I did it anyway. I had always got on reasonably well with her folks. I was deeply moved to get a note from her father Don saying how upset he was at the break-up. In part it read, 'Hell! I don't know what to say. I'm totally in the dark. Kim has always expressed her feelings for you in a very positive way — saying just a few weeks ago that she loved you and that she felt you to be her best friend ... You're like a son to me and I love you.' Her father kindly invited me and my chum Pat Lynch to spend the upcoming Thanksgiving holiday — the most important holiday for American families to be together — with him, even though he knew very soon I would no longer be his son-in-law.

I later learned that Kim's mother, Ann, was annoyed when she dumped me — and that Kim was so upset that Ann did not back her up that they became even further estranged. Don told an interviewer, 'Part of the reason for the rift is that Ann criticised Kim for divorcing Ron. Kim went beserk when she found out what Ann had said. She needed her mother to say, "Honey, I will back you in whatever choice you make."'

Kim's instant relationship with Jon Peters quickly became common knowledge, though officially she insisted they were 'just good friends'. Of course, she was able to use that to boost the role of Vicki Vale into a bigger part than had been originally planned. Jon himself claimed he thought he helped her through the early days of our separation.

'She was emerging as a woman — taking charge of her own life and dealing with the responsibility of herself — and I think I may have helped encourage that,' he said.

Whatever the truth of their relationship — I don't know if it was a serious love affair or just a case of physical attraction because they had been thrown together – Jon took a special interest in her role, and encouraged her own input.

'Kim is almost the heart of Batman,' he said. 'She's a very creative woman and I've been involved a lot with creative women. She was a big help to *Batman* director Tim Burton and me. There's a confrontation scene between Jack Nicholson and Michael Keaton which didn't exist originally and Kim's input was crucial. She'd keep reminding me, "JP, it's a love story."'

Kim's romance with Jon quickly became the most talked about gossip on the set of *Batman*. During filming money was no object when it came to pleasing Kim. Jon forked out a staggering $40,000 for her during their week in Manhattan for the première of *My Stepmother Is an Alien* on a shopping spree because she couldn't find any clothes she wanted to wear in London for her part in *Batman* and he was constantly buying her gifts of expensive, sexy underwear. As time went by, more and more tales circulated about Jon's extravagances when it came to pleasing my estranged wife.

Their romance did not last after the filming of *Batman*, although Peter told Hollywood writer Marilyn Beck, 'We had an affair; we were very involved for six months. Kim and I are still very good friends.' By that time, Kim was already making sweet music with Prince, who did the movie's soundtrack.

But she seemed to keep fond memories of Jon, whom she called 'my sweetheart hoodlum'. She said, 'He made me aware, he helped me get on with *Batman* and with life. I got to know a part of Jon that I consider very sacred. We had a lot of fun.'

As soon as Kim hit me with wanting the divorce, I realised I was at a great advantage over her. I am sure she thought she was being clever, getting me out of London before she broke the news. But that meant I was in residence at Don Juan Place. Although there was no doubt that legally that was Kim's house, it was the marital home we had shared for more than eight years and I had nowhere else to go. So I decided to stay there. I was worried that if I moved into a cheap motel or something like that, when it came to trial they could argue that was the standard of living I had come to expect. But I was used to a big house with an Olympic-sized pool in the back yard, driving Porsches and flying first class. I did not have a pre-nuptial agreement but that was Kim's idea, and I think now she was coming to regret it. She had always kept us both living well since she started making good money. Kim was horrified that I had stayed in the house and demanded that I move out. I refused and the legal battles began. The actual divorce papers were served on me on Christmas Eve, 1988. It was a very different Christmas from the time we had flown back from London just for three days.

Much to my amazement, in addition to the divorce papers I got a Christmas card from Kim. It was her typical, jokey card, saying, 'Merry Christmas to my kind of people' on the front and 'Bad all year and proud of it!!!' inside. She also sent me a watch, to replace a watch of mine that she always wore and had kept when she dumped me, and a key-ring, along with a jacket I had bought years before in Nice, while we'd been in France filming *Never Say Never Again* and which she loved. It was touching to get the card, and heartbreaking at the same time. It was the first note she had ever sent me that was not signed 'LTF ... Longer Than Forever'.

It was a friendly, chatty note, written in red ink, that started, 'Ron, Hi! I just wanted to send you these couple of presents because I saw them and they reminded me of something you might like,' and ended, 'I care. I want you to have a beautiful Christmas ... I'll definitely call you — A wish on a star for you. Love always, Kim.' She did add her symbol of a cross inside a heart, but that could not make up for the missing 'LTF ...' The key-ring sounds like a trivial gift, but it was very thoughtful because it came apart to make two rings, so I could detach my car keys from my house keys. If I had had one like that when my Porsche was stolen, the thieves would not have got hold of the keys to Don Juan Place.

Kim was having a very different Christmas holiday in London from the one I was spending at home in California. Probably Jon's greatest excess that sticks out when it came to the astonishing lengths to which he went to please Kim was the way he set out ensuring that she enjoyed her Christmas away from home — not that she'd have had a particularly happy one in California as I was firmly in residence at our place in Woodland Hills. Jon spent $10,000 on Christmas baubles and had a film set dresser from Pinewood Studios, where *Batman* was being shot, decorate his flat festively so that it would please her.

Technicians working on the *Batman* movie were outraged. One crew member said, 'We were all horrified by the extravagance. We'd signed wage deals that in effect meant we could not claim any overtime however many hours we worked.'

While Kim and Jon were snuggling up in chilly London playing out their White Christmas fantasies, I went to a Christmas Eve party with a new girlfriend, but on Christmas Day I was alone watching American football on the television with the dogs keeping me company.

I couldn't believe Kim's first settlement offer. It was essentially, 'I'll give you $50,000 if you leave the house, get out of town and never go back to work in the movies.' Just as she had changed my name and described me as an artist in her interviews, to pretend my work as a make-up man had never existed, now she was trying to make me disappear altogether. Six months after we had separated she was saying we were already divorced and that we had been apart for two years.

'This freedom has been like the opening of a cage,' she said. I had obviously ceased to be Charlie in the Upstairs Room, because she also said, 'This voice I talk about one day tapped me on the back and said, "You just got to go through this, Kim, 'cause we can't protect you any longer." '

It was laughable and depressing at the same time. I told her people, 'I always said to Kim that she'd make a million dollars and she had made a lot more than that. Now it's *my* turn for a million.'

I had nothing to do all day with no Kim to look after, and in the beginning I was doing cocaine every day. And I spent $1,000 on phone sex lines in the first month I was alone, just to listen to strangers talk about what they would do to me. I always asked them, 'Where did you lose your virginity? Have you ever done it with two guys? Have you ever done it with two girls?' They always told me the things I wanted to hear. Sometimes I told them I was married to Kim Basinger. I don't expect they believed me but they would talk about *9½ Weeks* and sex scenes. I thought talking to these girls was a big joke.

My lowest moment came a few weeks after the break-up. My

friend Ron Lang had just bought a house on Lake Tahoe, which is on the California–Nevada border, and suggested that I take it for a long weekend to get away. Pat Lynch and I went up there to kick back, play some tennis and go gambling. Ron's house was on the Nevada side of the lake in a community called North Shore and at night Pat and I would hit the casino at the Hyatt Regency Hotel. I was doing a lot of cocaine and drinking heavily and over a three-day weekend I lost $14,000 on the tables. I was spending so much money that they considered me a high roller and insisted that we move into the hotel. They gave us complimentary suites and all our drinks and meals were free and they even gave us tickets for a title boxing match. Of course, that meant we had no need to do anything but gamble and so I kept losing. I was also giving $100 tips to waiters and waitresses who kept plying me with free drinks while I was at the tables. Actually, I became close friends with Bob Ellsworth, who is head of the hotel's entertainment and hospitalities division. Even though I'm not so crazy any more, he still entertains me at the hotel's up-market Hugo's restaurant whenever I'm in the area. We play golf together and he calls me Mr B, but in his mind that's because he thinks of me as Mr Basinger.

Luckily for me, only a couple of days after my disastrous gambling escapade I bumped into a girl I knew, Leslie, who was 31, younger than Kim. I was 50, and it was good to know I could still attract younger women. Leslie had been our travel agent and had also arranged for Phil Walsh to become our personal trainer. Leslie had dated him for a while. Apart from sex, Leslie did two great things for me. She introduced me to a girlfriend, Jana St James, whose real-life love affair with author Robert James Waller inspired him to write the tragic romance novel *The Bridges of Madison County*. In fact, when I met her, Jana was called Jana Furrer but she wanted to change her name. I'm so good at changing names — having had to please Kim — that she asked my advice and I suggested St James after the club in London.

Jana had worked for a sex chat line and lasted two days. She told me how it was all faked, which I knew already, but she drove it home. After that, I never called them again. And Leslie was in rehab, a member of Alcoholics Anonymous and Cocaine Anonymous. I realised she was the girl for me going through this divorce because I'd need a clear head. Because of her influence, I was able to quit drugs and alcohol cold turkey. I didn't even touch a drop on New Year's Eve, when Leslie and I went to Cabo San

Lucas, a vacation port in Mexico, on her father's yacht. Her father got stuck into the booze and I was jealous, but I didn't give in to the temptation. Leslie was a great friend. I still have a picture of her in Kim's bed in Don Juan Place, and I showed her 'home movies' of Kim and me, which really turned her on. Leslie and I have remained good friends to this day.

Although Jon Peters and I were friendly enough in London, at least I thought we were at the time, his name cropped up later in less pleasant circumstances. Kim was coming back to California on a visit during a break from *Batman*. She called me and said, 'Would you please get out of the house. I'm coming back on Monday and I want to see my puppies.'

I said, 'Fine, come on. You're welcome here but I'm not leaving.'

I didn't hear any more from her and she never showed up. I went to see my attorney the following Monday and he told me he'd had a call from her lawyer before the weekend. The lawyer said, 'Listen, we may have a problem. I can't control Jon Peters. He's a big guy. Get Ron out of the house. We have no idea what he's planning to do, but he says he's going to get Ron out of the house, that he'll take care of it.' So Con replied, 'Bring him on. Ron's not afraid of him.' But he didn't warn me what was going on. As it turned out, nothing happened, but I told him it would have been nice to have had a bit of notice that I should have been expecting an unwelcome visitor.

I happened to know that Jon had been a tearaway as a youth growing up in the San Fernando Valley. He had been expelled from Junior High School and put on probation for stealing a car, and he had constant rows with his stepfather. Eventually, his own mother turned him over to the California Youth Authority when he was just 13, because she could no longer control him. He spent a year in detention, doing hard manual labour on a road gang and learning to box. This was the character who could have turned up on my doorstep without warning.

After that, however, Kim and I came to a temporary compromise. We had a second, smaller house on Cushdon Avenue in West Los Angeles. It was close to the 20th Century Fox and MGM studios, and Kim had bought it with the intention of converting it into an office. When Kim first complained about me being in Don Juan Place, I told her attorneys, 'Well, give me the other house and I'll go and live over there.' They said, 'Oh no, Kim said you'll never set foot in that house.' So a month or six weeks went by and I was still in residence in Woodland Hills. When it became clear that I wasn't going to leave, even with Kim back in California for that visit, they relented and suggested that I move in to Cushdon while we thrashed out the details of the divorce, so that Kim could have free access to Don Juan Place. The problem then was that the house was a mess. We had never got round to renovating it, the bathrooms were awful and there wasn't a proper master bedroom. I said Kim would have to pay to fix it up and make it fit to live in. We arranged to have a conference meeting in the Cushdon bungalow so that we could assess what work needed to be done and reach an agreement. Kim came along with her sister, Ashley, who gave me a big hug, Kim's business manager Mitchell Freedman and a builder, David Sheard, who had done the renovations at Don Juan for us, who was going to do the work. Sheard got the contract because Kim's people knew he would put in a reasonable bid to ensure he would continue to work for her. It was all very cordial but I wasn't sure I trusted what was going on. I hid a tape recorder in my pocket, and made sure I named the date and time as we talked. We all walked through the house agreeing on the work that needed to be done.

A couple of weeks later, Freedman called. He went over the work that was to be done and said they had not agreed to a lot of what I wanted. I put the tape recorder to the phone mouthpiece and pressed play. After a couple of moments, I fast-forwarded it to the end. What he never realised was that I didn't have the middle part of the conversation, because I hadn't been near enough in the room all the time and the acoustics were bad, but he thought I had it all on tape. Freedman responded by saying that in California you need someone's permission before you can tape them. But he knew he was on a loser, even though legally he was correct, and I bluffed him and won.

Perhaps it was the tape that made them believe I had kept a detailed diary of my time with Kim. Stories began swirling through television shows and magazines that I was threatening to sell the diary for millions of dollars if Kim did not give me a juicy settlement. Some reports had me demanding $20 million not to reveal my detailed notes of her supposed steamy affairs with Peters, Prince and even Michael Keaton. I never said a word and let Kim and her lawyers make what they wanted of the stories. In fact, I had kept very sketchy diaries, mostly detailing our travel arrangements, but I'd also got books full of notes that I'd scribbled out at various times, notes from Kim, pictures, videos and most importantly all my memories of happy and sad times together, but there was no actual detailed diary.

There were also stories that I was threatening to keep all the animals, though the reports never seemed to agree on what sort and how many there were. I would not have done that to Kim because I knew the animals were her life. But I was sad that she did not let me keep Dooboy, who had always been my dog. She didn't even keep him; she gave him away to her sister. He was a great fella with long blond hair. My friends told me she couldn't bear to keep him around because he reminded her too much of her blond beach-boy ex-husband. She wiped Dooboy from her memory, just as she did me.

I now had somewhere to live, at least temporarily. At first I didn't change my lifestyle at all, apart from dropping the drugs and booze. I took a girlfriend to Hawaii and went on a trip to Arizona. I got limos to take me to and from the airport. I was bored so I took up golf. But it couldn't last. I was used to dealing with American Express bills for $50,000, for airfares and so on, and just writing a cheque to pay them off. Now I had been cut off from our joint bank accounts and credit cards and had no income. I still had credit cards in my own name so I lived on them for months, charging everything because I didn't have any cash, and as a result I built up massive debts.

When Kim first asked me to get out of the business I was happy to do anything to please her. To be honest, it bothered me not being a breadwinner but we always knew Kim would end up making more money than I ever could and not working also meant I could spend all my time with her. When she started the divorce, she wanted to pay me off and for me to stay out of the make-up world. But when I would not accept that, her lawyers started saying that I didn't need a lot of alimony because I could support myself. In fact, keeping me away from work backfired on Kim. In my business, you have to work a minimum of five days every two years to stay as a union member in good stading. I had never given that a thought until I got a letter from my union IATSE — the International Alliance of Theatrical Stage Employees — saying I was out. They said they had written to me with a warning in 1987 but I never got that letter. They wrote again in 1989 and I can only think it didn't get forwarded to me. That was a shock because I always thought I could go back to work if I needed to. I lost the health insurance I had through the union, too.

So, still smarting from what I thought was such a mean

settlement offer from Kim, I thought I'd live on her money for a time while I worked out what to do. I didn't feel guilty about that at all; after all, I had given up my career for her. And even though I had been paid the one year I was her official manager, we had a cash-flow crisis and her business manager asked me to return all the money. I had just put it in the bank and was happy to give it back to Kim. I took up riding and golf, both of which I still enjoy. I play golf off an eight handicap, which isn't bad considering I didn't start playing until I was 51. And I have a fine paint horse, brown and white, called Reno, who I ride Western style. We finally settled on $9,000 a month spousal support which seemed a lot, and I also had a half-million dollar house and figured I would make some money on it. This was 1989 and some people were making more on property appreciation thatn they were from their jobs. What I had not bargained for, of course, was that while we were thrashing out the deal, I was living on plastic, and when I got my first lump sum from our community property that went to pay off my credit cards and the taxman. I refinanced the house on Cushdon Way and had to pay $3,800 on the mortgage, but property immediately went into a slump and I ended up losing it. I never had any spare cash.

I did get offers of work in 1993 and 1994, but I couldn't accept them because they were union jobs and I was off the union roster. But I realised my alimony would come to an end in 1997 and that I had to do something to get by, so I asked the union what I could do. They gave me a whole list of rules. The first work I did was on a non-union job in South Carolina, when a friend hired me. That didn't help at all getting back my IATSE card, but I wanted to see if I was still handy. Then, at the end of 1996, the solution came along. There was a new television show called *Pacific Blue*, a sort of *Baywatch* for bicycle cops at the beach, which was a union production but no members wanted to work on it because the pay was so bad. It was long hours and a lot of work, but I had a different agenda from my colleagues, so for me it was perfect. I did 61 days at soemthing like $15 an hour and that got me back into the union.

Then I was offered a pilot for a new television series, *The 119*, about a fire and rescue squad, and I did that for about a month in 1997. I also worked on the Dustin Hoffman film *Mad City* for one day. I didn't actually do Dustin, but I made up Alan Alda and Robert Prosky. I was originally asked to do the whole movie, but that was before I was back in the union so I couldn't accept the work. And I picked up two or three days on the Samuel L Jackson and *L. A. Confidential* star Kevin Spacey movie *The Negotiator* in early 1998. That summer I was hired to work on *The Big Brass Ring*, starring Nigel Hawthorne and Miranda Richardson and based on a script originally written by Orson Welles. It was shot in Los Angeles and, by a strange coincidence, I found myself working alongside my old friend, hairdresser Rick Provenzano. By this time, he had been dropped by Kim, but was doing a lot of work with Alec. However, it was very slow going trying to re-establish myself in the movie industry despite my track record. I'd been out of the business for so long that people didn't know me any more. The guys I'd worked with were older than me and had retired. Also, when I started out all the make-up artists were men; now, they were manly women. I was also wary of working with people who had worked with Kim at first, even if they were willing to work with me. I felt it would be too awkward and that I'd feel uncomfortable making up her friends and I was sure they wouldn't like having me working on them. However much Kim tries to ignore our years together, we will always be part of each other's lives in some way.

In March 1990, Kim was a presenter at the Oscars and on a whim I sent her some flowers and a note. I was astonished to come home a few days later and hear her sweet Georgia lilt on my telephone answering machine — particularly as she seemed to think I wouldn't instantly know who it was.

'This is Kim Basinger,' her message started. 'Hi. I just wanted to call you and tell you that I just got back into town and I missed your flowers. They died. But I just wanted to tell you that this note meant more to me than anything in the world, and coming from you, you know exactly what I'm talking about. I appreciate it with all my heart. I'll talk to you soon. Call me some time at the office, home or whatever, okay? Thanks. You know what I mean. Bye.' That was the last time she ever spoke to me directly — and I *didn't* know what she meant. I never did call her and she's never directly contacted me since. The only communication from then on was through our lawyers. Years later, though, after she won her Oscar, she wrote to my old friend Linda Lang, out of the blue, saying how much she missed her friendship.

Although I was shocked and distressed when Kim told me she wanted a divorce, I soon realised I found the idea very liberating. Ever since the Richard Gere incident we had been living a lie, however much we tried to gloss it over. I looked back over the last four years of our marriage and realised that I'd been going downhill with the drinking and the cocaine. It was a substitute for happiness. We had good times when we were high, but I realised I was just acting the part of a husband. We were faking it. For the marriage to work, I would have really had to become the Svengali people thought I was and taken over control of her life. Instead, I taught her to be stronger, and it destroyed what we had. I would never have left her out of my own choice, but I wasn't happy. Because we had managed to put the past behind us so often and for so long, my biggest fear in the first weeks of our separation was that she was going to come back and say she had made a mistake and expect to go on as we had before. I didn't want that. I wanted to be free. I wanted to become the real Ron again. I was riding high and I knew I was going to get some money out of it. But after about six months I went into a major depression. I thought I was a failure, that I had failed our marriage. I wallowed in self-pity. I felt I could have kept the marriage going. 'Why didn't I hang on in there?' I aksed myself. I also played the videotape I had taken of the Richard Gere letters, and that made me angry. That lasted for about six to nine months. Later, I thought, 'You goon, for not making this thing go. You could have been a partner in a multi-million dollar deal and had mistresses on the side.' I guess in the end I had enough integrity not to do that.

Years of playing sport had beaten down my right arm. It was difficult to raise it high, and two of the fingers were numb a lot of the time. I went to see Dr Robert Kerlan, the top sports doctor who was Walter Matthau's close friend, and he recommended surgery. I thought it was a great idea; if the divorce went to trial I'd be a more sympathetic figure with my arm in a sling and nobody could suggest I could go straight back to work. I also went to see a psychiatrist for extra ammunition. He told me I was facing four major traumas. As well as going through a divorce and facing delicate surgery, my mother had died just a few months earlier and my car, the Porsche Kim bought for me, had been stolen and found later, completely burned out. I went to see the psychiatrist once a week and knew that would look good in court. One of Kerlan's associates actually operated on me and although he did a good job, even now my arm gives me constant problems.

It never did get so far that I had to produce my team of doctors, though it was very bitter in the end. Because of all of Kim's nervousness and insecurities, I never believed she'd have the courage to go to court. Her lawyers tried to bluff it out. They said,

'She's an actress, she'll perform well on the stand.' But what they did not know was that Con and I had dinner with a friend of hers who told us Kim was absolutely terrified of the prospect of going to trial. We also heard that her lawyers were saying, 'There's no way a judge will be sympathetic to Ron. He's a man who's young, handsome, in good shape. He's been sleeping with Kim Basinger for 10 years and now he wants to get paid for it.'

That was pretty outrageous. I'd given up work at Kim's request and Californian law says a non-working spouse is entitled to alimony. The wind was taken out of their sails a bit at the compulsory settlement meeting that every couple in California has to go through before the divorce case proceeds in the hopes of finally reaching an amicable agreement rather than taking up the court's time. When we were trying to establish that I was entitled to a cut of her future earnings under the concept of goodwill, her team scoffed, but the judge said, 'I've never seen goodwill applied to a divorce before — but if it ever was, this could be the case for it.'

There were some funny moments throughout the divorce proceedings. Kim had to start signing her own cheques after so many years and sometimes the bank refused to acknowledge her signature at first. For years, I'd been writing her signature for her on the cheques so it was my handwriting and not hers they recognised as the real Kim Basinger. On one occasion, her lawyers collected all the cheques I'd ever written, stacks and stacks of them, and said they were going to go through every single one for me to justify the expense. They got very excited over one cheque for $3,500 for a model train. That was very funny, because it was one of the few that was actually signed by Kim. Jon Peters had given her a bracelet worth $450,000, and I think the train was a thank-you present for that. The funny thing is she'd never worn the bracelet. When Jon gave it to her, Kim was actually on the telephone talking to one of the very few friends I'd been allowed to stay in touch with, Linda Lang. Linda and her husband Ron were the very first people to whom I'd introduced Kim at the start of our relationship. Over the years, Kim had become very friendly with them herself.

'Oh my God,' Kim screeched down the telephone from London. Linda, who was at their main home just outside Palm Springs, thought Kim was being attacked or something and, being so far away, was helpless to rescue her friend.

'What's going on, Kim?' Linda asked anxiously.

Then Kim started to giggle her familiar girlish laugh. 'It's Jon. He's just given me a diamond bracelet,' she said. 'Now what am I going to do with an expensive bracelet? I don't wear jewellery.'

Linda said, 'Well, you could always give it to me.' She was joking and would never have said it if they'd been face to face because Kim was always very generous. You only ever had to say to her, 'Oh I like that sweater,' or 'I love your blouse,' and she'd take it off and give it to you straight away without a second thought.

During the divorce, we wrangled over cars because I hadn't replaced my Porsche but I had just bought Kim a Mercedes 450SL and suggested she give it to me. She actually hid it so I couldn't find it and drive it away! The weirdest moments involved arguing over what share I should get of her *Batman* pay and points since I was only on the film with her for a short time. This was a serious matter for me because *Batman* was poised to be one of the biggest money-makers of all time and the higher a proportion I could get the better my future income would be.

At first, her team argued that I should drop the whole thing because *Batman* would never make any money. 'If it's never going to be worth anything why are you arguing over it?' I countered. Kim then demanded something in exchange — a billowing white cape she had bought for me a while before and which I had never worn. It simply wasn't me, and never would be. I was astonished and said, 'Yes, of course she can have that.' Ironically, although *Batman* is now the 11th-biggest grossing film of all times in terms of the American box office, at $251.2 million, it still has not officially made a profit thanks to the 'creative accounting' so prevalent in Hollywood.

Kim did stick with the case and take it a lot further than I ever expected her to, although at first it didn't look as if she was going to turn up for the compulsory settlement meeting which was to mark the end of our marriage. Con and I got to court before Kim and her team were expected to arrive. While we were waiting for her, a man walked in with a camera. We'd been trying to keep the proceedings quiet and our hearts sank because we thought the paparazzi were on to us. As it happened, there was another celebrity hearing going on that day, and we were safe. Then Balaban turned up without Kim and said he had Kim's full power to agree to a deal, but Judge Richard Montes was furious and insisted that she turn up. He turned to Balaban and said, 'You go call her and we will all wait. I want her here in person to agree to anything.' When she finally did arrive, she was with a little boy of about five, who had dog bites on him. That was weird. She never gave any explanation for the boy's presence and to this day we never did work out who he was.

During the meeting, which was held in a small room to the side of the main court in the huge Los Angeles Superior Court building, Kim wouldn't talk to me or look at me and that hurt. She would not even acknowledge my existence on that final day when we left the room and she was in the corridor in front of me. I called out, 'Kim,' and wanted to tell her that I wished her luck, I was sorry it hadn't worked out and I hoped everything would go well for her. I didn't feel any animosity towards her. But she ignored me. She didn't even turn her head. I will never forget her blonde hair swaying from side to side down her back and the noise of her high heels tapping on the stone floor as she strode purposefully away from me down the courthouse corridor with that small boy. I felt that it wasn't just the court building that was cold, but her heart as well. When I finally left the building, I was so shaken up I couldn't remember where I had parked my car and had to search the whole multi-storey car park for it.

We had finally thrashed out our divorce settlement at that meeting in December 1989, just over a year after we split, which was pretty fast by Hollywood standards. Probably the fact that we did not have any children to fight over helped. I did not get everything I wanted, but it was certainly a lot more than Kim offered me to start with. Judge Montes ordered us not to make the terms of the settlement public, but when Kim went bankrupt four years later, my monthly alimony of $9,000 became public knowledge from her financial records.

I was sad at the way Kim spoke about our marriage while we were going through all this. True, the relationship had been falling apart but we had had such happy days at the beginning and that's what I wanted to remember. I wasn't particularly hurt by her flings with Jon Peters and Prince, but it upset me to see our time together put down.

'I just hadn't realised how detrimental the relationship was to my total mental and physical and creative health,' she said, a comment that hurt me deeply because I had always put her first. 'It was very, very smothering. My stomach was tied up in knots. My life was on hold. Finally, I had to say to my husband, "Now, we have to let each other go. I can only hurt you by staying here." The last five years of my marriage were a joke. It was a marriage in name only. We weren't even living together full time the last two years.'

But that wasn't exactly the position. We had been living together. Admittedly, we'd slept apart during the making of *My Stepmother Is an Alien*, but we'd seen each other virtually every day. She'd returned home after the shoot was finished and she'd taken me to London when she started work on *Batman*. Nevertheless, in the same interview, she went on, 'You can die and not be dead but just be breathing ... the person that had grown inside of me had been running from one movie to the next and that's it. It was like living in a surrealistic painting for eight years. I *saw* Christmases and I *saw* pumpkins and the glee showed in my face but behind it was not the emotion. I was just not allowing myself. And I don't know why.'

She also referred to our union as a friendship. She said, 'We were best friends and that's what we were. It was a safety net.' She'd add, 'That marriage was a mistake. A big mistake. Because two people were lying.' In one interview I read in *Cosmopolitan* magazine, it said, 'Ron was a guy who was much older than me; he really was much more ahead of the game than me with *everything*. I mean, he'd tried everything in life; he'd done everything.'

She would say that I took over the role of her protector and that our relationship was all about control — meaning me controlling her. That's certainly not the way I remember our lives together or the way it finally ended. I was the one who was told to give up work, change my name and, in the end, get out.

Kim said she had no regrets when it was all over, as I didn't, but she doubted if she would marry again. 'I love the institution of marriage and I will always believe in it,' she said. 'I just don't know what it is. I love love and I love to give love and I'm for honesty and truth. I don't think anybody should get married before they're 30 and even then I'd think twice about it. I don't think I'll ever get married again — I just don't see myself as a typical wife and mother.'

I was not the only person who was confused by Kim's view of things. In an interview to promote *Batman*, she bragged about buying her father a beach house and her mother a Mercedes. I knew Kim had given her dad a flat. But Ann Basinger didn't remember ever receiving a Mercedes and said she would not even want one.

Batman was a very exciting time for Kim. As well as her meeting Jon, she fell for superstar Prince when he arrived in London to do the soundtrack. And once again, when the film came out, her reviews were good, even though many critics found the film as a whole very dark. Liz Smith, the columnist who spilled the beans on Kim and Jon, wrote, 'Kim Basinger is one of the few truly beautiful sex symbols who manages to come across as a real, caring, intelligent person. I thought the love scenes were wonderful.' And in the *Wall Street Journal*, reviewer Julie Salamon wrote, 'Mr Keaton's best moments come into play when he's with Vicki Vale (Kim Basinger), the photographer who's hell-bent on unmasking *Batman*. By her side, Mr Keaton gets to smile a little, though even here he's a straight man for Ms Basinger's deft comedic delivery (and she looks stunning in the fabulous clothes designed for her by Bob Ringwood).'

Kim said in an interview, 'The whole atmosphere on *Batman* was very sexual. I really got turned on by the black outfits Michael Keaton wore. When I felt them I went weak. They were all black, gooey and shiny — they hypnotised me. It was a wonderful experience.'

Kim was thrilled to meet Prince, especially because he promised to make her old dream of releasing a record come true. Once *Batman* was finished, in the summer of 1989, she flew to Minneapolis with him and moved into his $10 million Paisley Park complex, where he had a studio and projection room, to record an album together. They were also said to have plans to do a music video and produce movies together. Kim was very excited. 'I was a singer long before I was an actress. Now people will be able to see what I do.'

In November 1989, Kim finally released a record with Prince, the maxi-single, *The Scandalous Sex Suite*, featuring heavy breathing and suggestive talk between her and Prince, which was an expansion of a number Prince wrote for *Batman*. It lasted 19 minutes and was divided into three parts — 'The Crime', 'The Passion', and 'The Rapture'. In some ways it was a kind of audio version of $9\frac{1}{2}$ *Weeks*, with the two of them acting out fantasies. 'Are you afraid?' Prince asks Kim softly. 'I guess I'm a little nervous,' she replies. He says, 'It's getting warm ... Let's go to the bedroom.' The music was jazzy with lots of saxophone.

They were a reclusive couple, as we had been. But unlike us, there was a price on their heads. They seldom ventured out in public, so when they dropped in at Chaya Brasserie, a trendy French/Italian/Japanese restaurant on the Los Angeles–Beverly Hills border in January 1990, pandemonium broke out when paparazzi photographer Kip Rano, who happened to be having dinner there, grabbed his ever-present camera and took their pictures. Bodyguards leaped up to hustle him out of the restaurant and Kim and Prince were furious. 'They overreacted to a simple snapshot,' said Rano. 'They looked very happy.' They were such a hot couple that the top American tabloid newspaper, the *National Enquirer*, was said to have paid Rano more than $100,000 for the snap showing them sitting side by side, a bearded Prince wearing a black blazer and Kim dressed in a loose grey jacket.

Their relationship hit the rocks that same month when Kim abruptly backed out of *Graffiti Bridge*, Prince's sequel to *Purple Rain*, and did not attend the American Music awards with him as had been arranged.

Prince was furious. 'Prince is a control freak and he thought he could control Kim,' a film industry insider said. 'But he found out he couldn't completely.' They got back together for a while and visited his luxury apartment in Paris, and there was talk that Kim was so serious about their relationship that she gave him a diamond ring.

Bizarrely, five years later, Kim's brother Mick, who had a major falling-out with her over Braselton, the town she 'bought', claimed he had actually kidnapped her from Paisley Park because her family were worried about the relationship.

'It was as if Prince had some bizarre hold over her,' Mick said. 'She was acting strangely, as if she was possessed by him. She treated him almost as a cult-like figure. She seemed to be under some kind of sexual spell.'

Mick claims he launched his kidnap plot when Kim told him Prince was driving her through red traffic lights at 100mph, just for thrills.

'I decided the only course of action was to go to Kim myself and physically get her away from Prince, using force if necessary,' he went on. He and Kim's assistant at the time went to Minneapolis when they knew Prince would be away and Mick said he ordered Kim into his car while the assistant packed up her belongings, then drove her to the airport. 'Kim turned to me and you could see the relief on her face,' he said. 'It was like she'd been possessed and we'd had to exorcise the demons.'

It wasn't only Mick who sensed demons around Prince. The Artist, as he likes to be known, took an instant dislike to our Brazilian maid Fatima. He told Kim to get rid of Fatima because he felt she had too much control and influence over her. Coming from South America, Fatima understood about Black Magic and the occult. She was into voodoo herself and accused Prince of being into witchcraft. They embarked on a strange ritual war of the underworld, each casting spells on the other. Fatima accused Prince of being dark and being in league with the devil. In the end, she out-lasted Prince, but her spell-casting wasn't strong enough to out-last Alec Baldwin. When the Irish Catholic actor appeared on the scene, he asked Kim to let her go, because he also felt she had too much influence over Kim.

Kim also had flings closer to home after we broke up. She had a brief affair with our personal trainer, Phil Walsh, the one-time Australian bodybuilding champion and the man for whom Kim had swapped sloppy work-out clothes for Spandex. That fling ended when Phil learned she was still seeing Prince. She snuggled up to her vet, Dr Todd Tams, who had a practice in West Los Angeles. His girlfriend, Kathy Borden, with whom he was living, called me up and said, 'Kim's taken my intended away. We've written a book together, we're supposed to get married, what am I supposed to do? What do you suggest?'

I said, 'Hey, just go home and Kim will get rid of him.' Sure enough, a few weeks later he went running back to the girl.

I wasn't at all surprised to learn that she'd also briefly picked up again with Richard Gere. But I was astonished to learn that she had a wild fling with a toyboy fashion designer in early 1990, shortly before she met Alec Baldwin. Alexio Gandara told the British newspaper the *News of the World* they enjoyed five nights of sensational sex, including one in a hotel suite with another couple in the next room. He claimed Kim fantasised about being a virgin submitting to his every desire, and that certainly rang true of what I knew of Kim.

'Kim made love with a passion,' said Gandara, who claimed he had no idea who Kim was when he first flirted with her at a Hollywood club. 'She made it clear that she liked to be dominated. She was acting the little girl, the virgin, while I was her teacher — the big, bad master who wore only black. She particularly liked me to playfully pull her hair. As we wrestled around the bed she gasped, "You're my master. I'll do anything you say. You are in control." '

According to Gandara, when she asked him what it was like to make love to a famous actress, he told her, 'I'm not impressed.' I was astonished. *I* was impressed the first time I made love to Kim and she was nobody in those days — and I'd bet I'd had more women back then than Mr Gandara had when he met her. He also claimed Kim talked about making him famous by wearing his clothes, and introduced him to Michelle Pfeiffer at a party. But after five nights together she told him to stop calling her.

'Maybe I was just a fool — a plaything for her to satisfy her fantasies and whims,' he lamented. Kim had certainly changed from the shy homebody she had been with me, if she was really hitting Hollywood parties and nightclubs and hanging out with other actresses. But I was fascinated by one comment he made, when he said she did not talk about her recent loves, Prince or Jon Peters. He said, 'The only guy she ever mentioned was Ron, her ex husband.' I wonder what she said about me.

Chapter 15

I was still in a daze from the shock of the news that Kim was divorcing me, and all the arguments with her business people and lawyers, when she dropped another bombshell. She 'bought' Braselton, a little town in Georgia near her childhood home. We had visited it during our years together, but she had never mentioned any ambition to buy the place. And I did not believe she had $20 million to splash out on such a wild scheme. My lawyers were looking at her finances, trying to sort out a divorce settlement for me, and there was no sign of that kind of cash. Until the last year of our marriage, I had handled our joint finances and I knew she had not salted that sort of money away. Her total film income by the time we split was $9,066,000, and once we reached a deal she was so strapped for hard cash she had to pay my share of community property in instalments.

The tiny town with a population of 500 was owned by the Braselton family, who had been trying to sell it for years. There were three branches of the family descended from the town's patriarch, William Braselton, who had founded the town in 1876, headed by cousins Henry, who was the Mayor of Braselton, Herbert, who ran the 102-year-old Braselton Bros Store, and Herman. Henry Braselton said that Kim planned to restore the dilapidated downtown area and turn it into a tourist attraction as well as planning residential and industrial projects and possibly a movie studio.

He added, 'The reasons we wanted to sell was our ages and to divide up the holdings of the three families. We're not getting any younger.'

Herbert Braselton explained that Kim's offer was attractive

because it was cash. The family had had a number of offers, but most bidders wanted to pay over 40 years. Since the average age of the selling Braseltons was 71, that was unacceptable.

'To people in their 70s and 80s, that doesn't interest them,' he said. 'We got a cash deal. Miss Basinger and her backers are good people. We've checked them out and they've got good banking and construction backgrounds. I think our forebears would be happy. We shed some tears today. But we're glad to get somebody we trust that will do this place proud.'

Kim and her partners were actually buying Braselton Improvement Company, which owned 1,800 acres and a number of commercial buildings, a bank, a shopping centre, and about 18 rented homes, but not privately owned houses, the city streets, the water system or the cemetery, and had no right to interfere with the town council. Kim actually bought 95.1 per cent of the bank, with the rest becoming the property of the pension fund of Ameritech Corporation, a Chicago-based telecommunications company. The identity of Ameritech was kept secret at first, and the whole company was named Basinger-Braselton Ltd. Much of the town, whose small fortunes had been built on cotton, had seen better days; many houses were run down, with sagging roofs and rotting porches. But it was close to the Interstate 85 highway, between Atlanta, Georgia, and Charlotte, North Carolina, and had the potential to become a dormitory town as Atlanta — which would be the site of the 1994 Olympic Games — expanded.

When news of the purchase broke, it was literally the talk of the town. Many residents were excited at the prospect of Hollywood types dropping in on their down-home lifestyle, and thought the Kim connection would bring a much-needed infusion of cash. There was talk of major development to turn Braselton into a kind of Hollywood East, complete with a Disney-style theme park to be called Kimwood, like singing superstar and actress Dolly Parton had done with Dollywood in Tennessee — though Kim always denied that. Other proposals people discussed excitedly included a hotel, country club, a golf course and recording studios, all of which would have provided building and landscaping work to start with and then ongoing employment in a poor and needy rural area.

'I have high hopes,' said Linda Phillips, who worked at the Braselton Bros store. 'I feel like it will be beneficial to all of us with families here. My whole family, my dad, my brothers and sisters, all live on one street, Piedmont Avenue.'

Not everyone was so enthusiastic, however. Farmer Gerald Gooch was indifferent to the prospect of rubbing shoulders with stars and said, 'I'm undecided what it all means. I've been so busy with 18,000 laying hens I haven't had a chance to talk to anybody.'

Still others were appalled by the idea. The population were overwhelmingly staunch Methodists and the town was dry, by local ordinance, but Kim's reputation had gone before her. Henry Braselton's brother, Kit, who owned a hardware store, agreed with the sale for practical reasons.

'We have no young Braseltons who want to carry on this operation,' he said, but added, 'I saw *Playboy* and I could feel myself turning red, I was so shocked. I'm a church-going conservative and I don't usually appreciate that kind of picture.'

Another old-time resident was so outraged at the thought of banking at a financial institution whose owner had bared all for Hugh Hefner that he immediately closed his account. Yet another sniffed, 'She wants to put a movie studio here. But if they're like her movies, it'll be pornography.'

Although Kim was later to say she had never really bought the town and was simply a figurehead for the investors, at first she happily chatted about the town as if it was all hers, and said she had great plans for it.

She said, 'To the younger Braseltons, I just put it straight. I said, "These are the acres where we all parked all summer long, every summer. And I'm here to preserve these fields." But with the older Braseltons, I said, "These are the lawns where I'd walk with my boyfriends." And they said back to me, "Yes indeed, a lovely place to court." '

In her now-famous comment to *Vanity Fair* magazine, she went on, 'Court? These are the fields where I learned oral sex!'

That prompted her father, Don, to send her a package containing a yellow tennis ball, a roll of waterproof surgical tape and a note that read, 'When you give an interview and the feeling of being outrageous is present, please place this ball in your mouth and then tape your mouth shut. If you are still able to say 'oral sex' after doing this, then you are hopeless.'

Kim never became a major figure in Braselton, though she appointed her brother, Mick, as Chief Executive Officer of the company. She was seen so seldom that people talked about 'Kim sightings' the way some people claim to see Elvis Presley. Mysterious sightings included rumours that she had helicoptered in to dine privately at a local vineyard, that she had driven through town in a Chevy Suburban truck and, most bizarrely, that she drove up to a family home in a chauffeur-driven limo and made the chauffeur go and buy a cantaloupe melon from the residents. Brother Mick claimed she was a regular visitor, but kept her visits secret to avoid publicity.

'You have to understand from Kim's perspective,' he said. 'It's uncomfortable. She works her tail off to get to the position she's in and then she has to wear sunglasses to disguise herself.'

One visit she definitely made was in 1989, when she took an impromptu tour of a Mitsubishi electronics factory, by far the biggest employer in the area, not just for Braselton but for the other small towns in the area. She signed lots of autographs for the thrilled workers. Ironically, however, Mitsubishi was not one of the Basinger-Braselton tenants! She did send autographed pictures to some residents, including one to a baffled motor mechanic, Terry Kitchens. In her familiar purple scrawl, it was signed, 'The best-looking mechanic in Braselton.' But he had never met her. He was a great fan of hers and was to support her later, though even he became disenchanted before Kim's Braselton endeavours reached their sorry end.

In March 1990, Kim was named an Outstanding Georgia Citizen and was presented with a commendation by the Georgia Secretary of State. But by March 1991, the Braselton backlash had begun. According to the *Wall Street Journal*, she had to be replaced on the board of the Braselton Banking Co because she did not attend meetings. And she did not even pick up the keys to the town. Mayor Henry Braselton said sadly, 'We've got a key all ready for her. We just haven't been able to get her here to pick it up.' Jackson County Elementary School asked her to speak to a graduating class but she didn't show up. A new hotel, the Braselton Inn, opened up soon after Kim's big announcement, hoping to profit from the rich new tourist trade that never materialised. And the manager, Sam Sloan, tried unsuccessfully to get Kim to commit to a five-kilometre charity race. 'I would have scheduled it any time to fit her convenience,' he said plaintively.

The promised development simply did not happen. Decaying buildings were pulled down but not replaced, and when Basinger-Braselton wanted to demolish two older buildings, the council stopped the move and demanded historical and architectural studies to see if the structures should be restored rather than destroyed. And tenants were very unsettled because the maximum lease the new company would grant was just 90 days. The reason for that was so they could move quickly once they had made their plans for the land. However, they didn't make any plans.

Kim addressed the rumours that people in 'her town' were unhappy. 'My town is a huge concern of mine,' she said in 1991. 'There are plans going on, none of which I can talk about. But I will say this: I hope to employ thousands of people. This is not Dollywood at all. No offence to Dolly. This is going to be a major, major playground. We hope to bring in a major musical park. It's going to be a huge surprise. Also, I hope to build a music recording studio, seven or eight recording studios. This is the area to do it because it's so fast-growing, right on the I-85 where the trucks can get off. God's little 2,800 acres. And I'm going to buy a bunch more land so it's going to be bigger.' Of course, the land she already had was only 1,800 acres, but Kim always did have a capacity to forget details.

By 1992, there was a lot of grumbling. The biggest stores, which had been owned by the Braselton family, were closed and no new ones opened up to replace them. The car showroom closed, as did the garden tool rental shop. Even the video rental shop, the only entertainment in a town without bars, went as well. In all, more than a dozen businesses shut their doors, and many residents moved away. Town clerk Angela Colley, whose duties included issuing building permits and checking plans, said, 'People are frustrated. They see nothing but houses torn down. I haven't received a single plan for anything. These are country people. They thought we were getting big investment but it was just the opposite. I guess we'd settle for having the grocery store back now. There's no place to buy anything. A lot of old people have to rely on rides to Winder, which is two miles away.'

Herman Braselton lamented, 'She promised to make us all happy, but that hasn't come true at all. I wish she'd pass it on to someone else because this town is dying. We trusted her because she was the local girl. But the film studio hasn't happened. Nothing has. More than anything we wish she'd just tell us what she was up to. She wanted us out of the stores and now we don't get consulted on anything. She said there would be no industry here that used pollutants.'

Mick Basinger blamed low sewage capacity for lack of development, saying, 'Kim's goal is not economic. It's more philanthropic. She wants to put something back into the community.'

By this time, Kim had a lot going on in her life and it was hardly surprising that Braselton was not her first priority. Her relationship with Alec Baldwin was growing stronger but she was embroiled in the legal row over the film *Boxing Helena*, which would eventually drive her into bankruptcy. But the problems of a woman who had backed out of a job that could have made her millions of dollars, and who later went bust claiming to live in a 'modest' million-dollar house, made bitter reading for Braselton residents, who were asked for their views when Kim hit the headlines.

After the *Boxing Helena* verdict, Meltzan Schumake, manager of the local diner, said, 'She wanted to put Braselton on the map. She said her name would attract thousands of tourists. I remember her saying, "Just wait — by the time the Olympics come, you won't be able to move for tourists." She has done nothing for this town. Sixty per cent of our 418 folks are on welfare and without jobs. Most children are on assisted-meals programmes.'

Mayor Henry Braselton, who had welcomed her so enthusiastically, was clearly disillusioned. He said, 'We can't wait to see the back of that woman. She has taken everything that we hold closest to our hearts and destroyed it. We are good Southern folk with a sense of pride. If anyone can survive this we can — but it's no thanks to her. It would be nice to have someone with a heart running this town again. Provided there's still a town to run.'

One of Kim's residential tenants, Joyce Higgins, complained she was living in a slum. 'We were better off before she came in here making these pretty promises and then breaking them,' she complained. 'She told me I'd get a new back porch. But it's still rotting away and infested with rats. Kim Basinger don't care about us. She's only been to this town twice. And she's never been to our house even though she owns it. She promised that all our homes were going to be made decent places to live in. But look at this place. Who in their right mind would call this a decent place?'

Joyce, who shared the house with her invalid mother, said she had to patch holes in the walls with paper and rags to keep out the rain, but despite repeated claims to the property management company, nothing was done. She said, 'When we paid our rent to the Braseltons, they'd come and see us when we complained. They were good people. Now we just get ignored.'

Even her mechanic fan, Terry Kitchens, was less than enchanted by her, though he tried to look more on the bright side. He said, 'The bank was a family affair when the Braseltons ran it. If things were a bit tight you could always get a line of credit. Nowadays, things are impersonal and unfriendly. Most people blame her for things that have gone wrong. They thought she'd make them rich. But she's done good things, like pulling lots of weeds, cleaning up things.'

By the time Kim went bankrupt, residents sounded as if they were heartily sick of her. Jeff Forrester, manager of Dado's restaurant, said, 'I don't think what she does affects what happens here one iota.' Resident Danny Grindle added, 'It's not exactly the buzz around town. There ain't a damn thing happened since she bought the place.'

Kim was equally disenchanted with Braselton. She started distancing herself from being the owner, and blamed the poor economy for the lack of development. She also revealed that she and her brother Mick had had a major falling out, which cannot have helped the situation.

She told *Movieline* magazine in 1994, 'I didn't buy the town. I just searched for two years so a corporation could buy this town. A company in Chicago bought it and I was only going to be the supplier of the dream. There was never any idea of a "Kim's Wood" — I don't even know what that means. A take-off of Dollywood I guess. My dream was for artists — record people, movie people — to make a major career centre on the East Coast. An auditorium for artists to play their new stuff and an in-house radio station. There's a hungry crowd down there in Georgia. It wasn't a stupid dream. Unfortunately, at the time the economy was going straight down and dreams became expensive. It's dead. Totally dead. It's a really horrible story.

'My brother's been very involved there. Only I'm not involved with my brother and haven't seen or talked to him in three years. I gave him a good two-and-a-half years to come clean and say how we've not spoken, because I did not any longer want my name associated with Braselton and I felt it is being misused. I really do love the people there. Braselton is a beautiful area and it needs to be preserved and I pray that people do right by it. It's not a nice story, this story about Braselton. That on top of this other stuff that's been going on these last three years, it was just one more thing I probably should not have got involved with. But I have no regrets. I learned a lot.'

The rift with Mick was clearly very bitter. He was to claim later that it started as early as 1991, when he wanted to concentrate on working in Braselton. He said he had been taking care of financial affairs for Kim and wanted to hand her business matters over to professionals. He said he had written the new team a note warning them that Kim could be difficult and advising them to 'Document everything you do with Kim because I guarantee you, when something goes wrong she'll blame you.'

Mick insisted, 'I didn't mean it as an attack on Kim. But Kim went nuts when she heard about the letter. She sent me a very curt note back, saying, "I am shocked you have undermined me and are hanging out our dirty linen in public." She cut me out of her life. I was horrified. After all the years we'd worked together she was just cutting me dead.'

She refused to return his calls and Mick finally visited Kim and Alec at a holiday home in North Carolina to try to patch things up. He saw her through the front door but she refused to speak to him and got Alec to send him away.

Mick said, 'He just shrugged his shoulders and looked embarrassed. He told me, "She won't see you, Mick." That was the last time I saw my sister.' For good measure, he added, 'She is the most selfish, arrogant, pompous woman I know.'

And when Kim told *US* magazine that she had severed her ties to Braselton and stopped speaking to him, he wrote the magazine a brief letter.

'Let's be real honest. One does not quit talking to a brother because of a failed business deal. I know the truth about Kim Basinger, on a number of fronts, and it's not very flattering.'

Mick was not the only family member on the outs with Kim by this time. She and her mother, Ann, had stopped speaking, too. Neither of them has ever explained what caused their estrangement, but Kim's sister Ashley said it was connected with Braselton. Kim lamented, 'She's completely cut herself off from me and anything that's gone on in my life. There's a lot of envy involved.'

Ann, who had always encouraged Kim, said bitterly, 'I don't want any part of her life.'

Although Kim was claiming by 1994 to have cut her links with Braselton, she still owned the bank, which was auctioned off in September of that year as part of her bankruptcy settlement. The minimum bid was set at $810,000, but it was sold, to another bank, for $1.5 million.

'It's a little gem of a bank in a little gem of a town that just got caught up in a Hollywood-sized mess,' said Jack Dunn, Georgia's Banking Commissioner. 'I imagine it teaches us all a good lesson that banking and acting don't mix.'

Bizarrely, Mick Basinger spoke for his sister at the time and said she was happy to sacrifice the bank to honour her debts. 'There isn't a personal attachment to the bank,' he said. 'Kim has no interest in being a banker. Never did.'

Bank President Carol Clark lost her job after the takeover.

Kim now had no real links to the town, and Ameritech decided to cut their losses by putting it up for sale again for $10 million, half of what they had paid for it. But the locals still associated her with their misfortunes. In January 1995, the prestigious *New York Times* ran a scathing article headlined THE BASINGER BANKRUPTCY BOMB. Carol Marie Cooper wrote, 'Instead of becoming a tourist attraction tied tightly to Ms Basinger's name, Braselton is now just another asset in her bankruptcy — and one with an uncertain future. The folks of Braselton, population 450, learned that getting too involved with an actress can be dangerous.'

Residents who were tenants of Basinger-Braselton began to fear for their future as rumours swirled through the town. Their $60 a month ramshackle cabins were not much, but they provided a roof over their heads.

Pensioner Tom Brown, who had lost his job when the hardware store closed, said, 'I ain't got no place to go. I heard that they will tear down my place and build something fancy on it when the land is sold. Folks figured this town would become mighty rich being linked with her. It just didn't happen that way. Now folks are whispering that eviction notices are being drawn up.'

His daughter, Clara Mae, added, 'Where folks used to be pleased about Kim and her interest in this place, now there is only anger. I think she feels sorry for letting people down.'

Betty West, another tenant, said, 'She came with so much promise and nothing was delivered either before or after all her trouble with the movie company. There was a really nice woman who worked for the Basinger-Braselton group. When she left she told me, "Betty, there may be eviction notices. The land has got to be sold and what the new owners will want to do with it is anybody's business." '

Tenant Bill Gables commented, 'She got folks' expectations all riled up. All they did was tear down a few rickety buildings but didn't put any new ones back up.'

Even Terry Kitchens found it hard to stand up for Kim. He said, 'I was feeling more for Kim than I was for myself when I heard about the bankruptcy and would have done anything I could to help her. But now she's out of it and we're left in the lurch. Big businessmen don't feel anything for small country folk. We're just numbers on a balance sheet. If they say, "Move out," I get 30 days to load up. I haven't heard anything yet — but I'm keeping my fingers crossed that I can stay put. I was born and raised in Braselton and I want to stay.'

Kim was furious at the *New York Times* article and got her lawyer to write a letter of complaint, which read in part, 'To blame the plight of the residents of Braselton on Kim Basinger is both intentionally deceptive and deliberately irresponsible.' Kim herself said, 'I am sympathetic about Braselton's problems and I have always tried to do what was fair and honest — and I believed helpful — from the very beginning. I care about Braselton and its people. But the *New York Times* article is a cruel, unfair and completely inaccurate picture of what has happened.'

Her bankruptcy lawyer, Leslie Cohen, added. 'Kim's lawsuit had absolutely nothing to do with Braselton's troubles. The problems in Braselton grew out of a nationwide declining real-estate market that led to a decision by the Ameritech Pension Fund, which managed the investment in which Ms Basinger was a limited partner, not to go ahead with its development plans.'

Kim's sister Ashley put it more succinctly, 'What went wrong is money and greed. The Braselton thing hurt everybody because everybody wanted a piece of the pie. It has just about torn this whole family apart. I am really happy that my husband and I didn't get involved. Kim wanted to bring in a lot of businesses so she could offer people in the surrounding area and Braselton itself a lot of jobs. She also wanted Braselton preserved. She didn't want all the old buildings and the stores torn down. Mick wanted something else entirely.'

Kim still has fond dreams of what might have been if the dream had not turned into a nightmare when Ameritech finally sold Braselton in 1995 for just $4.3 million. She told *Detour* magazine, 'We had plans for an arts centre, an animal preserve. The Braselton situation probably did more harm in my life than anything I can think of. I thought my being in the public eye would help get the town going and raise money but I left it in the hands of other people and it just went downhill from there. I've never seen $20 million. It was an excellent business opportunity for up the road, years from now. At the same time, I never wanted my name involved. My involvement was purely, at its inception, out of saying, "God, no, don't let anyone come in here and turn it into an industrial park." I've never really heard about people in the town having any animosity towards me. I think they know that it was not in my hands, that the controls were in the hands of the investors. I didn't have the money. I had the dream. You know, a dream can be expensive.'

Chapter 16

Apart from being 6ft tall, the same height as me, in Alec Baldwin Kim could not have found a more different man eventually to make her second husband. Alec is four years younger than Kim, while I am nearly 15 years older than her. He was brought up on the East coast of the United States; I've lived on the West coast all my life. The son of a famous movie make-up artist, I had mingled with Hollywood celebrities from as early as I can remember. Alec, the second of six children, is the son of a high school social studies teacher and football coach. He grew up in a household where money was always tight and professes to have had no desire to act until he got to college. He was intensely interested in politics from an early age. I never wanted to act but went into my father's business because it was a good way to make easy money and meet beautiful women. I've never had an ambition to run for public office.

Alec got his acting start appearing in low-budget, daytime television soap operas filmed in New York in 1980, then progressed to two seasons on the television series *Knots Landing*, which was filmed in California. On the show, he played bible-thumping evangelist Joshua Rush, who eventually jumped to his death from a tall building. He returned to Manhattan to do his first stage play — *Loot*, by British author Joe Orton — for which he won a Theatre World Award in 1986. Movie directors started noticing his on-screen potential because of his camera-friendly good looks and the wicked twinkle in his eyes. By the end of the 1980s, he was the hottest supporting co-star around, thanks to films like *Married to the Mob* and *Working Girl*.

Disney executives had high hopes of turning him into an established leading man when, in February 1989, brash young producer David Permut brought them an original script from comedy king Neil Simon. It was a period piece with the feel of *Gentlemen Prefer Blondes* or *The Front Page*. Permut had already had a read-through of the script with director Herbert Ross and Alec. Permut, who had worked with Kim before on *Blind Date*, thought she'd be perfect for the female lead.

Penny-pinching Disney, a studio notorious for wanting to keep film production costs down, refused Ross' pay demands to direct and appointed Jerry Rees, a protégé of then Disney chairman Jeffrey Katzenberg. Jerry had started drawing cartoons at the Mouse Studio's Burbank operation as a high school try-out and went on to make his only previous feature film, the award-winning animated movie *The Brave Little Toaster*.

Kim was introduced to Alec just three weeks before they began filming the ill-fated comedy, which turned into no laughing matter for anyone involved, although they had spoken on the phone when he called her while she was staying at Prince's Minneapolis house to discuss the film and they'd literally bumped into each other — but not spoken — while Kim was making *My Stepmother Is an Alien* and Alec had visited the set. When they met, at a script reading meeting at the Beverly Hills Hotel, she obviously knew nothing of his acting background. She admitted, 'In mid-sentence, I turned to him and said, "Can you act?" ' To smooth things over and get to know each other better, they agreed to have dinner the following night at Morton's, a Los Angeles restaurant famous as a popular place for movie industry titans' power meetings.

No sooner were they seated than Kim informed Alec that she was a vegetarian. Quick-thinking Alec, anxious to be on good terms with his soon-to-be leading lady, replied, 'So am I.' He followed her lead, and instead of ordering his usual veal dish, ordered a vegetable platter. Kim was delighted and asked him, 'Are you a vegan?'

Slightly confused, he said, 'What do you mean?'

'You know, people who don't use any leather products. No belts or leather shoes or wallets or luggage.'

His ploys became more ambitious as he strove to please her ever more. 'I am a vegan as a matter of fact,' he said, convincing her that his shoes and belt were imitation leather. It wasn't until some time later, when she found take-out hamburger wrappers littering his car, that she realised she had been fooled.

Kim and Alec hit it off so well that, at the end of the meal, they left together. They decided to retreat to his place in nearby Brentwood. According to witnesses, as they stood outside trying to decide which car to take, Alec borrowed a line from the movie they were set to make and told Kim, 'Mine's bigger.' Unfortunately for Alec, the vehicle had broken down. They had arrived in two cars but still left in one — hers. She drove him back to her house in Woodland Hills. Taking him by the hand, she led him through the main building, past the swimming pool and into the guest house that we'd converted into a gym and music room. She called it her 'sanctuary'. Kim recalled, 'We came back to the house. We were talking. He kissed me and then asked me if I wanted kids. I told him he was psychotic. That was the beginning.'

It should have been a match made in movie heaven for the Walt Disney Studio executives making *The Marrying Man*, a 1940s and '50s comedy about a young toothpaste heir, Charley Pearl, who meets and falls in love with Las Vegas lounge singer Vicki Anderson — who also happens to be the moll of the gambling capital's founding mobster, gangster Bugsy Siegel — and ends up marrying her four times during a stormy relationship. But the best laid plans of Mouse and men went astray as the dream couple turned into a nightmare duo because of their volatile relationship, stormy behaviour and tantrums during filming.

It was the beginning of a journey into bedlam. Although they fell head-over-heels in love off-camera, their on-screen sparks failed to ignite. For the critics, it was more fizzle than sizzle. Kim and Alec should have been deliriously happy to have found each other but in reality everyone, including them, was unhappy about how filming went and the atmosphere on the set.

Kim said, 'Making the movie was the worst situation anyone could imagine — ever. I thought hell was below us, but it fell right on my head.'

Up until then, she had always insisted that making *Never Say Never Again* had been her worst experience. She added, '*The Marrying Man* took such a long time to shoot. The director and I didn't get along. It was not only creative differences. It was a very tough situation.'

It was ironic that Kim and Alec should fall so heavily in lust and, eventually, love. She had threatened to pull out of the project when she learned the identity of her leading man. She had demanded Kevin Costner as her co-star and a salary to match the $3 million he commanded in those days. As a result, Disney were going to replace her with Julia Roberts. After some negotiations,

Kim got near to the fee she wanted but not the co-star. Who knows what would have happened if she'd completely won? Ironically, Kim was supposed to star in *Sleeping with the Enemy* after finishing *The Marrying Man*, but that part eventually went to Julia. Kim's decision to back out of *Sleeping with the Enemy* should have been an indication that things were troubling her. On the same day, she also fired her agent and lawyer. Later, she was sent the script for *Basic Instinct* but said, 'I didn't find the character interesting.' And when she was offered the role that eventually went to Meg Ryan in *Sleepless in Seattle*, Kim claimed; 'The timing was wrong.' In those early days after we split up, Kim seemed to be out of control and in need of someone to guide her.

Although Disney has a reputation for its strict policies of sticking to budget on production costs and tight shooting schedules, matters got out of hand because of the inexperience of the director and over-zealous studio executives who were desperate to follow up their then current romantic blockbuster, *Pretty Woman* — which starred Julia and Richard Gere — with another hit. As it turned out, the consequences of their over-enthusiasm and rush to judgement, believing that you can match any old two good-looking actors, put them in a comedy and you'll have a hit on your hands, should be taught as a recipe for disaster to would-be movie executives at film school. While *Pretty Woman* had grossed the studio a whopping $178,088,702 up to the end of 1997 from the American domestic box office takings alone — and earned $11,280,591 on its opening weekend in March 1990 — *The Marrying Man* only grossed $12,454,768 up to the same time, and took a disappointing $4,030,749 in the United States during the weekend it opened in 1991.

Things went rapidly awry and tales of the lengthy hold-ups caused by rows over cellular telephones, chair-throwing and other tantrums, huge demonstrations of egotism and blatant displays of sexual exhibitionism became the talk of Tinseltown. Problems were written in the sand long before the cast and crew arrived to start filming in the desert. Alec had just finished playing Jack Ryan in the movie version of Tom Clancy's *The Hunt for Red October* opposite Sean Connery, though the movie that was destined to make him an international star had not yet been released, when he signed to make *The Marrying Man*. It appears that Katzenberg, now a partner in Dreamworks SKG with Steven Spielberg and David Geffen, may have set the tone of discontent that was to follow by reportedly joking to Alec — whom he was paying $1.5 million, a million less than Kim — 'We could get a gate guard to do the same job you do.' The unfortunate remark stuck in Alec's memory.

For her part, Kim had a spectacular falling out with legendary playwright and screenwriter Simon, whose lengthy list of hits includes *The Odd Couple*, *California Suite* and *Barefoot in the Park*. Kim has always fancied herself as a writer and she wanted some changes in the script. A month into filming, she is alleged to have said to the critically-revered writer, 'It isn't funny. Whoever wrote this scene doesn't understand comedy.' Simon has denied that the insult was quite so brutal even though it is a story that has circulated Hollywood ever since. But he does admit that they had 'a discussion that was an argument'. Whatever the depth of the insult, it is a fact that up until then Simon had been on the set virtually every day but after that *discussion* he rarely returned to the set during the rest of the shoot.

A consummate Hollywood professional, Simon has said very little about his views on Kim. But of the incident, he did say, 'She didn't say it to me. I heard about it. My problem with Kim was different. My problem with her is she never came to any rehearsals, and I can't fix something or rewrite it unless I hear it. Alec Baldwin, I must say, was wonderful about that. Alec is an actor from the theatre and he came to every rehearsal. Kim didn't come. She's a movie star and she's treated differently. Actually, she's quite good in the film. She really is.' Others were not so diplomatic in their views towards her.

She often held up production due to lateness. Frequently, her explanation was that she had been washing her hair in the must-have Evian water that had to be supplied as written into her contract.

Her tardy time-keeping had begun before filming. She was five hours late for her make-up test, and because she had refused to give her home telephone number to the production staff, the crew had to call her agent to reach her. When she did finally arrive, she tried on one outfit, did a single test, then got back into her own street clothes and left. She was only on the set for about two hours. Yet when she saw the results of the test, she demanded that the director of photography, Ian Baker, who had previously filmed *A Cry in the Dark*, be fired because she was not pleased with the way she looked. Even though she was the one who was late and did only one take, Kim got her way. The cinematographer got his full $120,000 salary and the budget started to escalate from that moment on.

Kim was late for song rehearsals even though she desperately wanted to establish herself as a singer and hoped that Disney would release an album of musical numbers from *The Marrying Man* when the movie came out, to showcase her talent. She was extremely worried about rehearsing her first big on-screen number, Cole Porter's classic *Let's Do It*, in front of the rest of the cast, so she asked Jerry Rees and replacement director of photography, Donald Thorin, to come to the set early so they could go through it together in private. Even though Jerry and Don had been working very late the night before, they agreed and arrived promptly at 7.00am. Kim turned up five hours later. Most directors would have blown up at that but that was not Jerry's style. He was a soft-spoken man, a vegetarian who came from a long line of vegetarians, a bearded, reflective person. She became even more annoyed when she discovered that Disney wasn't planning to release an album of the movie's soundtrack after all.

There was so much disruption on the set of *The Marrying Man* — which was released in Britain under the title *Too Hot to Handle* — that in Hollywood Kim's reputation went from being the great blonde hope to huge trouble in a size six dress. She was rumoured to have set the foundation for her new reputation as Tinseltown's bad blonde bimbo on *My Stepmother Is an Alien* and she poured the concrete on it making *The Marrying Man*.

Movie sets are great places for gossip about who is having an affair with whom and who is feuding. There's a lot of tittle tattle going on. On this occasion, it didn't take long for the crew's suspicions to be confirmed. Filming started in Lancaster, California, a desert town about 80 miles outside Los Angeles, on 29 May 1990. On the fourth day, Kim and Alec were sitting in a car between takes, waiting for the next scene. Crew members listening in on the headphone intercom system couldn't believe what they were hearing. Kim was telling Alec in the most graphic detail what she planned to do to his body when they were making love that night. Nothing was left to the imagination. Crew members are pretty hard bitten and have seen and heard just about everything imaginable, but even they were shocked. Explaining what they'd heard, one embarrassed sound man said, 'Think of the dirtiest things you can think of.' The tension on the set was further enhanced by what crew members described as Kim's 'sexual obsession'.

A few days into filming, Alec moved into our house in Woodland Hills. Initially, Alec had been very punctual but as soon as they started living together that was all said to have changed. And it wasn't all a bed of roses. They had a very tempestuous relationship in the early days. A crew member said, 'If they were in a good mood at home, they came to the set in a good mood. If they were bad at home, watch out.'

I had always been concerned that Kim look after her lily-white skin. I insisted that she stay out of the sun and whenever she was outside that she wear a wide-brimmed hat and use plenty of sunscreen lotion. There were several scenes shot in the desert and, on the set, her obsession with staying out of the sun became legendary. She and Alec used to drive around in a convertible with the top up. Every time she left her trailer, she insisted on having an umbrella to keep her in the shade. Directors Guild trainee Michael Ryan Baxter recalled, 'When Kim came out of her trailer, I opened an umbrella and handed it to her. She'd carry it and then hand it back to me as she got in the car or on to the set or wherever she went. Her skin was really sensitive.' People thought she was being awkward but I completely understood why she did it.

Jerry Rees admitted that there were genuine and legitimate tensions between the cast and the studio. He believed that Disney made films to 'the more-cooks-make-a-better-broth theory'. As a result, too many middle-level executives were having a say in what was going on. He said, 'Collaboration is fine, but film by committee is a whole different ball of wax. It's not how I operated and it's not at all what those actors were used to. So there was frustration.' He found himself having to calm people down and get things focused again when the stars became upset by executives interfering in what they regarded as the creative process.

As an example, Jerry recalled, 'Repercussions came back from the studio people that Kim was spending too much time getting ready for her scenes. My position as director was that I was glad that she cared enough to be a bit of a perfectionist. I got footage the studio should have been very happy with when she got in front of a camera. So when I would talk to them, I would say, "Look, you're putting her in a position where she cannot win. If she doesn't give you enough time, you say, 'She should have spent another half-hour — the hair isn't quite right!' If she gives the hair and make-up and wardrobe people the time they need, you say, 'She shouldn't have been in the trailer that long getting ready.' So which do you want?" Then it was taken further. The time she took to get ready would be tabulated, and they would try to charge it against her fee. To have an actress come to the set who has just received a paper charging her for this when she was trying to get ready ... It's kind of like having someone applying a cattle prod to a group of people in the morning, then handing them over to me and saying, "Have a nice day." '

He also admitted that the shooting schedules were too tight and that agreements for sets and other details were reneged upon.

Both Kim and Alec took their frustrations about the working conditions out on their director, any of the big brass at Disney who were unlucky enough to be on the set and anyone else who unfortunately got in their way. Kim hated to be stared at and she would explode if she saw an extra whom she thought was looking at her.

Set director Jim Duffy said, 'She'd carry on and refuse to do a scene unless they got rid of all the people. If you're classy, you just tell the Assistant Director to deal with it, but she'd scream and holler.'

As production proceeded, so the screaming and carrying on got worse. A crew member said, 'We'd come to work and go, "Gee, it took her 45 minutes to have her first yelling fit today." At the beginning of the film, we were catering to Kim because we knew she was a prima donna but we weren't catering to Alec because he was a nice guy. But then he wanted to get the treatment she was getting.'

The arguments became more and more trivial. On one occasion, Kim and Alec became irate because Disney refused to refund the caterers for reusable plates that the cast and crew had inadvertently thrown away. As a result, the caterers had swapped the hard plastic plates they had been supplying for cheaper Styrofoam ones that were non-biodegradable. Kim announced to the assembled gathering that 'Disney is a polluter'.

One afternoon, they refused to start filming a scene because they did not want to stop and then return to it in the morning. Jerry complied with their wishes and, from that moment on, he was no longer in control. A production staff member recalled, 'It was only a little incident but what happened from that day on is that the actors began to realise they had a great deal of influence. We had given them an edge and they took it and ran with it.'

Jerry became so exhausted that he was rushed to a hospital emergency room with pneumonia, a 105 degree temperature and dehydration. He was so ill he was kept in hospital for two weeks towards the end of the shoot. Despite his attempts at being placatory, Jerry admitted, 'There were concerns up front from the studio people that Kim would not have the patience to sit through what it really takes to do period hair.' To be fair, throughout the times I did her make-up, I never once had a problem with Kim.

Crew members also found themselves distracted by Kim's underwear — or rather her lack of underwear. Even though there were times when she was annoyed at being looked at, on other occasions she acted like an exhibitionist. Long before Sharon Stone's *Basic Instinct*, Kim knew how to uncross her legs and give the lads a smile. Sitting in her director's chair, Kim would drape her legs apart for all the world to see. A crew member recalled, 'Once I turned around and it was like "Woooo!" She saw me look and asked, "How are you?" I replied, "Today, I'm doing a lot better, thanks." '

Alec started out under control but got progressively more hostile as the filming continued. He had a huge showdown with unfortunate Disney executive Jay Heit, who unluckily for him was using a mobile telephone on one occasion and bore the brunt of Alec's displeasure. Alec frequently threw his own cellular telephones, which were supplied by the studio to the stars as perks, at the walls and anything else which happened to be there. A technician recalled, 'He didn't like it when his phones cut out so he would slam them against the wall. I don't know how many phones he smashed to smithereens.'

When one phone cut out he was so furious he threw a director's chair so hard across the set that it narrowly missed electrician Mark Banuelos. 'He came out of his trailer and this director's chair came flying by me,' Mark said. Alec later apologised in front of the crew and asked how he could make it up to him. 'Tickets to see Santana,' came the reply. The sparky got front row seats. Heit, however, was not so fortunate. Alec caught him talking on the telephone on the set of a bar room scene. With a theatrical backhanded gesture, Alec sent the glasses and ashtrays flying. He yelled, 'The phones are not working in my trailer. You gotta phone, why don't I have a phone? Goddammit, I want a phone.' With that, crew members recall, Alec snatched Heit's telephone and dramatically threw it to the floor before storming off. On the way, he kicked over a case full of camera lenses causing cost-conscious Disney to get Panavision technicians to assess the damage and threaten to charge it to their uncooperative co-star.

Kim and Alec nicknamed the Disney executives they regarded as enemies 'Phone Monkeys'. As a prank, a crew member had T-shirts made with a picture of a monkey talking on a mobile telephone with a slash across it.

Disney's dislike of Alec was nothing compared to their loathing for Kim. They threatened her with possible legal action over her lateness. But her most outrageous action was her demand to see a psychic — in Brazil. At least, that was the story that did the rounds at the time and I could easily believe it. Our housekeeper Fatima, who had stayed on long after I'd left the Woodland Hills house, had introduced Kim to a spirit doctor in Brazil. Fatima was really into this guy — she still is — and believed he had healing hands and could do just about anything. Kim, with her weird ideas that dogs were really aliens and that Charlie in the Upstairs Room was her guiding force, really took to him. About four weeks into filming, she was said to have suddenly informed the director and producers that she had to go to South America to consult him. Disney executives had their own prediction; if she went to Brazil, she would have to pay $85,000 a day to cover lost production costs while she was out of town. Kim didn't need to be psychic herself to realise they meant it and changed her mind. But she was bitter that she had not got her way. A production member recalled, 'After that, she wanted to prove a point.'

In fact, years later, Kim said that the story was false, a smear campaign launched by vindictive Disney executives. She had wanted to go to South America, but it was because she had written a script for an animated film and the famed Brazilian animation director Mauricio de Sousa was helping her. Disney had agreed to give her two weeks holiday before shooting ever started, so she decided to go to Brazil. But obviously she did not want to tell her bosses at the world's most famous animation studio why she was going.

Whatever the truth was about her planned trip to Brazil, one thing was clear — Disney and its stars were at war and the battle that ensued throughout filming was bloody. The studio executives did like the footage they were seeing, and besides, by this time they had spent so much money that they were committed, they could not afford to cut their losses and pull the plug on production even though they'd have loved to see their stars swept down the plug hole with the bath water. Eventually, it was decided to ease up on the confrontations, let Kim and Alec have their way and just get the project finished. Set director Jim added, 'Word came down from head office, "Hands off Kim Basinger". She could have whatever she wanted.'

Kim and Alec were in control. Crew members were banned from rehearsals and Kim started rushing through her scenes. Time and again, this led to scenes having to be re-shot because they were out of focus or there was some other problem. Funnily enough, having to re-shoot scenes infuriated Kim even more. To add to the frustrations and lengthen the filming time still further, Kim insisted that her hair and make-up be touched up after practically every take instead of when a scene was wrapped, which is standard practice. The additional beauty work took as much as 30 minutes a time.

Kim and Alec appeared to be doing what they wanted rather than listening to the director. If Jerry Rees asked Kim to do a particular scene again, sometimes she'd agree, sometimes she would not. Often she'd say adamantly, 'One more time and that's it.' On one occasion, Alec insisted that a night scene be filmed during the day, adding huge production costs to create darkness, just because he didn't want to work in the evening. Another time, they decided that a bedroom love scene be filmed in a bathroom even though it wasn't in Neil Simon's script.

Defending their behaviour, Kim said, 'We just wanted to stand up for what we believed in as far as the characters were concerned and the movie that we were promised to do. It never happened. It was *who's going to control who.*' Later, she did confess that work on the movie was 'a creative tragedy'.

Anyone might have expected a director to stand up to his stars and for his movie and throw his own tantrums, but it just wasn't in Jerry's personality. When line producer David Streit tried to assert some authority and bring things back in hand, Kim had him banned from the set and he spent most of the last month of production sitting in his office. By the end of filming, movie trainee and umbrella holder Michael Baxter was the only one allowed to knock on her trailer door and he had to act as a go-between, passing messages back and forth. He said, 'It was funny because I was the low man on the totem pole and yet I'd have to go up to the producers and say, "Kim doesn't want you knocking on her door." '

Towards the end of the original shoot, Disney executives again changed their policy of going easy on Kim and Alec. They wanted some scenes re-shot but Kim and Alec refused until they had completed everything else. Fearing that at the end of the day, Kim and Alec might just walk away without completing the retakes, the executives dug their heels in and insisted that the re-shoot be done immediately. Alec became so annoyed that he hit the wall of his trailer with his hand hard enough to make an enormous dent in it. Part of the dispute was over a wedding chapel scene in which Kim's and Alec's characters were forced to marry for the first time by sinister mobster Siegel, played by Armand Assante. Disney wanted it done again, Alec refused, and when the executives informed him that they intended to charge him the cost of the crew for filming the original shoot, he offered to write them a cheque on the spot. Eventually, Katzenberg got his way and the scene was done again.

In the end, the movie wasn't wrapped until nearly a month after its original 52-day shooting schedule and cost $6 million more than the original $20 million budget. And it wasn't only Kim and Alec who had their noses put out of joint over the film. Neil Simon was also upset. When Disney asked him to rewrite the last 20 minutes of his story, Neil declined. He said he was too busy because of the impending opening of his Broadway play *Lost in Yonkers*. So the studio went ahead and had a completely new ending hastily scripted without his involvement. Kim and Alec were secretly called back for 10 more days of work in January 1991 and the deed was done. It was rumoured that Disney had to pay for a lavish holiday for Kim and Alec to persuade them to do the extra filming. As it happened, test audiences didn't like the replacement ending, and when the film was released in April 1991, the original one was used.

Simon found himself in hot water over *The Marrying Man* almost from the outset of the project. His longtime friend Alan King, of Odyssey Films, claimed that he'd bumped into the writer at a tennis tournament in 1988 and told him the story of shoe magnate Harry Karl — one-time husband of actress Debbie Reynolds — who met, married and remarried starlet Marie 'The Body' McDonald four times. Their bizarre relationship titillated American tabloid readers in the 1950s. Neil thought that it was a funny story and could form the basis of a comedy script. Then King discovered that a division of Disney was about to make *The Marrying Man*, from Simon's script. He handed it over to his lawyers to deal with and eventually his ex-pal and Disney settled by paying him a six-figure sum.

Producer David Permut should have realised that *The Marrying Man* wasn't going to be a picnic then. He had just signed a deal with Disney to produce the movie under its Buena Vista wing when his secretary persuaded him to take a short holiday in Hawaii. Permut, a fast talking workaholic who was 35 at the time, was relaxing in his seat as the plane took off and he prepared himself for his first holiday in 10 years. He opened his copy of the entertainment trade newspaper *Daily Variety* to read well-respected gossip writer Army Archerd's column. To his horror, it detailed King's complaint. He wasn't 10 minutes into his break when he found himself hitting the airplane's phone in front of his seat, trying to establish the seriousness of the situation and the legitimacy of King's allegations. The five-hour flight seemed to go on longer than forever. When he landed in Honolulu, he got straight on to another flight and returned to LA. He recalled, 'I was in Hawaii for 26 minutes and I came back paler than when I left.' Little did he realise that was the easy ride.

The Marrying Man firmly gained the reputation for being one of the unhappiest movie sets of all time. One senior production crew member said, 'Honest to God, if I were destitute and living on the street with no food and somebody offered me a $1 million to work with Kim and Alec, I'd pass.'

That basically summed up what the critics thought of the movie as well. And, for once, not even Kim got off lightly. Duane Byrge, of the *Hollywood Reporter*, wrote, 'If only they would have filmed the reported childish on-set insanities instead of this limp dud, *The Marrying Man* might stand a chance of sating moviegoers' whet appetites. Instead, this romantic comedy is likely to be left deservedly standing at the box office altar. One would have to unearth the Playboy Clubs to dredge up a sexual sensibility and story philosophy as dated and out-of-it as this Buena Vista release.' He added, 'In a career as splendid and bountiful as Neil Simon's, it's not surprising that among such a considerable body of scintillating work there lurks the occasional low point — and this is the pits.' Commenting on Kim, he concluded, 'While Basinger is to be commended for parting her large pouty lips to a degree usually only attained by Mick Jagger and certain species of tropical fish, her sultry singing style — abrupt hip sashays, unexpected shoulder scrunches, and other mechanical novelties — perhaps can only be appreciated by the ace Disney animators who viewed the rough cuts of Jessica Rabbit's shimmying in *Who Framed Roger Rabbit?* before the final, smoothing-out phases of her movements were drawn in.'

Richard Schickel wrote in *Time* magazine, 'Basinger is something of a problem. She is a very self-absorbed actress who gives the impression of a woman trying to get in on a joke she does not quite understand.' And *Daily Variety* observed, 'Disney's *The Marrying Man* is a stillborn romantic comedy of staggering ineptitude.' *Variety* also noticed similarities between Kim and Jessica Rabbit. Its review said, 'Basinger, replete with vocal coach and choreography by no less than Jeffrey Hornaday, gives a mechanical impression of a competent singer while grabbing herself during the numbers in a manner more like the animated Jessica Rabbit (of *Who Framed Roger Rabbit?* than Mae West. Unlike her obvious inspiration, Michelle Pfeiffer in *The Fabulous Baker Boys*, Basinger fails to integrate the singing stunt organically into her characterisation.'

Kim's desires to be a singer fell on deaf ears with the critics and Disney executives wished they could divorce themselves from Kim, Alec and *The Marrying Man*.

Chapter 17

When Kim took the witness stand during her breach of contract court case over dropping out of the film *Boxing Helena*, I was amazed. She had dreaded going to court during our divorce and I was convinced that she would have done anything to avoid it this time. On the other hand, I can understand why she didn't want to settle the case, for two reasons. Actors and actresses often drop out of projects without being sued — as, in fact, Madonna had done with this one. Second, knowing Kim the way I did, I was sure she had convinced herself in her own mind that she had never been committed to the film. Sadly for Kim, however, the jury were not convinced by her performance in Los Angeles Superior Court and she was ordered to pay the film's producers $8.9 million.

I couldn't believe my ears when I first heard stories about *Boxing Helena*. It had to be a joke — a movie about an obsessed doctor who cuts the arms and legs off the woman he loves and keeps her in a box! David Lynch's daughter, Jennifer, was said to have dreamed it up when she was 19, and spent years trying to get it made. There were rumours that somebody big, like Barbra Streisand, was interested in it, which was astonishing. Then it was announced that Madonna had got the part. That was about the time when she was doing her book, *Sex*, and I figured if anyone was outrageous enough to play such a part, she was the one. But even she got cold feet about it and dropped out.

Then in February 1991, I heard that Kim had accepted the part and I was completely taken aback. Kim had taken risks with films like *9½ Weeks* and *Fool for Love*, and had a highly developed comic touch that played well in *Nadine*, *Blind Date* and even *Batman*. She'd done thrillers and expanded her repertoire by singing in *The Marrying*

Man. A film like *Boxing Helena* would certainly take her in a different direction, but it simply didn't fit the pattern of work I expected her to do. It certainly was not worth taking a pay cut to $600,000, which is what I heard she was being offered — though there was a complex financing deal which would have raised her pay to $3 million if the film made a profit — and that is a very big *if* in film speak. So I wasn't surprised when she thought better of it in June.

Jennifer Lynch thought differently, however, and immediately announced plans to sue Kim, her Mighty Wind production company and her agents, ICM. Main Line Pictures, which eventually made *Boxing Helena* with *Twin Peaks* star Sherilyn Fenn as the girl in the box, brought the suit for breach of contract, demanding damages of at least $5 million and asking for an injunction to stop Kim working for anybody else during the time she would have spent making their movie. They targeted ICM because they believed the agency had persuaded her to drop out of the film because, the suit said, 'the character that Basinger had contractually agreed to play would not be good for her public image.'

When Kim was first approached about the film, her agent was Bill Block at Intertalent. Since then, she had switched to Guy McElwaine at ICM, who would not have been entitled to any commission if his client went ahead with a film set up by his predecessor. Main Line and Lynch were adamant that Kim had committed fully to the film, to the extent of getting changes made to the script. The suit claimed the company and its president, first-time producer Carl Mazzocone, 'in good faith tried to satisfy Basinger's every whim with respect to revisions of the movie script, the role and conditions stipulated in the actress' already final agreement'.

Jennifer Lynch complained, 'We were days away from shooting and Kim's leaving hundreds of people unemployed.' That was ironic, because at the same time Kim was full of mysterious plans for Braselton and talking about her scheme that would create thousands of jobs.

Kim always acknowledged talking to Lynch and expressing an interest in the role. But she completely denied accepting it. Her entertainment lawyer had talks with Main Line. But her trial lawyer, top Beverly Hills attorney Howard Weitzman, the man who had successfully defended failed car magnate John Z DeLorean on cocaine charges, insisted right from the start, 'Sometimes studios jump the gun, without deals being signed, sealed and delivered. They proceed at their own risk when doing so. There never was an agreement on how the character would be portrayed between the director/writer and Kim. There was never any signed agreement.'

Main Line were particularly furious because they had advertised the film to foreign distributors as starring Kim, and on the strength of her name and reputation they sold overseas rights in advance, at the Cannes Film Festival, for $7.6 million, with another offer for American rights of $3 million. But when Sherilyn Fenn replaced her, the distributors balked, and the producers could only raise $2.7 million.

My prediction that Kim would go for an out-of-court settlement proved wrong and in February 1993, nearly two years after she had backed out, the case went to trial. The first drama came during jury selection, when prospective jurors were told that *Boxing Helena* might be shown as part of the evidence. It had not yet been released but had been screened at the Sundance Film Festival with an NC-17 rating, meaning that nobody under 17 could watch it legally and that mainstream cinemas would refuse to show it. Four jurors asked to be excused because they did not want to watch a film with an adult rating. It was cut to get the rating lowered to an R, meaning people under 17 could watch it with an adult, before its general release.

The trial lasted five weeks and provided the public with an insight into a side of Hollywood most people had never dreamed of — the 'handshake deal'. It is common for multi-million dollar films to start rolling with nothing in writing — but it is equally common for actors or directors to be 'attached' to a film for a while and then walk away. In opening arguments, Weitzman said Kim agreed to meet Lynch because she was intrigued by the script and would be interested in helping a first-time, female director if the role was right for her. He said, 'Miss Basinger started out thinking that this might be an opportunity to help this young lady, but she nonetheless had reservations. Miss Basinger will tell you that she felt the nudity in the sex scenes was gratuitous, that they were unnecessary. And she never got any satisfactory answers from Jennifer Lynch. She never agreed to act in the film, no contract was signed. The decision she had to make was: if she were to do an offbeat film and if it wasn't done correctly, it could ruin her career.'

He could not deny that Kim had made *9½ Weeks*, but he said she had reached a stage in her career where she could choose not to do nudity or graphic sex scenes. 'Miss Basinger will tell you that the films she did in 1984 and 1985 were what most women had to do to get ahead in this business.'

But Lynch's lawyer, Patricia Glaser, said Kim did indeed have a contract. 'You have a star who abused that star quality, an ego run amok,' she said.

Jennifer Lynch told the court Kim told her she loved the script and said, 'I can't wait to get in that box.' After a second meeting, Kim hugged her, and Lynch said, 'I didn't take that as her way of saying, "I hate everything you just said to me." '

Lynch said the finished movie with Sherilyn Fenn had more nudity than the version she wanted to make with Kim, but that, as far as she was concerned, she had never tried to deceive Kim into gratuitous nudity. She said, 'I knew as I went into our second meeting there were some things she wanted to change. And I told her that I would not shoot anything that she was uncomfortable with in regard to nude scenes.'

Carl Mazzocone insisted that Kim had agreed to make the film as early as 11 February 1991, and she had signed a 'deal memo' on 27 February that year, listing 13 points of agreement, including limited script approval for Kim. Typically in Hollywood, actors and film-makers agree contract terms in conversation or on the phone, and the producers draft a 'deal memo' spelling out the terms that the final contract will have. It is quite common for filming to start before the contract is actually drawn up. Her oral agreement said she would have a $3,000-a-time hair colourist, a treadmill and video player in her 'star size' dressing room and a limo with a telephone, which sounded exactly the sort of perks Kim would ask for. And the plaintiffs also pointed out that they had got hold of ten of Kim's earlier film contracts and six of them had never been signed. Mazzocone claimed Kim's new agent Guy McElwaine had told him he needed to change her image after all the negative publicity over *The Marrying Man*, and that *Boxing Helena* was not a suitable film to do that. Mazzocone warned McElwaine that Kim had a deal with Main Line and that there would be legal problems if she backed out. 'He didn't seem impressed,' he said. Eventually, ICM was dropped from the case.

Kim sat quietly throughout the testimony, betraying no emotion, with Alec by her side most of the time. When she finally took the stand, however, he was not there. She explained why she had agreed to meet Lynch. She looked pale and strained and had a terrible cold that made her cough and sneeze throughout her evidence.

'When I read the piece I just felt I had to meet the mind behind this idea,' she said. 'I think it was probably the strangest piece I ever read — and well constructed.' But she maintained she had never agreed to go ahead with the film.

Weitzman asked her, 'Do you believe you ever agreed to render acting services in *Boxing Helena*?'

'No, I did not,' she replied firmly. And she said she changed her mind after asking for comments from '15 or 20 people I admire in the entertainment industry and the overwhelming response was, "this is a joke"'.

Kim said Lynch made changes in the script but that the character was still not acceptable. 'Lynch had an argument for every single idea I had come up with,' Kim said. 'She was very, very stern about her vision of Helena.' And of the last script changes, made days before she backed out of the film, Kim added, 'I told her they were laughable. I told her it was like bad television, the worst television writing in history.'

In closing arguments, Weitzman appealed to the jury, 'What we have here is a failure to communicate, that's what this case is about. I believe Carl Mazzocone believed he had a deal with Kim Basinger, maybe because he wanted to believe that or needed to believe that. And what we do know is that Mr Mazzocone hit the ground sprinting once he thought he had a deal. But it just doesn't make sense that a star like Kim Basinger, with all of her experience in this industry, would meet with Jennifer Lynch for a total of two-and-a-half hours and suddenly come up with a deal. It's just not logical.'

His legal opponent, Glaser, countered, 'No one's saying Kim Basinger had to act in this film if she decided she didn't want to, but once she had committed to the project she would have to pay the piper upon backing out. Carl Mazzocone mortgaged his house to get this picture done. And now the picture is $2.1 million in debt. All because Kim Basinger breached a deal memo. You have heard expert witnesses testify that deal memos are custom business practice in Hollywood. Considering the pace of business in this industry, relying on short memos is the rule, not the exception.'

It took the jury of four men and eight women less than two days to find against Kim and on 24 March 1993, they ordered her to pay Main Line $8.92 million. That was $7,421,694 for breach of contract and an extra $1.5 million for denying the existence of the contract in bad faith. Weitzman told the jury, who still had to consider punitive damages, 'Your multi-millon dollar award is almost double Miss Basinger's net worth. You have pushed her beyond her means.' The jury decided not to award punitive damages after Kim's lawyers told the court her net worth was $5,387,382.19.

Kim, visibly shaken, was ushered out of the courtroom with Alec through a back door, leaving Weitzman to comment and promise to appeal. 'I think Kim was shocked,' he said. 'Kim Basinger to this date, as she testified under oath, did not believe she entered into any agreement with Carl Mazzocone or Main Line Pictures. I think it was the star versus the little guy and the jury didn't like the star. She makes too much money. She's too pretty. Her boyfriend is too handsome.'

Lynch and Mazzocone, not surprisingly, were delighted with the verdict. A beaming Mazzocone was close to tears as he said, 'Everything about making a movie is an uphill battle and today I was vindicated for all the pain I was caused. I'm a little guy and I stood up for my rights and for the rights of other independent producers.' Lynch added, 'I feel like I just woke up from a nightmare I've been having since the day Kim Basinger left the picture. It's been two-and-a-half years of pressure and it's been horrible having negative feelings surrounding my first movie before I even made it.'

The court case itself was not the only ordeal Kim had to face as a result of her disastrous association with *Boxing Helena*. Bizarrely, during the trial, she and Alec were invited to a party being thrown for Judge Chirlin's clerk, Syndy Scaife-Richard, who was expecting a baby. They felt they had to go but Kim said it was awkward for her being forced into making small-talk and signing autographs for strangers in those circumstances.

'They were all very nice but I felt very uncomfortable being there,' she said after the trial, when she spoke about the party for the first time. 'I wasn't sure what to do. We took pictures with the judge's mother. I felt like I had signed up for an episode of the television sitcom *Night Court*'.

Weitzman was also furious about the party invitation, which was not revealed until later. 'Kim shouldn't have been invited because it made her feel as if she had to show,' he complained. 'This woman was a defendant in a case, on trial for her financial life. She shouldn't have been put in that position.'

Weitzman was also unhappy that Lynch and Mazzocone invited both the judge and the jurors to the première of *Boxing Helena*. Juror Chawn Sanders recalled, 'I remember after the trial, Jennifer and Mr Mazzocone told us they were inviting us to the première. I remember walking out of the courtroom thinking, "That's strange. How can they have a première when they kept saying during the whole trial they didn't have enough money to finish the movie?" We had been under the impression they couldn't get it sold, and now they were having a première?'

The verdict caused a furore in Hollywood. Weitzman said, 'We interviewed jurors after the trial. Two said there was a deal because Kim said she loved the script. Two said there was a deal because she continued to talk to the director while her lawyer was negotiating. One said it was a deal even though nothing was signed. And they all admitted that $9 million was a number they just made up.'

Alec Baldwin sprang to Kim's defence in an article he wrote for the *Los Angeles Times*, saying, 'This verdict is not a victory for anyone in this business, a business where the climate of deceit and distrust, self-serving and self-seeking is high enough already. Now simple expressions of good faith and courtesy ("I loved the script!"; "Of course I'd like to do it") will necessarily be replaced with a level of caution and calculation few artists are trained in. The statement "I love this movie and want to do it" always had an unspoken, "if we can agree on material terms and conditions" attached to it.' And Martin Bregman, who produced Kim's film with Val Kilmer, *The Real McCoy*, also stuck up for her, using a financial argument rather than discussing Hollywood customs.

'I've never known an actor or director to make a deal with a producer who's getting his financing by selling territories without getting his or her salary placed in a bank trust fund. You don't make a deal with first-time people if the money isn't guaranteed.'

Two months after the verdict, Judge Chirlin granted Weitzman's plea to throw out the $1.5 million bad faith portion of the award but ordered Kim to pay more than $700,000 in lawyers' bills. Kim could not afford it, and she declared bankruptcy, claiming assets of $4,918,233 and liabilities of $11,031,089. She filed for what is called Chapter 11, which meant that her assets could not be seized to pay her debts, but that she had to come up with a suitable financial plan to pay her creditors over time which a bankruptcy judge would approve. Meanwhile, her finances — including the alimony she paid me — were laid bare for the world to see. Her interest in Braselton was listed as 23,775 shares in the Braselton Banking Company, worth $900,000 and 50,000 shares in Braselton Planning Inc, with a current market value of zero. The house on Don Juan Place was worth $1 million and the furniture and household effects were valued at $592,000. She had $327,000 in her pension plan, jewellery worth $192,000 and three cars. She had to reveal her monthly expenses, including $7,000 on pet care and personal expenses, $6,100 on clothes, $8,900 on home maintenance, $4,000 on entertaining, $3,100 in gifts to charities including Comic Relief and the International Fund for Animal Welfare, and $1,000 for gas, electricity and water, which totalled $43,100.

Her income from her production company, Porch Swing Productions, was $187,000 a month, on which she paid $72,000 in taxes and social security. And she had another $7,000 in interest and dividends.

Against that, she owed Main Line Pictures $8,921,694 and the Harris Trust and Savings Bank, trustee for Ameritech Pension Trust — her partner in the Braselton investment — $911,300 from a loan. Her other debts included one to her old business manager Mitchell Freedman, who was claiming $145,000 for a breach of contract suit filed in May 1992, and $30,000 to the British taxman for her *Batman* payments. Even though Kim and I had been divorced for more than three years, a copy of every document in the bankruptcy was sent to me, thousands and thousands of pages.

Bankruptcy Judge Geraldine Mund gave Kim a tough time. She ordered her to come up with a plan to pay the full amount she owed Main Line — plus 10 per cent interest. Kim claimed it would take her 15 years to pay that amount, a statement hotly contested by Main Line's lawyers, given that she could earn $3 million a movie. The judge was scathing about Kim's description of Don Juan Place as 'modest', noting that the gardener's bill alone was $600 a month. 'That's a pretty good house,' she said. She also asked if Kim had a licence to run a kennel, given her high pet expenses, and threatened to throw the case out altogether, leaving Kim no protection from her creditors.

'Time is running out here,' she said at the second hearing in the case. 'I will have no hesitancy to dismiss this case. Good faith is an absolute requirement of a debtor in possession.' She rejected Kim's first proposal to pay Main Line all her earnings for the next three years, saying it was 'vague'.

'There has to be something more than, "I'll pay you over three years if I make any money," because that's what you have right now.'

Main Line then dropped a bombshell and demanded to know if Kim planned to have a family. Her bankruptcy lawyer, Leslie Cohen, said, 'Main Line argued that her plan should be denied because Kim could get pregnant. They wanted assurances that she wouldn't start a family as a way of avoiding payments.' Main Line also wanted the right to compel Kim to accept roles she was offered, even if she did not like them.

Kim must have had as emotionally upsetting a Christmas that year, 1993, as I had had five years earlier, when I was served with divorce papers on Christmas Eve. The day after Christmas she switched from Chapter 11 bankruptcy to Chapter 7, meaning her assets could be sold to pay her creditors. But her house and furniture were exempt so Main Line would only make a fraction of what they were owed — and Kim's future earnings would be safe.

Kim, whose beauty on film will last longer than forever...

Top: Kim and I joke around in a happy moment during a break from filming on location.

Bottom left: Sexy Kim busts out in a titillating pose – almost in costume as Memo Paris in *The Natural* in 1983.

Bottom right: Kim saying 'Hey dahlin' to the camera during a break from filming *Blind Date* in 1986. She is wearing a dance workout shirt she was given during the making of *Never Say Never Again*.

Kim, always a water babe, wearing the famous *Never Say Never Again* swimsuit.
In fact, she was given the fabulous tiger-faced outfit by the *Playboy* organisation.

Top: Animal-lover Kim feeds sheep in the countryside on one of our last days together in a break from the early filming of *Batman* in 1988.

Bottom: Kim wearing her Athens High School cheerleading sweater.

Top: The tunnels on Kanan Road, Malibu, which terrified Kim because of her agoraphobia. I took pictures like this to help her overcome her fears. After therapy and months of encouragement she plucked up the courage to drive through them by herself.

Bottom: My beloved dog Dooboy in the garden at our Woodland Hills home. As usual, he was dripping wet after a swim in the pool.

A portrait I took of Kim during our early years together.

Top: Kim and I have a lazy afternoon celebrating Independence Day in our backyard.

Bottom: A disconsolate Kim prepares to return to North Carolina for additional footage of *No Mercy* in 1986. It was a difficult moment for both of us because of the turmoil over Richard Gere.

Top: Kim and I enjoying a cuddle.

Bottom: On my Dad's boat in Playa Del Rey, California, soon after we were married.

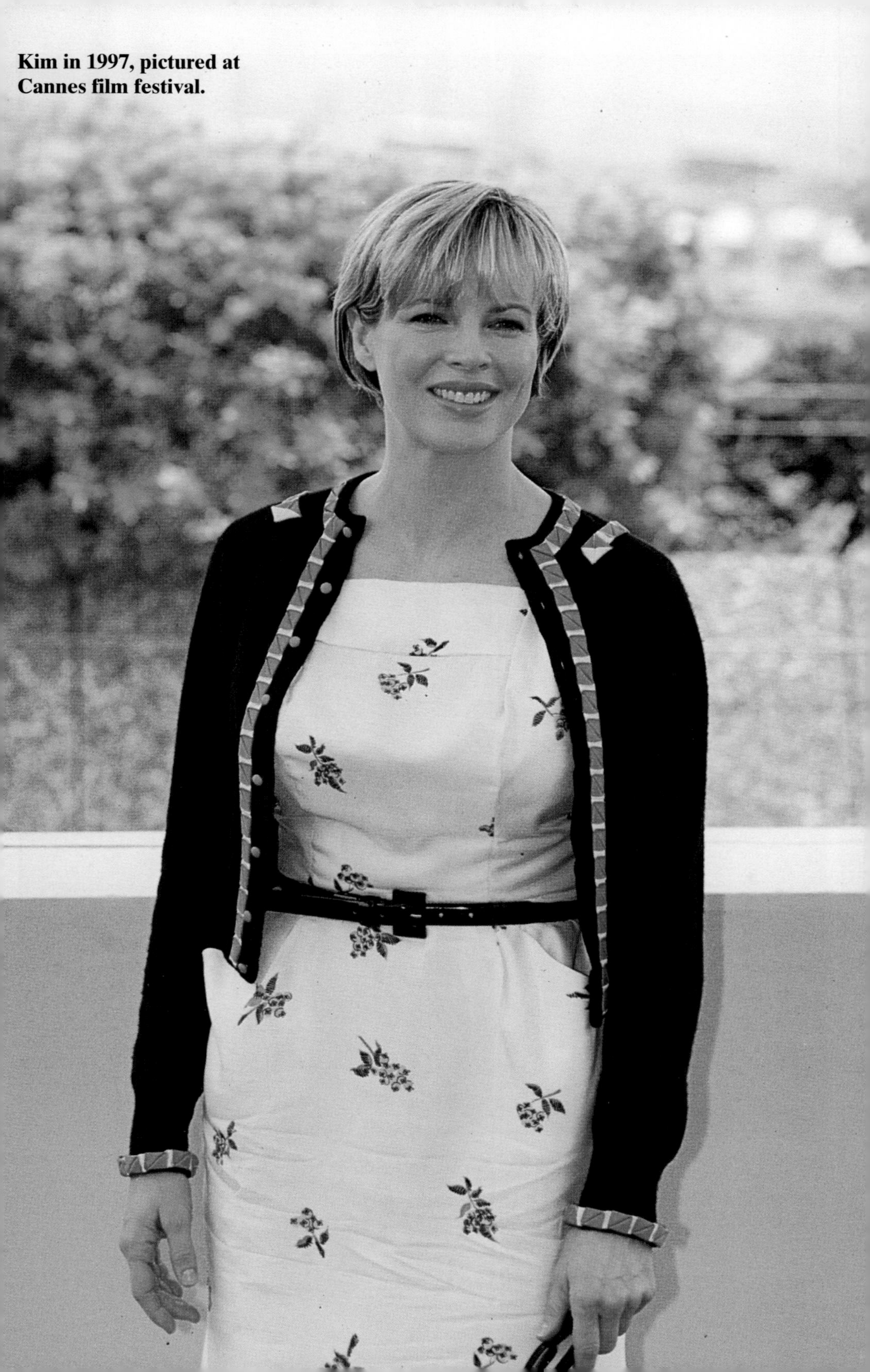

Kim in 1997, pictured at Cannes film festival.

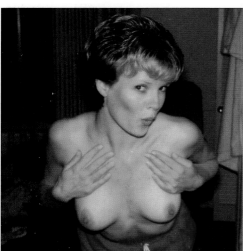

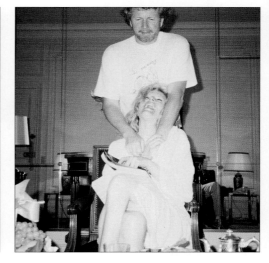

Top: Kim and her favourite dog Macaroni, relaxing at home in Woodland Hills.

Bottom left: Kim shows off some of her assets during a break from filming *The Man Who Loved Women* with Burt Reynolds in 1983. This was one of the shots she put into the 'goodies books' she made for me.

Bottom right: Kim and me having lunch and a laugh at the Royal Monceau Hotel in Paris during the publicity tour for *Nadine* in 1987.

Top: A portrait shot I took of Kim while filming *Mother Lode* with Charlton Heston.
Bottom: Kim stretches back during a relaxing moment.

The famous white slip picture from *9½ Weeks* that Kim sent out to fans – but they didn't know that I signed many of the autographs.

Top: My Mom Beverly, sister Sherry and Kim celebrating Christmas 1984 at our home.

Bottom: Kim at the gates of the Woodland Hills house. She put up the yellow ribbon to celebrate the release of American hostages, 1981.

Kim as the man-eating temptress in the made-for-television movie *Killjoy*, which aired in 1981. After *Hard Country* Kim went back to television work because we were short of cash.

Top: Hamming it up for the camera during one of our happy moments in Kim's trailer.
Bottom: A sexy publicity shot of Kim, from *9½ Weeks*.

Kim as Lynn Bracken in *L.A. Confidential.*

Not surprisingly, Carl Mazzocone was furious. He claimed, 'In the three years Kim wanted to give us and her other creditors, she'd probably stay home and make a family and, when the three years are up, go back to work. Then we'd be left out in the cold.'

The bankruptcy was put on hold until the *Boxing Helena* appeal could be heard. But Kim did not have any respite from the court case. In a bizarre twist, it was revealed that the court clerk whose party she and Alec had attended, Syndy Scaife-Richard, had written to Kim after the trial, a strange note which was actually penned on the day Kim married Alec. The court clerk actually asked for a loan of $125,000 to buy herself a house. Although the letter was addressed to Kim, she said she would like Alec to make the loan because of Kim's financial and legal woes.

'Dear Kim,' she wrote, 'I have a really big favour to ask of Alec, but out of respect for you and your relationship with him, I thought it would be better to convey my request through you.' She said a professional sportsman she knew had backed out of a promise to lend her the money and went on, 'You and Alec are the only other individuals I know who might have and be willing to loan this large amount of money. Hopefully, I have not tarnished your opinion of me by making this request. It was very hard for me to set aside my pride and write this letter. I have great respect for you and will respect your decision, whatever it may be. All transactions shall be CONFIDENTIAL.'

Scaife-Richard even spelled out the terms of the loan she wanted — five per cent simple interest, payable over 22 years — and enclosed a photograph of herself and her three children. She followed up the letter with phone calls and a second letter. Kim's lawyer told Judge Chirlin about the request, and the clerk was disciplined.

The *Boxing Helena* case went to appeal in September 1994, and the verdict was overturned on a technicality — a ruling that Judge Chirlin did not give the jury clear enough instructions. Kim was delighted and said, 'I am delighted with the court's decision. I continue to maintain that there was no contract.' Winning the appeal did not get Kim off the hook as far as her bankruptcy was concerned, however. On the day of her victory, the Bank of Braselton, in which she had a 95.1 per cent interest, was sold at auction for $1.5 million, the first time in Georgia history a bank was sold in bankruptcy court. Kim had offered Main Line $3.8 million, plus an extra $2.2 million once all her other creditors had been paid off. Once again, however, Judge Mund rejected the settlement — this time saying the sum Kim proposed paying was, 'Too rich'.

Kim had always been adamant that she would not settle the *Boxing Helena* case with Main Line. 'People ask me, "Why don't you settle?" ' she said. 'This whole town is about settling. But I won't give anything to anyone when it's a complete and total lie. I didn't do anything wrong.'

But finally, in December 1995, with the *Boxing Helena* retrial set to start, Kim and Main Line announced they had settled. Main Line got $3.8 million, payable in instalments, and her other creditors would get a proportion of what they were owed.

Kim issued a formal statement through her publicists saying the settlement was not a sign that she admitted any wrongdoing, 'The United States Bankruptcy Court has approved a compromise with the Bankruptcy Trustee and Main Line Pictures which will dismiss all claims against Kim Basinger. Ms Basinger does not plan to appeal the ruling, as the dismissal totally exonerates her and will allow her to keep her personal assets.'

I was delighted for Kim that it was all finally over, and that she had had the strength to fight so long and so hard.

Chapter 18

In addition to the tantrums on the set of *The Marrying Man*, Kim's reputation in Tinseltown as trouble with a capital T was further enhanced by her performance as a presenter at the Academy Awards ceremony in 1990. Apart from being criticised for her fashion sense — she turned up in a weird evening dress she had personally designed — Kim offended the members of the prestigious Academy of Motion Picture Arts and Sciences, who vote for the Oscar winners, by lambasting them for ignoring director Spike Lee's movie *Do the Right Thing*.

Kim had been asked to be a presenter several times but had always turned the offers down because of her nerves, but within months of us splitting, she seemed to have developed a new-found courage. I've always believed that in the beginning I was there to give her courage whenever she needed it, but finally she gained the courage to not need me any more. She told an interviewer that she changed her mind about going to the Oscars because 'All of a sudden, it was like God came down from the sky and went, "You cannot keep running from these situations".'

Regrettably, her new-found bravery also seemed to give her permission to shock her peers. Kim said the reason she felt she had to attack the other members of the Academy was because 'One night, soon after I'd seen *Do the Right Thing*, I was sitting in bed, watching members of the Academy — the voters — being interviewed on TV. Some of these people were talking about films they obviously hadn't even seen, and one of them was *Do the Right Thing*. Over and over again, they said, "Oh, well," just dismissing it. I've never been so sick to my stomach.'

At the awards ceremony, which was being watched by tens of millions of television viewers around the world, Kim told the members that by recognising films such as *Driving Miss Daisy* and *Born on the Fourth of July* but failing even to nominate *Do the Right Thing* they had made a big mistake. At the end of the event many people shunned her.

It was the first year that Russia was getting a live television feed of the Oscar ceremony. Over her gown, Kim wore a jacket which only had one long sleeve and on it she had the dressmaker emblazon *'To Russia with Love'* so the Russians could read it. As a result, she became the object of ridicule within fashion-conscious Hollywood.

However, the way she dressed and her outburst obviously caused her no long-term damage, for the following year she and Alec were invited to present the Oscar for the Best Original Musical Score, which went to John Barry for his work on Kevin Costner's *Dances with Wolves*. Among others attending the 63rd Annual Academy Awards in 1991, at the Shrine Civic Auditorium in downtown LA, were Madonna escorted by Michael Jackson, Julia Roberts with Kiefer Sutherland, Nicole Kidman and Tom Cruise, and Cindy Crawford with Richard Gere, who at the time was co-starring opposite Kim in *Final Analysis* which was her next film after *The Marrying Man*.

The critics pouring cold water on *The Marrying Man* did not dampen the fire burning between Kim and Alec and, despite her new reputation, Kim continued to be offered 10 new movie projects a week. I found a certain irony that after *The Marrying Man*, she had chosen the thriller *Final Analysis*, which threw her back into the arms — at least on screen — of co-star Richard, who played her psychiatrist and lover.

Originally, *Final Analysis*, which had Kim playing a troubled murderess and also starred Uma Thurman as Kim's sister and Eric Roberts as her hoodlum husband, was to have been filmed in New York, where Kim was spending most of her time living in Alec's apartment, but a union strike caused the location to be switched to San Francisco. Alec had signed to film *Prelude to a Kiss*, which was being filmed in Chicago, so if *Final Analysis* had gone ahead in Manhattan it would have been easy for them to commute to be together much of the time. However, even being so far apart did not cause Kim to fall again for Richard, who by this time was dating stunning model Cindy.

Alec missed Kim so much he sent her a special token to display his affectionate feelings for her. He alerted the cast and crew of *Final Analysis* that he had hired a plane to pull a banner with the words 'I love you, Kim' across the sky behind it. But when the moment came, Kim didn't want to be bothered with being dragged outside her trailer as she wasn't working. Finally coaxed out, she was flabbergasted by what she saw. *Final Analysis* director Phil Joanou recalled, 'Kim smiled and turned red and said, "I can't believe this." '

In return, Kim wanted to make sure that while Alec was in Chicago filming, he thought about her each day. So every morning, she had one perfect rose in a vase delivered to him at the movie's production office. Each rose was accompanied by a card — she was always good at sending cards — with only one word, a new one every day, which combined with all the other cards to form an ongoing message.

Kim started carrying a mobile phone and gave the number only to Alec. One night while on a trip to LA she was in the ladies' powder room in the then trendy but now defunct Nicky Blair's restaurant on Sunset Strip when it rang and other women in there were treated to Kim cooing into her handset.

Alec, who had previously been engaged to *Northern Exposure* actress Janine Turner, was so smitten by Kim — he even quit smoking at her request, though later he took up smoking cigars when it became the hot trend in Hollywood — that there was no doubt he was destined to really become a marrying man. Prone to addiction, he was so obsessed by Kim that he joined Co-Dependents Anonymous, a group that helps partners deal with their obsessive romantic feelings for the person they love.

Kim also became a slave to love. She said, 'Love is the most important thing in my life. If doesn't matter who you are. If you're a movie star you need love as much as someone who works in a factory. I believe love is the most important thing in anyone's life.'

Even though Kim and Alec were working on opposite sides of the United States and Richard was on hand to give her temptation, their relationship lasted and they flew across the country to spend time together whenever they could.

Making *Final Analysis* was not without its share of high drama and scandal. Kim brought in lawyers to prevent her body double, Shelley Michelle, who was 11 years younger than her, revealing the secrets of her sizzling movie love scenes with Richard and Eric Roberts. It was Shelley's astonishing body that audiences actually saw in all the naughty scenes but coy Kim was keen to keep that information under wraps. Kim has always had a thing about the back of her hands, her feet and her legs. She always hated the look of them. These days she has it written into her contracts that they are never filmed. She used to tell me she had 'farm girl's hands'. Kim had her legal eagles send off a furious letter to her stand-in when Shelley, who by this time had insured her own legs for $1 million, started talking about the part she played in getting the movie made. After receiving the legal threat, Shelley would only reveal, 'They told me to say that I only doubled for Kim's arms and legs.' In fact, Shelley claimed there was a lot more of her than that which appeared in the movie. The filmmakers used Shelley's breasts to double for an opening shot in the film, and she later stripped off in front of Eric, Kim's screen husband. Shelley, who also stood in for Julia Roberts in *Pretty Woman*, first became Kim's double in *My Stepmother Is an Alien* but later Kim denied she ever worked on that film. Kim's legal gag worked and Shelley fell silent.

I was amused to hear about a feud between Kim and her co-star Uma. It appeared they became incredibly jealous of each other. They were both concerned about who was getting on best with the director. Kim was annoyed because she felt Uma was becoming too chummy with Joanou and as a result was getting the better scenes. Now, when had I heard of that happening before? It must have been galling for Kim to see a much younger actress playing the tricks she was so good at.

Although Richard, who was also an executive producer of the movie, wasn't happy with the way *Final Analysis* turned out, it was well received by the critics, who once again raved over Kim. Duane Byrge wrote in *Hollywood Reporter*, 'Mature audiences should lap up this *Double Indemnity/Body Heat* update.' And he went on to say, 'As the diabolic blonde, there's never any question that Basinger fits the part to full-figure dimension. She's sultry, cunning and victimised all at once.' *Daily Variety* proclaimed, 'Succeeding much better than most attempts at reproducing old-fashioned Hollywood thrillers, *Final Analysis* is a cracking good psychological melodrama in which both star power and slick surfaces are used to potent advantage.' And *Box Office* magazine said, 'Basinger, in a role that calls for a feline seductiveness and a ruthless streak, does some of her best work.' It did moderately well at the box office and has enjoyed more success as a video to rent.

As their relationship progressed, Kim and Alec divided their time between Alec's homes in New York and the Hamptons on Long Island and Kim's home in Woodland Hills. Alec, who suffered a heart-attack in the mid-1980s brought on by his addiction to drugs and booze, admitted that he had been fighting personal demons through the making of *The Marrying Man*.

Alec, who was said to have beaten his addictions six years before he met Kim, spoke of how he had become a tantrum-tossing wildman, once again strung out on drugs and alcohol. His voice chastened, he admitted, 'All of a sudden, after *The Hunt for Red October*, I was a star. I went from making $200,000 for that picture to being offered millions. But I didn't handle it well. I went crazy.' He confessed that he had got so bad he was sneaking drinks and drugs into his dressing room. 'I would swear to myself that I wasn't gonna get drunk or high but before noon, out would come the booze or drugs,' he said. 'I was as crazy as you can get and still be sort of functional. I made it to work, did my lines and did a respectable job. But God only knows how I did it. Luckily, I was healthy enough to pull it off, at least for a while.' Thankfully, he recognised his problems before it was too late and sought help. I wondered how Kim coped with that; although she had occasionally enjoyed coke with me, she was never close to addicted and often pleaded with me to stop.

He praised Kim for giving him 'the strength and desire to keep on going'. Recalling the bad times, he said, 'A typical breakfast for me used to be two fried eggs over easy and a Midori [a melon-based, 46-proof liqueur]. For lunch, I'd have a sandwich and vodka and tonic, and for dessert I'd have some more hard liquor. Dinner would be some fish and steak and some more booze and cocaine.'

Years later, in 1998, Alec became a good example to his younger brother Daniel of how it is possible to beat addiction to drugs and alcohol. Daniel, who starred in the television series *Homicide: Life on the Street* was arrested at the luxury Plaza Hotel in Manhattan after guests reported hearing a commotion. His room had been trashed and he was found naked and confused, a porn video playing loudly on the television and empty vials littered about the room. He was handcuffed and rushed to St Lukes-Roosevelt Medical Centre, where he was treated for an apparent overdose of crack cocaine and was said to be in critical condition. The family started gathering as soon as news of the overdose reached them, and Kim and Alec were soon at his bedside. Alec, no doubt thinking back on his own wilder days, urged the rest of the family to take an understanding view. Daniel was charged with two drug offences and released on $1,000 bail. Four months later he agreed to plead guilty to a reduced charge of disorderly conduct in Manhattan Criminal Court and was given a conditional discharge and ordered to continue treatment for drug abuse.

Despite their intense feelings for each other, all was not completely smooth sailing during the early days of their romance. Writer Graydon Carter, who lived in the same Manhattan apartment building as Alec, said at the time, 'Not a week goes by when we don't see them in a shouting match on the street. Either Kim or Alec often drag some belongings into a cab then taxi back a few hours later for a tearful reunion.'

Kim insisted that their often public rows were because they were two highly-charged and fiery people. She said, 'There's an enormous amount of electricity between us. Sometimes the current gets overloaded and there's a short — but things are back to normal in no time.'

After making *Prelude to a Kiss*, Alec, who has always loved performing in the theatre, went into rehearsals for a Broadway production of Tennessee William's classic play *A Streetcar Named Desire*, in which he appeared opposite Kim's old rival Jessica Lange.

Early in their relationship, Alec introduced Kim to politics. Alec has always been interested in politics and, in fact, as he has aged he has often expressed ambitions to change career and become a politician. A staunch liberal Democrat, in his younger days he made telephone calls for the likes of Jane Fonda's former husband, Californian politician Tom Hayden, and Alec even attended the 1988 Democratic National Convention. Mark Weinberg, a former press secretary of Ronald Reagan who became friends with Alec when they were at George Washington University in Washington, DC, believes he will run for public office. He said, 'He really cares. There's a passion and maybe even an anger about some of the things that are wrong in the United States — the disparity between the haves and have-nots. He gets angry and morally outraged when the Government doesn't meet its responsibilities to its citizens. I think the energy he would bring to government would be well received and effective.'

Although Kim, who loved to sing, was always phobic about performing in public, she was persuaded — thanks to a little white lie — by friend and record producer Don Was to perform at a New York fundraiser for Democratic Presidential candidate Jerry Brown in March 1992. Once she'd discovered the truth, I'm sure Kim, who had never even registered to vote when she was with me, went ahead with it anyway partly to impress Alec with her political commitments.

Kim recalled, 'I'll never forgive him for this. He calls and says, "Kim, there's this little cocktail party thing that the B-52s are going to do. Kate's the only girl, because Cindy is out. They need a girl singer. Come to New York and learn the B's lyrics." Instantly, I wanted to help him out. He says, "Oh, Kim, it's just a little cocktail party for about 50 people, I don't know, maybe 100." So I say, "OK." I come in and we rehearse for three nights and had a lot of fun. So it's the night of the "little cocktail party" as he described it to me, and we get to the place. It turns out it holds like 3,000 people and it's a Jerry Brown benefit — *Jerry Brown*. My heart just dropped, and I almost fainted. I'm standing in the green room with all these famous musicians, and I'm just glued to the wall, terrified I'm going to have the runs or something. I walk out and the reception is amazing. All of a sudden, we break into the first song and I just went with the flow. I had the best time. I had the best time I have ever had in my life ever since, since ... since I won the Athens Junior Miss Pageant.'

I've always thought that maybe Kim protests her innocence on this occasion a little too much and she did have some idea of what was going on.

The rock band B-52s introduced her as their *new singer* at the $20-a-head event held at the Ritz. Bounding on stage, like a typical rocker, Kim stunned her fans by appearing with her hair cut to a short bob. While Don Was, who in addition to being a world famous record producer is also an accomplished guitarist, played, Kim gyrated, sang and sweated the night away. I was amused to learn that during performing the B-52s' hit song *Love Shack*, lead singer Fred Schneider turned to Kim and asked, 'How about you, lady, who are you voting for?' to which Kim cooed, 'Oooooooh, Jerry.' Candidate Brown took the stage to announce, 'This is the most unusual, energy-filled political rally that I have seen to date.' Kim's explanation for her startling new look was, 'I cut it because I was out of my mind. I'd already cut it off emotionally so I said, "Why not take the scissors and whack it?"'

Kim kept up her interest in Democratic politics after that remarkable start. Her crowning moment came in the summer of 1998 when she and Alec played host to President Bill Clinton, less than three weeks before he was due to give evidence about his relationship with former White House intern Monica Lewinsky. The President was staying with neighbours Steven Spielberg and his wife Kate Capshaw, and attended a fund-raising dinner at their $1.75 million farmhouse at Stony Hill in the wealthy area of New York's Long Island called The Hamptons. Dozens of Clinton supporters forked out $5,000 a head for the privilege of eating indoors with the President and Hillary Clinton, while hundreds more paid from $250 to $1,000 to dine outside under marquees pitched on the lawns of the five-acre estate.

I was astonished to read in one report that the menu included foie gras, probably the carnivorous delicacy most loathed by animal activists because of the way it is produced by force-feeding ducks and geese until their livers become massively enlarged. The rest of the menu of shrimp, lobster and smoked salmon sounded much more likely.

I later learned that when Kim and Alec found out that foie gras really was on the menu, chosen by the Democratic party organisers and announced just a few hours before the bash was due to begin, they threatened to call the whole thing off. Ingrid Newkirk, president of People for the Ethical Treatment of Animals, told the *New York Post* that an enraged Alec called her to tell her what had happened. 'He was very upset about it,' she said. 'He called someone high up — very high up — in the Democratic National Committee and said 'Can you imagine what it feels like to have a metal pipe shoved down your throat?' He was adamant about it. He asked for the foie gras to be pulled from the menu, and it was pulled.' So the party went ahead after all.

The guest list included celebrities like Tom Hanks and his wife Rita Wilson, Robert DeNiro, singer Billy Joel, the Spielbergs and homemaking guru Martha Stewart, but after the party, top gossip columnist Liz Smith reported that the biggest names to turn up were actor Chevy Chase and Sony records boss Tommy Mottola. She also reported that guests complained because the grounds were sloping and women got their high heels snagged on the grass and people who had paid $1,000 got the same food and service as the $250 crowd. And she also took a swipe at the memento given to the high rollers who ate inside the house — a Le Sportsac backpack with the presidential seal embossed on it. She made the acerbic comment, 'It is made of parachute material. Fitting for this beleaguered presidency.' One person who was not invited was Alec's brother Billy, who appeared in the films *Backdraft* and *Sliver*. According to the *New York Post*, Billy was furious at not being asked to attend, allegedly because of a political falling-out between him and Alec. Ironically, although Kim and Alec had owned the secluded estate for several years, they had just spent two years renovating the house and had not got round to furnishing it. 'The weird thing is that the house is empty,' Alec laughed before the event. 'The Democratic National Committee didn't care. They said they'll bring in local decorators. They'll decorate the whole place temporarily, even bring in flowers and food.'

Despite the Lewinsky problem, the President looked relaxed and appeared to enjoy his weekend rubbing shoulders with the glamorous stars of Hollywood East, away from the pressure of Washington.

Kim was far from relaxed at the event however. She was so nervous about entertaining such high-profile guests and being thrust into the middle of so many people, that she was hit by one of her panic attacks, I later learned. 'Hours before the party, Kim was doubled over with nausea, anticipating the swarm of people who would be arriving,' a friend told a magazine after the event. 'She told Alec,' "I don't think I can get through this," and he said, "Honey, I'll be with you the whole time — it's going to be OK. Remember — you won an Oscar." Kim put on her best performance, but her friend said she hyperventilated and had to rush to the bathroom to compose herself. 'At one point she was in the kitchen clutching her chest,' her friend said. 'And at other times she was sweating and wringing her hands nervously. But she made it through the affair and at the end of the night Alec gave her a big hug.' Kim told her friend, 'I wanted everything to be perfect for the Clintons and I put too much pressure on myself.' Of course, the foie gras fuss can't have helped her nerves.

When *A Streetcar Named Desire* opened the month after her singing performance for Jerry Brown, Kim, dressed in a pink suit, was on hand to support Alec. Backstage, she appeared more wound-up than the cast. She said, 'I was so nervous — I'm glad it's over. I'm so proud of all of them.' Alec should have been delighted with the reviews, which called him everything from electric to magnetic in a role owned by Marlon Brando, but he was described as appearing 'wrung out' by the strain of his performance.

Following her success at the Ritz, Kim headed into a recording studio in London that summer where she was reunited with Prince. If he was concerned, Alec had no need to fret; Kim only had eyes for him. Kim worked with Prince on songs and a video at a studio with Don Was' group Was Not Was, but at the last minute she pulled the plug on the project and the album, which was to be called *The Color of Sex*, was never released. Kim, who technically still owes Warner Brothers an album because of her contractual obligations, even had famed photographer Herb Ritts shoot the cover for the album.

Kim said, 'Who knows if it would have ever made a dime or not? I wrote a lot of stuff on the album. There's some things on it I'm very proud of, and there's some things on it I think, Kim, what *were* you thinking? Even the title, oh God.' She also said, 'It wasn't my heart, that was my problem.'

Just as I had realised very quickly that Kim was the girl of my dreams, Alec had done so as well. One evening he was said to have prepared a gourmet meal for the two of them at his posh New York apartment on Manhattan's Central Park West. He lit candles and incense to add a special, romantic feel to the event. As the evening progressed, he took hold of Kim's hand and, looking deeply into her eyes, he asked her to marry him. 'He was as nervous as a schoolboy,' a friend revealed. But the night did not go as he had hoped. Kim told him, 'No, Alec, I can't. I love you, but I'm not ready to get married again now.' He was devastated. Then his pain turned to anger and he told her he was fed up of feeling that she was taking him for granted. There was a distinct edge to his voice as he told her that she had better think about her answer because he wasn't prepared to wait forever. The following day, he returned the $100,000, pear-shaped engagement ring that she never even set eyes on to the jewellery shop. But love was to prevail for them eventually as Alec stood by her and gave her support throughout the dramas of *Boxing Helena*, bankruptcy and Braselton. Eventually, Kim did agree to marry him *kind of* in her non-committal sort of way, but she would never actually be tied down to a firm date.

Early in our relationship, I'd introduced Kim to the classic Disney movie *Song of the South* and it became one of her favourite films. So I wasn't surprised when next she took an unusual career move. *Song of the South*, based on the Uncle Remus stories about Brer Rabbit, was the first movie to combine animated cartoon characters with real life actors and it appealed to the innocent and childlike side of Kim's character. *Song of the South* was a Walt Disney film and won an Oscar for Best Song with 'Zip-a-dee-Doo-Dah', but it is never shown today because it is perceived as being politically incorrect towards African-Americans.

Even though she always expected her fee to rise as her career progressed, Kim couldn't resist a $1.7 million offer for just six weeks work to appear in the bizarre semi-animated movie *Cool World*.

The film also starred Irish actor Gabriel Byrne, as a cartoonist who falls in love with one of his creations. Kim played that cartoon character, Holli Would, who eventually comes to life with disastrous effects. The movie was directed by controversial filmmaker Ralph Bakshi, who also made the X-rated cartoon *Fritz the Cat*.

Kim found herself at the centre of a controversy over another body double when the film was finished. Sexy body double Jenine Jennings accused Kim of pulling strings to keep her from getting the proper recognition in the film's credits. Jenine was outraged that she did the dancing and acting for the animated sections — the animators used her outline on which to draw over their cartoon cutie — in *Cool World* but Kim, who took over as Holli when she became human, got the only credit for playing the character.

'I worked very hard,' complained Jenine, who was just 21 when the film was made. 'But I was told by the producer that Kim would never allow my name to appear as Holli.'

It was a no-win situation for Jenine. She had to slink around in skimpy costumes and do steamy love scenes with Gabriel while illustrators pencilled over her image to draw in Holli and she was never actually seen on screen; as far as the audience was concerned, Kim was the one and only Holli Would. Jenine did get listed in the credits as choreographer and music consultant.

Both the producer and director quickly came to Kim's defence. Producer Frank Mancuso Jr said that Kim had nothing to do with decisions over the credits and he denied that Kim caused problems. He insisted that the real problems were technical, such as Gabriel Byrne having to respond to a cartoon he couldn't see or touch. And director Bakshi said, 'Kim was a doll who did everything I asked her to. I don't know how these rumours spread.' And he joked, 'I never slept with her, either.'

Although her life was in turmoil because of all the legal problems she was battling, July 1992 became a high spot in her life. Kim received her star on the Hollywood Walk of Fame, the pavement shrine's 1,959th. It was a particularly fine occasion as she was presented with the prestigious accolade on the same day that the *Cool World* movie makers won a legal victory about her. Superior Court Judge Stephen O'Neil gave the OK for a giant cartoon likeness of her to adorn the landmark Hollywood sign. The caricature had outraged local residents when it had been put up two days before Kim got her star. The judge decided the LA authorities acted properly in giving Paramount Pictures a permit to attach the 75-foot cartoon figure of Kim to the letter D of the world famous sign. People who lived near the sign, which is situated in the Hollywood Hills section of Griffith Park, objected because they feared the cut-out would attract large numbers of fans and tourists. They sought a court injunction barring the city from issuing permits for advertising on the sign. But Judge O'Neil rejected the request, saying the caricature was 'an insignificant, inconsequential interference' to recreational use of the park.

Kim said working on *Cool World* was 'a whole load of fun. I was actually very impressed by my cartoon counterpart who, of course, is nothing like me at all!' But the critics found nothing cool about *Cool World*, which also starred Brad Pitt as detective Frank Harris, whose job it was to keep humans and 'doodles' apart. The movie, which cost $30 million to make, bombed at the American box office taking in just over $14 million from cinema ticket sales.

USA Today movie critic Susan Wloszczyna wrote, '*Cool World* is not an especially nice place to visit and you definitely wouldn't want to live there. A brutal, bombastic blend of cartoon and live action that strives to be the hipster's *Who Framed Roger Rabbit?*, it can't even make it as a *Ren & Stimpy* knockoff. There's no "happy, happy, joy, joy" in this out-of-toon town.' *Daily Variety* concluded, 'Style has seldom pummelled substance as severely as in *Cool World*, a combination funhouse ride/acid trip that will prove an ordeal for most visitors in the form of trial by animation.' *Variety's* reviewer found the film 'visually dazzling but utterly soulless'.

Unfortunately for Kim, her next movie outing was even less successful at the box office and not at all a happy experience. From playing a cartoon bimbo in *Cool World*, she went on to become Karen McCoy, a reformed cat burglar who is forced back into crime after leaving jail, in *The Real McCoy*. Kim's character reluctantly teams up with a handsome but incompetent hold-up artist, played by Val Kilmer. An evil rival-in-crime of hers, played by Terence Stamp, claimed to have kidnapped her young son to force her reluctantly to break into one of America's most tightly guarded banks, storing $18 million as the sought-after prize. The movie was set in Atlanta, Georgia, near Kim's home town and directed by Australia's Russell Mulcahy, who had previously made *Highlander*. Entertainment industry insiders snidely joked at the time that Mulcahy might be taking on the impossible casting two stars with enormous reputations as divas *extraordinaire*.

Kim was enthusiastic about her role, saying, 'The movie was a gift after all I have been through. I did not have to think about my accent. I could just be myself. Also, I got to play the lead and Val Kilmer is the equivalent of the dumb blonde. That makes a big change for me and is the way I like to look at it.'

Despite an early setback — she broke a bone in her foot and filming had to be delayed briefly — she threw herself into work heart and soul, even visiting women in jail, including murderers, as part of her research. She said, 'It brought home to me how life can be *really* tough. They were going to be pushed out of prison with the clothes they wore to court, their belongings and $25 to make something out of their lives. It made me think that my own problems are pretty small.'

The script required some extraordinary physical contortions and Kim did them all even though she was injured. She said, 'I was in agony when we started. I got a flexible cast so I could move around. But in a lot of the scenes I was actually in a great deal of pain.' Despite this she regained her reputation as a joy to work with.

'We were warned, "She'll be difficult",' a crewman said. 'But there were no tantrums. She was always on time, prepared, friendly, accessible. We were all shocked.'

Producer Martin Bregman, who had also worked with Alec Baldwin making *The Shadow*, said, 'Kim was terrific, a real pro. Never late, always very prepared, always very helpful and never an ounce of trouble. She was a classy, nice woman, who always brought cookies to the crew.' He added, 'She is an old-fashioned actress. She's very quiet, easy to deal with. Of all the actresses I've ever worked with, Kim was one of the easiest.'

Terence Stamp said, 'There seems to be a lot of animosity towards her but my experience with her was so delightful that there's something not quite right about what they say. From my own experience ... she was really bright, her ideas about the script were intelligent, thoughtful. She was really caring.'

Right from the start, Kim had been the director's first choice to play the part of Karen McCoy. He saw her as a female Steve McQueen and was pleased with her performance. But she blamed herself for the film bombing. She said, 'This film was originally a love story that turned into a caper movie. I blame myself in part for this. I fought to get Val Kilmer in the movie but he just wasn't into it. It just fell apart.'

The critics hated the film. The LA *Village Voice* announced, '*The Real McCoy* is real bad entertainment.' David Kronke wrote in the *Hollywood Reporter*, 'If this is the real McCoy, audiences will want to root for the Hatfields.' Chris Willman in the *Los Angeles Times* said, 'The only real-seeming thievery in *The Real McCoy* is of the audience's good will.'

After Kilmer, Kim wanted a leading man she knew she would enjoy working with, so when Alec was offered the leading role in a remake of Sam Peckinpah's 1972 action thriller *The Getaway*, which originally starred Steve McQueen and Ali MacGraw, he persuaded her to join him as his co-star. After all the problems making *The Marrying Man*, the irony of them working together again escaped few in the entertainment industry. They predicted that if history repeated itself, studio bosses might tell Kim and Alec to retitle their movie *The Go Away*.

Chapter 19

Kim and Alec were acutely aware of their difficult reputations after the débâcle of *The Marrying Man* and their opportunity to set the record straight came on a film that had its own early troubles. Anyone might have thought that it would have been relatively easy for a producer to do a remake of his own hit film, but in the case of *The Getaway* it took David Foster years to overcome a mountain of complications.

'The history of the new *Getaway* is rather amazing, a legal involvement and entanglement beyond belief,' Foster said at the time.

But he did succeed in overcoming all the legal and financial hurdles and filming began in early April 1993. Once Foster chose Alec Baldwin to take the role originally played by the late Steve McQueen, Alec lobbied hard for Kim to co-star as they were anxious to work together again.

In an interview, Kim said, 'We want to prove we're not the difficult actors some people say we are.' Almost certainly because of Kim's then ongoing financial headaches, she and Alec struck an unusual financial deal with Foster and his co-producers. They were paid $4 million to be split between them at their discretion. Unbeknownst at the time the deal was thrashed out, history would repeat itself; while making the original, Steve McQueen fell in love with his co-star Ali MacGraw, who was then married to producer Robert Evans, and married her — and between the time filming of the remake was completed that summer and the new *Getaway* was released in February 1994, Alec and Kim would become man and wife.

After the disappointments Kim had experienced making *The Real McCoy*, it was ironic that her next character was also called McCoy, this time Carol, who, with her just-out-of-jail convict husband Doc McCoy, finds herself being chased by the cops across the blazing Arizona desert after a bank robbery. Walter Hill, who wrote the original script and the screenplay for the remake, was to direct but dropped out and eventually New Zealander Roger Donaldson ended up in the director's chair. Also in the cast were James Woods, Michael Madsen, Jennifer Tilly and Richard Farnsworth, with whom Kim had worked before on *The Natural*.

Ali MacGraw was extremely upset that a remake was to be filmed so soon after the original — only 22 years between them. However, she calmed down when she was assured that the story had been changed significantly.

It amused me to note that in the remake of *The Getaway*, the sex scenes were so explicit they shocked test audiences and had to be toned down, because in the original, McQueen's character was impotent. But that certainly wasn't the case the second time around. In fact, in one scene things were so intimate that Kim and Alec insisted their steamy bedroom romp be filmed by remote control cameras with no crew members present. Two cameras were positioned over the bed in a small room and left running while the naked pair did their love scene. A member of the crew said, 'The sex scenes were very authentic. They were filmed over three days and the set was totally shut down. Alec and Kim were naked and no one was allowed in the room. They wanted absolute privacy to make it look realistic and the word later was that they did just that. In fact, they did it so well that some people who saw the rushes were fooled into thinking Kim and Alec really had sex for the movie cameras.' Kim described their on-screen love making as 'my hottest love scenes since *9½ Weeks*'. But she insisted that there was more play than passion on the set. She said, 'We were just cracking up. We're in this clinch, and it was like, "Honey, can you move your arm? Ouch, you just elbowed me in the stomach." Love scenes are choreographed, not sexy, even with your real partner.'

In scenes that were filmed with a cameraman present, Kim admitted, 'We did a lot of pretty heavy stuff. The steadicam operator would be going up and down our bodies, panning in and going back. When they cut, he would put the camera down, and lean against the wall and go, "Oh, my God." He was so embarrassed.'

Kim predicted that everybody who saw the film would ask, 'So, is this what you guys do at home?' She was adamant that it wasn't.

When she said that, I thought to myself that things must have calmed down in Kim's bedroom since the time we were together.

It wasn't just the sex scenes that Kim and Alec wanted to ensure were realistic. In another scenario in the film, they had a brutal fight. They insisted on doing it themselves with no stunt doubles to take the painful blows.

The movie, which had a crew of around 180 and used a staggering 2,500 extras, came to a climax with a dramatic petrol tanker explosion. Shot in Phoenix, it caused enormous logistical problems. Toni DiJorio, who worked for the city's movie co-ordinating office, said, 'We had to cover all our bases in terms of businesses and home owners within a two-mile radius, alerting and re-routing vehicular and pedestrian traffic. We alerted the airport so that pilots flying over would not worry that the fire and smoke were from a terrorist bombing.'

In a bid to keep the mood light and squash their previous reputation, every Saturday, to mark the completion of another week's filming, Kim and Alec bought pizza for themselves and everyone on the set. *The Getaway* finished its 12-week shoot on time and there was no need to return for any re-shoots. Foster had nothing but praise for his co-stars with a reputation for difficult behaviour. 'They were pussycats,' he said.

Co-producer Larry Gordon admitted that he'd received telephone calls from colleagues asking about his experiences working with Kim and Alec. He told them, 'Zero problems. I mean *zero*. And this was a tough shoot, six days a week in the desert. Lots of action. But they were total pros and I love them both.'

To say there were no problems was an exaggeration; there were complications — there always are making a movie — but the ones that had occurred shooting *The Getaway* were not of Kim and Alec's making. They were mainly caused by the relentless and unforgiving heat which had caused sensitive Kim major skin concerns. Kim had dealt with it in her usual way. She said, 'I just made sure I was well covered with cream — and there was a regular supply of umbrellas.' But Kim wasn't prepared for what happened to her while shooting promotional photographs to be used on posters for *The Getaway* a few weeks after filming was wrapped — she collapsed!

The trailers arrived at the site — a five-mile-long section of the California desert known as the El Mirage Dry Bed, a scorching strip which is the second-hottest place in the United States — early in the morning, followed by Kim, Alec and famous photographer

Herb Ritts, and their entourage, who flew in by helicopter. Everything was set up by one in the afternoon but it was too hot so they had to wait until around 4.00pm to start shooting, when it was still a gruelling 103-degrees.

During the first couple of takes, Kim, who was wearing high heels, grabbed a bag and ran towards the camera. In the background, Alec looked on at her as he held a shotgun. Ritts snapped away, taking the same scene from various angles. He continued for some time. But suddenly, delicate Kim keeled over; putting her hand to her head, she fell to the ground. Alec and the crew rushed to her side fearing that sun-sensitive Kim had been felled by heatstroke. A witness said, 'One minute, Kim was posing for the camera, the next, she was flat on her back with half-a-dozen people hovering over her. After about 10 minutes of just lying there, she finally got up and went into her air-conditioned trailer. She stayed there for a good half hour.'

When the film was released, *Los Angeles Times* critic Kenneth Turan said, 'A perfectly respectable thriller that mostly manages to be as crisp and efficient as the crimes it depicts, this Roger Donaldson-directed *Getaway* compares favourably with the Sam Peckinpah original.' And he added, 'The best thing about this *Getaway* turns out to be that Baldwin-Basinger pairing as Doc and Carol McCoy, partners in crime and concupiscence. Though McQueen and MacGraw may have been just as crazy about each other, the new couple is much better matched in terms of on-screen charisma. Not only in the glamorous love scenes, which will make interesting viewing for future grandchildren, but also in angry confrontations and even quiet moments, Baldwin and Basinger's palpable chemistry brings a pleasant buzz to the proceedings.' *Daily Variety* wrote, 'The Getaway is a pretty good remake of a pretty good action thriller.'

Not every critic was impressed but overall the reviews were favourable and this time most people felt that the on-screen chemistry between Kim and Alec worked. *The Getaway* still did lacklustre business at the box office. Nevertheless, it was not a lost cause for Kim and Alec because it had restored their reputations as actors whom people could work with.

As was often the case, Kim's next movie project came out before *The Getaway*. She had a cameo role in the sequel to the highly successful *Wayne's World*. In *Wayne's World II*, a wacky tale in which comedian Michael Myers' Wayne character is told in a vision that he must organise a rock festival called Waynestock, Kim played a Mrs Robinson-type seductress called Honey Hornee, a hungry housewife who gets her claws into Wayne's gormless sidekick Garth, played by Dana Carvey, and initiates him into manhood. The movie had suffered a series of delays with Carvey threatening not to return to his role in the sequel because his partner Myers, who was writing the script, had not given Garth quite the right emphasis. But when the script problems were resolved, filming began quickly.

Shooting started in late June and the film was out in time for Christmas. It was a bit of light relief for Kim and easy money at a time when she needed it. She signed for it as soon as she filed for bankruptcy.

Dana Carvey personally asked Kim to play Honey. At first she turned him down, but he kept calling her and in the end she agreed. She found working on the movie a laugh a minute but she confessed shooting the love scene with Dana was difficult. She said, 'I honestly thought I was going to get fired because I could not keep a straight face. I never really looked into his eyes. I could never do it. I would focus on a piece of his hair and say, "Be really cool, Kim." And then when he started to kiss me, I just came apart.'

Kim was desperately concerned about her financial situation. She confessed to Alec, 'I still love you and I want to marry you. But not until I've paid off my debts.' But loyal Alec was having none of it. He declared, 'I can't wait that long. I'll help with the debts.' He was as good as his word; having negotiated the $4 million fee for The Getaway they shared it 50-50 and Kim no longer had an excuse to delay their marriage.

When Kim finally agreed to turn their engagement into an actual wedding, Alec gave himself just six weeks to pull it together.

Despite all the trials and tribulations Kim was enduring in her life, 1993 became a very joyful year for her. Kim actually described 1993 as 'the happiest year of my life'. In addition to proving she and Alec could behave on a movie together, they finally walked down the aisle together in a far more lavish wedding ceremony than ours had been.

But even then the journey to the altar was not without its almost disastrous deviations. Kim threatened to call off the wedding when she discovered Alec was planning to have lunch with his old flame Janine Turner. Janine was about to fly to Italy to film Cliffhanger with Sylvester Stallone when she received the invitation from Alec, who had split up with her years before. Ironically, Alec had wanted to open his heart to her and clear the air about his emotional problems dealing with people, as he had been advised to in the love addiction self-help group meetings he had been attending. But Kim didn't see it as a cleansing of the soul. She went berserk and the rendezvous never happened.

They spent the night before their wedding apart. Alec called the house where Kim was staying to talk to her sister Ashley every two hours to make sure she was OK and hadn't changed her mind. Then the phone calls came every hour and finally every 30 minutes. Kim recalled, 'He'd ask, "How is she? Is she there? Does she still wanna do this?" '

Finally, at sunset on the balmy evening of 19 August, Kim and Alec walked into a circle of smoothed sand surrounded by flickering torches at the water's edge on an East Hampton, Long Island, public beach, in front of the $2.5 million waterfront estate of their friend and fashion designer Josephine Chaus, to exchange vows. About 100 friends, including Paul Newman, Billy Joel, Christie Brinkley, producer Martin Bregman and Chynna Phillips — then Billy's girlfriend who later married him at another celebrity packed wedding in The Hamptons in 1995 — stood by the Atlantic Ocean to watch the 8.00pm seven-minute ceremony, performed by Justice of the Peace James R Ketcham, which included Kim and Alec tearfully reading the first love letters they wrote to each other. A witness revealed, 'Wiping tears from his eyes, Alec read, "The first time I saw you, I fell in love with you. I knew then I wanted to marry you and just hoped you would feel the same way. Miraculously, you did." '

Kim replied, 'I fell in love with you, too. When I met you, I knew I was meeting a very special person.'

The ceremony ended with thousands of pink, red and white rose petals being thrown in the air amid cheers and laughter as the bride and groom kissed. As they both said 'I do', they slipped plain gold rings on to each other's fingers. Then they kissed. A friend joked, 'The kiss lasted longer than the ceremony.'

Alec wore a dinner jacket and Kim was in a floor-length, virgin-white gown designed by John Hayles. She looked radiant. Her hair was partially swept up into a bun, which was encircled by tiny white flowers. I wish I'd done the make-up. Alec's younger brothers Daniel, William and Stephen acted as groomsmen. Kim was given away by her father Don and her sister Ashley was her attendant. They were the only members of her family to attend the intimate event. Kim's estranged mother, Ann, snubbed the ceremony. It revealed just how bitter Kim's feud with her folks had become. She is now estranged from almost all of them.

Their wedding took place during the year that the United States was hit by terrible flooding, which had caused massive destruction to the American heartland. Instead of wedding gifts, they asked that their friends and family make donations to the American Red Cross Midwest Flood Relief or, for animal-lover Kim, the American Rescue League, which had been saving animals in the flood.

As Kim and Alec swayed in the evening glow, the band singer crooned, 'When somebody loves you, it's no good unless he loves you, all the way ...' Four helicopters from television news stations swirled overhead and reporters on the ground were kept 25 feet back from a curtain that hid the unfolding events. *The Getaway* producer Foster admitted, 'I've never seen a guy more in love, so protective.' But staunch Catholic Alec probably summed it up best, when seconds after hearing Kim pronounced his wife, he turned to her and said, 'Other than God, I love you more than anyone in the world.'

Dinner was catered by an Italian restaurant in a marquee outside Chaus' home. Guests dined on organic salad, potato and leek soup, shrimp cocktail and a choice of New York strip steak, roasted garlic chicken or grilled salmon — an odd selection for staunch vegetarians. During the meal, Alec lifted a glass and proposed a toast, 'To my beautiful new wife, my family and friends. Thank you all for coming to celebrate the most important day of my life.' The highlight of the feast was a six-tier wedding cake. The night ended with a huge fireworks display on the beach and the couple retired to their suite in Chaus' mansion. And Kim was quick to tell everyone that they hoped to start a family 'a lot sooner than most people expect'.

They had kept the wedding so secret that they had not sent out the invitations until five days before the event. Even then, Alec faxed out the invitations making up a fake story about it being a whale watching and pie eating contest. No one knew the truth and the location until after they replied.

Kim and Alec enjoyed a low-budget honeymoon far from the glitz and glamour of Hollywood. They remained in East Hampton, spending their days with friends and taking romantic strolls by the shore. Then they packed up their blue Jeep Wagoneer sports utility vehicle and headed to Pennsylvania's Pocono Mountains, a favourite honeymoon haven for people who live on America's East Coast. There they rode bicycles, strolled by a lake and generally relaxed. It was as if they'd put all Kim's troubles behind them.

I have to admit, I was hurt when in an interview Kim said, 'My first marriage was about protection and not seeing clearly. This one is about clarity and having gone through a lot of things together. This one is about being in love and being attracted to this human being, really loving him, who he is.'

Kim has always had an ability to turn her back on things she doesn't like or unpleasant memories. Before long, she will have successfully obliterated them from her mind. I knew that it wouldn't take long before — in Kim's mind at least — I'd never existed. Even so, I wish her no harm. In fact, quite the contrary.

As it happened, I too ate Italian food the night Kim and Alec married. I had played golf during the day and was going to my favourite restaurant, Primi's, just a couple of minutes walking distance from the house on Cushdon Avenue in West Los Angeles that Kim had been forced to sign over to me, when — partly because of the three-hour time difference between the East and West coasts — I heard on the radio they had married. I am glad to say I had a date with a beautiful young lady or I might have been sadder than I was. Over dinner, I raised a glass and gave a toast to Kim and Alec to wish them well. Hopefully for Kim, this time round I prayed her marriage would last LTF ...

Chapter 20

Kim and I were once driving along the freeway going from one location to another when a dog darted out into the fast lane.

'Stop the car,' she shouted. 'We've got to save that dog.'

I said, 'I can't stop — we're doing 65.'

Fortunately by that time, the dog had got off the road, but Kim's reaction was typical. This was on location for *Hard Country* and we were not even dating yet, but from my earliest acquaintance with Kim I knew she was mad about animals. A strict vegetarian from her teens, she loved all creatures great and small.

The first time I went to her house on Don Juan Place I met the founders of her pack of dogs. There were two big outdoor dogs, Zeke, a Siberian husky, and Elvis, a giant Malamute who had hip dysplasia. You could always rely on Kim to go for the lame dog — literally. Then there were her indoor dogs, Pekineses Macaroni and Noodle. The little dogs didn't like me because they saw me as an intruder taking over Kim's affections. Also, they were used to sleeping on the bed and I kicked them off to sleep in the kitchen. Kim had hated being separated from her pets during that first location shoot in Bakersfield, but she knew as her career developed she would be forced to leave them behind a lot. To remind her of them when she was away, she started wearing the Pekes' spare collars, one pink, one blue, on her wrists like bracelets. She hardly ever wore jewellery; a reminder of her dogs was more important to her than gold or gems. After *9½ Weeks* she wore the miniature handcuffs I gave her on one of them. She even used to slide rings on to the collars, which began to look like charm bracelets.

Whenever Kim was away from home, however briefly, or if I had to return early from a trip to sort out any problems, Kim would always send me cards and she'd write, 'Kiss the babies for me' or 'Give my love to the babies'. The 'babies' were the dogs. Then she'd sign it 'LTF ... Me' and put her familiar heart with a cross in the middle at the bottom of the message.

Soon after I moved in, Macaroni went missing. Kim was absolutely distraught and for two days I did nothing but scour the hillsides around our house for any sign of him. Finally, I found his poor little body. In those mountains there are a lot of coyotes which often venture into built-up areas, scavenging for food, and small pets are always at risk. I buried him where I found him and went home to break the news to Kim. She didn't believe me; she thought I had made up the story, not to be mean, but so she would at least know what had happened to him. Her biggest fear was that he had somehow got picked up by someone who would sell him to a lab for experimentation. She would not be convinced he was really dead until I dug him up and showed her the body. She was heartbroken, but after a while hunted down an identical dog, which she called Mack Truck, but who went by the nickname Mac Mac.

We spent a lot of time at the vet's, especially with Elvis, who had to have surgery on his hips. One day we were there and a woman brought in a little Shih Tzu who was going blind. She told the vet she couldn't cope with her and wanted her put to sleep. Kim was horrified and said, 'You can't do that — I'll take her.' She was called Choo-Choo and she was a sweetheart. Kim spent a fortune on operations trying to restore her sight, but nothing worked. A cousin of our second housekeeper, Fatima, eventually fell in love with her and ended up taking her home.

Kim could never resist pet shops. I had to keep her away from them because we were getting too many dogs. One day we were in a pet store near our home and there was a little girl looking at three Shih Tzu puppies, three brothers, for sale. She wanted a puppy so badly, and Kim said, 'If your mom says you can have one, I'll buy him for you and pay for his vaccinations.' But the mother said 'no'.

They were cute puppies and we took two of them. The next day she sent me back to see if the little girl's mother had relented. The third puppy was still there and Kim told me to buy him as well. She could not bear to split them up. They were called Buddy, Barney and — Itsy Bitsy Teeny Weeny Yellow Polka Dot Bikini (Teeny for short). He was the smallest dog we had, with by far the biggest name. On another visit to the pet shop, we got the dog who was to become mine. He was a beautiful Golden Labrador, the last of the litter. He had been in the shop for a while and they were talking about sending him back to his breeder in Arkansas, because he'd got past the cute puppy stage. If he'd gone back he would have been destroyed so, of course, we had to have him. We called him Doolittle after the husband of country singer Loretta Lynn — we'd just watched the film of her life story, *The Coal Miner's Daughter* — and he became known as Dooboy. I had worked with Sissy Spacek, who played Loretta in the film, and we had become great hot-tub pals. We would soak in the tub naked, but there was nothing more. I knew her husband, Jack, too.

Kim always said I should write a book called the Zen Art of Picking up Dog Doo-Doo, because that was my job every day, and believe me, with 10 dogs that was no small task.

As well as the dogs we had a lot of wild cats living in our enormous back yard. They were descended from domestic cats who had been abandoned or run away and become feral over the generations. They were far too wild to handle or to get into the house, but we fed them every day. There was a mother cat we called Ophelia, but she was the only one we named. There were always a lot of kittens around especially in the spring, and Zeke used to attack them. Ophelia and the other mothers used to give birth on the flat roof at the back of our house, but inevitably some of the kittens would fall or jump and Zeke would go after them. There were times when we rescued a kitten still alive, and Kim would spend $200 or $300 in vet's bills in a vain attempt to save its life. Often the kittens died anyway, because it's a hard life with predators around, and we could not get hold of them to get them vaccinated.

When she could not save a kitten, Kim was devastated. And when Kim cried it was heart-rending to see her face. It made everybody else want to cry along with her. It was so sad to see her scrunch up her face. It was too much to take. She was so expressive and her eyes used to puff up so quickly.

One winter's day she had her black Corvette parked in front of the house. Kim had been out in the morning and because the engine was warm a cat had crawled into it. She went out again and for once she was actually driving. We went about two blocks and there was a dreadful thumping from the engine. We stopped and found the cat. It was dead, caught in the fan belt. Kim was completely broken up. She blamed herself and I could not console her. She never drove that car again. She gave it away to her brother Skip. And ever after, she would not get into a car without thumping it to warn any cats that were in it or under it to get away.

The maid cooked for the dogs. I wasn't allowed to eat meat — certainly not at home and even in restaurants Kim disapproved of it — but the housekeeper made 'people' food for our pets. Not just mincemeat and stuff like that, but gourmet meals, roasts and so on, served in porcelain bowls. I would see and smell the dogs' dinners and want them so much. Every now and then the housekeeper would slip me a piece of meat when Kim wasn't around, but I felt as if I had to sit up and beg for it!

As well as lavishing love and affection on her own animals, Kim was also concerned about how other people treated living creatures. While she was making *Nadine* in Austin, Texas, they were shooting at a house in a residential area and some people down the street were beating a cocker spaniel because she was fighting with another dog. Kim was outraged and at lunchtime she sent the hairdresser, Rick Provenzano, over to see if they would sell the spaniel. I have no idea if they knew who she was, or her co-star, Jeff Bridges. But they knew we were all with a movie company and must have a lot of money. So they demanded $250 — and Kim happily paid it. Rick took a shine to the pooch and Kim was happy for him to keep her. He called her Nadine, after Kim's character in the film, and kept her all her life as far as I know.

When Kim made *No Mercy* there was a mutt called Petey who was in one of the scenes. He wasn't a trained animal actor but a dog from the pound. He used to go for long walks on the beach with us, and my sister Sherry, who was her personal assistant, took a real shine to him. We didn't want him to go back to the pound and risk being put down, so she found a family who would take him in and give him a good home. They lived in an apartment on the first floor. When Sherry took Petey there to leave him, he saw her going and leaped out of the window to be with her. He wasn't hurt, but Sherry was so touched by his affection that she decided to keep him.

The first time we ever went to New York together, to meet the writer for her *Playboy* layout, she pointed out a beggar on the corner of 6th Avenue, a big black man who was blind. He had a German Shepherd, his best friend, between his legs. He'd been there for years, while Kim was in New York modelling. He had a cup on the ground and passers-by were putting money into it. Kim told me to give him some money — $20. I put it in his hand, and told him it was a 20 and he was to put it inside his clothes, not just in the cup, so that nobody could steal it. American notes are all the same size so I had to make sure he realised that I was giving him something larger than a buck. After that, whenever we went to New York, we always looked him up and gave him $20 or $50. Soon after Kim and I split up, Rick Provenzano called to say the guy had been knocked down by a runaway car and was in hospital, and they didn't know if he was going to survive. He also told Kim about the beggar and she sent him some money to help pay the hospital bills and look after the dog. Dogs were Kim's first love. Whenever we quarrelled I used to call her Cruella De Vil, after the evil dognapper in *101 Dalmatians*, and that always made her mad.

Also during our first New York visit, we were walking through Central Park and I suggested it might be romantic to go for a ride in a horse and carriage. She was horrified. 'Those poor horses are worked to death,' she said. 'I saw one drop down dead in front of me when I was living here. I'm not paying to exploit the poor things.' Years later, getting the carriage horses banned from Central Park was a pet programme for her and Alec Baldwin.

She continued collecting dogs when she got together with Alec. In fact, in an eerie echo of my first animal experience with her, she claimed later to have fallen in love with Alec the day he rescued a dog which had been knocked down on the Ventura Freeway.

They were staying at Don Juan Place during the making of *The Marrying Man* when they saw the accident. Alec slammed on the brakes, dodged the traffic and gave chase to the dog, a boxer bitch. He recalled later, 'Kim screams at me "Go and get the dog!" I had to run miles and miles to catch up with her. We wind up being an hour late for work. We take the dog home and four weeks later the dog has ten puppies in our garage.' They adopted her and called her Gracie.

The next summer, Kim spotted another beggar with a dog on the streets of New York, and when she got home to Alec's apartment she had an instinctive feeling that he could not take care of the mutt any more. She and Alec searched for him and when they found him he gave her the dog. They shipped him back to LA, but he did not get on with the rest of the pack and they had to find him a new home. Alec was obviously learning the lessons I had, for he said, 'I wanted to be sensitive to the whole thing. I have to live with this woman.'

He also had a lesson in Kim's bizarre beliefs, while he was starring on Broadway in *A Streetcar Named Desire*, with Jessica Lange. Kim gave him a pair of Shih Tzus to go with the two dogs he already had in New York with him. One of them was named Amelia and he told a friend, 'Kim thinks she's found the soul of Amelia Earhart in her.'

I don't know what happened to Gracie and Amelia, though obviously dogs don't live for ever. But in April 1994, she talked about her menagerie to television chat show host Jay Leno. She still had Barney, Buddy, Teeny and Mac Mac, as well as new family members Hussy, Dodo, Bob, Bebop, Chubsey and Noona. Noona had always been the nickname she called Noodle, one of her original Pekingeses, but he had died in 1985 when, sadly, we were away from home visiting her family in Georgia. She was heartbroken.

By the time of the Leno programme, she also had three tame cats, Eli, Tuffy and Moses, and had nicknamed three of the feral cats Black Kitty, White Kitty and Grey Kitty. Around this time, her brother Mick claimed later, she offered her mother, Ann, half a million dollars a year to move to California and take care of the brood for her! But Ann didn't want anything to do with it.

Kim made no concessions to other people's customs in her concern for animals. While we were still together we did a publicity tour for *Nadine*. We were driving past a French marketplace and there were coops with chickens in them. She didn't realise what they were. One of the French guys we were with explained they were destined to go to restaurants and she was horrified. She wanted to go back and buy them all and set them free! We talked her out of it, but that was quite a moment. I could imagine her sparking an international incident by accusing French restaurants of cruelty for wanting to buy their poultry live.

On that same trip, in Italy, she said to a woman she saw wearing a fur coat, 'How many babies did you kill to make that coat?' I don't think the woman understood, which was probably a good thing, although in Europe in those days I think they were a lot less sensitive about wearing fur.

When we went to Japan to promote *Blind Date*, we narrowly avoided outraging her even more. We were travelling with her body make-up woman, Kiori Miller, who was Japanese herself. That was great because it meant she could correct the official interpreters if they translated something wrongly to put a different spin on things or to put words into Kim's mouth. She had been an actress in Japan before she married an American and had a lot of connections. We travelled to Tokyo and Kobe and had great treatment thanks to Kiori.

One night we were taken to a traditional dinner, with Geisha girls and everything. They brought out a platter of fresh lobster sushi — so fresh it was still alive! Its back was cut down the centre and flesh was sliced but it was still moving. Rick Provenzano was with us, and he and I noticed this thing at the same time. We both knew Kim would freak out if she saw it, but we didn't want to offend our Japanese hosts by making a fuss. So we signalled to the waiter to bring it straight to us and we polished it off before she noticed.

The Japanese were fascinated to hear about all of Kim's animals. I guess the idea of living in a big enough space to have a whole pack of dogs was novel to people used to living in cramped, high-rise apartments. She also told them about our 'victory garden'. We had a big patch of land behind the second house in our back garden which wasn't being used for anything, so we decided to plant it. The first things that came up were radishes and we were so pleased I took a picture of them. We grew cucumbers and onions, stuff that was easy to grow and for a while we were really into it. Kim would be outside on her knees, digging and weeding away. And she dressed the part, in her favourite dungarees, a grown-up version of the farm girl she was as a kid. Then we were away on a long trip and the garden perished because we neglected it for so long.

Not all of our 'pets' were actually alive. Kim had about 20 inflatable ducks which bobbed up and down in the swimming pool — not 60, as has often been claimed. She gave them silly names like Yippie, Pidge and Stoop.

Although Kim was always concerned about animals and opposed to wearing fur, as well as being a vegetarian, she did not become a real activist until she met Alec. Alec is much more high-profile than I was and they are seen out in public a lot more. Also, Kim had overcome a lot of her shyness; she still referred to it, but as the 1990s progressed, she was able to do things like go to the Oscars, which would have been impossible for her in the early days.

There are dozens of different animal causes, but Kim became attached to two of them — the Performing Animals Welfare Society (PAWS) and People for the Ethical Treatment of Animals (PETA). That did not stop her taking potshots at any perceived cruelty that was not being targeted by these groups, but she concentrated mainly on the plight of working and performing animals and laboratory experiments on dogs.

She first went public with her mission in 1992, when she joined veteran American game show host Bob Barker and actor Richard Kiley to testify to the United States Congress who were reviewing the US Animal Welfare Act. They called for more humane treatment of animals in rodeos, zoos and circuses and animals working in films. In her videotaped testimony, Kim recalled a trip we had made to Florida to see her brother Mick in 1985, when she visited a number of small roadside zoos. 'We are speaking for those who cannot speak for themselves,' she said. 'This is a deep-rooted tear in the heart of society and the time has come for this misery to end once and for all.'

The year after she testified, Kim and Alec were honoured by the Carriage Horse Action Committee in New York for their efforts to get at least improved conditions for the Central Park horses, which were living in dilapidated, 100-year-old stables, if not a complete ban. Kim said, 'When I moved to New York to be a Ford model and I was walking across the park in the summer, I saw these horses for the first time. Ever since then I've been totally against carriage horses. I just feel passionately about the horses and I will until it's no longer a tradition in New York. It's a real dream for me to get these horses off the street. It's a new thing for me to speak up. But when you care for something so passionately, your fear just seems to subside.' Alec was clearly delighted by his bride's new-found ability to speak out. He told a ball thrown by PETA, 'Kim says a nation is only as strong as the way it treats its animals.'

She was not afraid to make herself appear unpopular. While the Atlanta Olympic Committee were making elaborate plans for the 1996 games, she launched a protest two years in advance about a scheme to release 2,400 pigeons as part of the opening ceremonies, after pigeon breeder William Thompson said, 'If live animals are released, they'll fly toward the Olympic flame and be roasted alive, or slam into buildings.'

Alec also tried to save birds on one occasion. In 1996 he and 26 other celebrities wrote to the Governor of Pennsylvania to protest against a traditional pigeon shoot in Schuykill County, held every Labour Day, the first Monday in September. And he led a 1997 protest against Charles Holbrook, a local politician in Clarkstown, New York, for wanting to kill Canada geese that messed up the town's parks with their droppings. The previous year, 251 of the graceful birds had been slaughtered.

And, in a throwback to *Playboy* days, Kim shed all her clothes for a photographer to appear in an anti-fur poster for PETA, which had a long-running campaign of models posing naked with the slogan, 'I'd rather go naked than wear fur.' Kim's poster, which showed her lying on her back with her hands over her breasts and her right leg bent to hide her crotch, proclaimed, 'Beauty Is Not About Wearing Someone Else's Coat' and 'Every fur coat means animals died a painful death by electrocution, drowning or being gassed.' It was unveiled at a dinner at a New York vegetarian restaurant that raised $50,000 for PETA. But the poster was only displayed in Europe so Kim's American fans were deprived of the chance to admire her.

She also joined forces with Golden Girls star Bea Arthur in writing to the government asking them to stop subsidising the fur trade. Kim was outraged to learn that the United States was spending $12 million a year to promote the sales of luxury coats made from American fur in the Far East and Europe, and pointed out that the money could be better spent on poor children. 'Let's show the next generation we've worked to stop violence and death instead of subsidising it,' she wrote. The unlikely couple actually persuaded the House of Representatives to pass an amendment to drop the programme.

By this time, Kim and Alec had bought a cow, called Henry, but she did not live with them. Parts of Woodland Hills are designated as 'semi-agricultural' and lots of people keep horses at home, but I think the neighbours in Kim's quiet cul-de-sac would have objected to a farm animal moving in. Henry lived on a farm sanctuary in Orland in Northern California. So Kim was understandably delighted when California's Republican Governor, Pete Wilson, signed a bill to bring in increased protection for diseased and crippled farm animals. 'We worked very hard to get this act, the first of its kind in the country,' she said.

Kim and Alec also went to the rescue of deer in North Haven, New York, near their summer home in The Hamptons. Residents planned to shoot a herd of 300 deer which had overrun the tiny town of 700 people. Mayor Jack Resier said, 'The deer are a nuisance. They're spreading Lyme disease, eating the shrubbery and causing numerous traffic accidents.' But Kim and Alec wrote an angry letter to the local paper, suggesting that some of the deer could be moved and the does placed on birth control. The letter had some effect for a while. In the weeks after they wrote, nobody applied for a deer shooting permit.

After her passionate plea for better treatment of zoo animals, Kim began to focus especially on trained elephants. In 1995, she was the star guest at a $125-a-head fundraising dinner organised by PAWS, to raise money to move two retired zoo elephants from Milwaukee, Wisconsin, to PAWS' retreat for old animals in Galt, California, near Sacramento. Two year later, she joined forces with former elephant trainer Pat Derby to lobby the American government for more humane treatment of the animals and a ban on making them work in travelling shows.

'I've seen 14 hours of secret elephant-training tapes, how they are made to salute with their trunks,' she explained. 'It's not natural, and when I saw them screaming, brought down on all fours, beaten till they pick up their trunks, I said to Pat Derby, "I'm in. I'm as committed as you'll find." '

They went to Washington and met Agriculture Secretary Daniel Glickman, Senator Harry Reid, a Democrat from Nevada, and Florida Democratic Representative Bob Wexler.

'We're not animal-rights crazies,' she said. 'With all the violence we have on the street, the way we disrespect human life, it's the wrong lesson for children that you can hit and abuse other living creatures.'

Later, in 1997, she took on the owners of King Royal Circus after Heather, one of their elephants, was found dead in the height of summer in a hot, poorly ventilated 40-foot trailer in a car park in the desert city of Albuquerque, New Mexico, with two other live elephants and eight llamas. She demanded that the US Department of Agriculture revoke the circus' licence, and the surviving animals were handed over to the city. 'How much more suffering will animals have to endure?' she asked at a televised press conference.

For her efforts on behalf of the elephants, she was given the PAWS Humane Achievement Award in 1997. She praised the work of PAWS and said, 'I'm just me and the only thing I can offer is access to people. I can help organisations that I'm a member of. That's all I am. I'm a member, not a spokesperson. But the Free the Elephants Campaign is something that is very near and dear to my heart. If my celebrity can be used for the greater good, all the ups and downs will have been worth it.'

The same year she was also outspoken in her support of PETA when they protested at experiments being carried out on beagles at the British-owned Huntingdon Life Sciences in East Millstone, New Jersey. The lab was testing a new Japanese treatment for osteoporosis made by the Yamanouchi Pharmaceutical Corporation. PETA alleged that the dogs were being given an experimental compound meant to strengthen the bones, that they were going to have their legs experimented upon as part of the testing, and that they would only be given one dose of pain killer. An undercover member of PETA also took videos of the dogs. Kim was appalled and offered to take all the beagles herself. In a passionate letter to Huntingdon chief executive Christopher Cliffe and to Yamanouchi president Singo Ogawa, she wrote, 'I beg you to cancel this cruel experiment immediately. I will personally adopt each and every one of the animals now held in small, barren cages in your laboratory. I cannot bear to think of the pain they will suffer as their legs are sawed and broken. The agony they will continue to endure for weeks of follow-up tests and X-rays is unimaginable. These 36 dogs represent a continuing breakdown of the ethical and moral fibre that has held our society together since the beginning of time. We are rapidly acquiring an all-too-easy and acceptable throwaway attitude when it comes to life.'

The publicity persuaded the company to back down. When Kim arrived at the lab hoping to collect the beagles, however, manager Alan Staple turned her away and said, 'It wouldn't be in the best interests of the dogs to release them before they are properly socialised. To transfer them now as requested by Ms Basinger would be irresponsible.' A few days later, the beagles were given to the American Humane Association, who housed them in nine animal shelters until good homes could be found for all of them.

Kim was particularly appalled by the proposed experiments on the beagles because the drug had already been tested in Japan. She firmly believes that computers could and should replace animals in drug tests of all sorts, with the added advantage of being more cost-effective. She said, 'I don't believe in any animal testing. There are other ways. You don't have to be an animal rights activist, you just have to care about one word — injustice. What right does man have to use the "lesser creatures"? Animals are great teachers. They taught me to be the mother I'm becoming because I've brought up so many animals in my life. Given what I know and what I've been presented by numerous medical professionals who have told me straight out over the past 10 years, there are so many alternatives that we need not have one more animal's life taken in a lab. Computers are the answer. And it's very, very expensive to have animals in a lab and watched for 24 hours a day. If you buy a computer it does not have to be fed, it does not have to have a technician to watch over it. How many times a day are you amazed by man's ability to be so inhumane? I have to get through all these tears about animals, though, so I can do something about it. Animals don't need your tears; they need your help. I would love to think that the definition of the word 'animal' will change somehow before I leave this planet. I don't know whether it will or not.'

Not all Kim's animal traumas were so public. She and Alec were at home in Don Juan Place on the morning of 17 January 1994 when the 6.7 Northridge earthquake woke them abruptly at 4.31am The epicentre was only six miles away, and Woodland Hills suffered a lot of damage. All the electricity was cut off and the house was a pitch-black obstacle course with debris thrown all over the place. Kim said, 'We were fine but our whole house was trashed and it was so dark inside the house that I couldn't see anything. It was absolutely terrifying but I needed to get to my puppies. I crawled on the floor in my pyjamas and bare feet over broken glass, smashed dishes and every can and box in the kitchen that had been thrown off the shelves. It was all there on the floor and I had to manoeuvre my way through it. The puppies had all run into a small bathroom and they weren't barking at all. They had completely shut down and weren't making a sound. They wanted to get outside of the house as soon as possible so I passed each of them to Alec and he took them outside. It was a horrible experience but we were OK, so that's all that matters.'

Kim will always love animals with a passion. Her campaigns are not just for publicity — I'm sure it is still hard for her to force herself to make public statements. But motherhood has lessened her tolerance for the sort of animals most people get rid of without a second thought, like cockroaches and rats.

We filmed *Nadine* in Austin, Texas, and that's tarantula country. We lived in a rented house and used to find them in the garden, on the steps and even in the house itself. They won't kill you but they are big and nasty. I had to get rid of them without hurting them. Kim wouldn't let me kill them. But after their daughter was born she told an interviewer, 'All creatures need to be treated with as much respect as human beings. We're all living things. But I have a baby and New York apartments are sometimes full of rats and cockroaches. I haven't had the experience but if one jumped on me, let me tell you that sucker would be dead in about one second!'

Just like any other animal, Kim's maternal instincts had taken over and her first reaction was to protect her offspring from other creatures — great or small.

Chapter 21

Turning 40 can be a traumatic moment for any woman and Kim decided to pass the landmark, 8 December 1993, in style. Not with celebration champagne, but a day of being pampered and primped. She booked herself a day of beauty treatments at the exclusive Frederic Fekkai Beauty Centre at the posh Manhattan department store Bergdorf-Goodman. And although it was her birthday, *she* was the one handing out presents.

First, she got a catering company to bring in a lavish buffet breakfast for the whole staff and other clients — four kinds of bagels, three kinds of toast, smoked salmon, cream cheese, fresh fruit and freshly squeezed fruit juice, mixed berries and assorted jams. Then, as her beauty treatments got under way, she handed out lavish tips. She gave her stylist $150 on top of the $275 charge, $100 to her $300 colourist and $80 to the hair washer. She also tipped the boy who delivered the breakfast. By that time, her hair had been washed and she had it bundled up in a towel, but she was still instantly recognisable.

A visitor to the salon said later, 'The delivery boy stood there with his mouth hanging open and couldn't even form the words "thank you". He was so in awe that Kim and a few of the staff started to laugh. He finally thanked her and left. 'Kim burst out laughing and said,"That boy looked like he'd seen a ghost. I should've put on my make-up. Now he'll tell all his pals that I look like a mess in real life!" '

Kim went on her spending spree, which also included $515 dollars on skin-care products and make-up, despite being an official bankrupt because, she said, 'I care about others and I love to make people happy. Giving makes me feel good. She spent the best part of $2,000 on her day of beauty, and paid for it on one of Alec Baldwin's credit cards. But it was still a cheaper trip to the salon than when we regularly spent $6,000 on round-trip, first-class air tickets from LA to New York so she could visit her favourite colourist.

Still reeling from bankruptcy and the humiliation of being asked about her plans for a future family, Kim flew to Paris to do publicity for *The Getaway*'s European release. While she was there, she bumped into her old friend and *Fool for Love* director, Robert Altman, who promptly offered her a role in his latest film, *Prêt-à-Porter*. It was an ensemble piece with a huge cast including Sophia Loren, Julia Roberts, Lyle Lovett, Rupert Everett, Lauren Bacall, Tim Robbins, Stephen Rea, Linda Hunt and Marcello Mastroianni, playing fictional characters from the fashion world — writers, designers, photographers — mingling with real-life fashion *cognoscenti* and stars like models Naomi Campbell and Claudia Schiffer, singers Cher and Harry Belafonte and high-voltage fashion designers like Christian Lacroix and Jean-Paul Gaultier playing themselves.

Kim's character, television journalist Kitty Potter, was the focal point of the movie. At various times, actresses as diverse as Meryl Streep, Anjelica Huston and Lily Tomlin had been considered for the role, but Altman was undecided until he saw Kim. He later said, 'I didn't know who Kitty Potter was going to be until the day Kim arrived, which was about four days before we started shooting. I look back now and can't imagine anybody doing it except Kim.'

The film had a sketchy plot about the murder of a top fashion designer during the Paris spring fashion shows, and was a black comedy skewering the posing and preciousness of the world of *haute couture*. Many scenes were shot at real fashion shows, with genuine buyers and journalists roped in as extras simply by turning up, and Altman's technique was to tell his actors to stay in character and ad-lib their way through fashion parades and parties, without knowing if the cameras were on them or not. Altman did not know what shape his final film would take; he watched the footage and used the best and most outrageous material.

Kim had always hated rehearsing but this went to the other extreme. She could not even enjoy the ritual of turning up for work in the morning and spending a couple of hours in hair and make-up psyching herself up to start acting. Even her wardrobe fittings were unorthodox. She explained, 'I was doing publicity for *The Getaway*; people were coming in from all over the world to do six-minute interviews. Then, during my lunch hour, Altman's people would race me over to a fashion house — two houses — fit me, and then it was back to the hotel for more press. The junket ended, I think, on Saturday morning and Sunday morning I was up for Altman. I was thrown into this role and so much of it was improvisational. The first day, Altman sat all the members of the cast down and said, "With this mixing of fantasy with reality, with your being at these real fashion shows and being a participant or part of the audience, I just want you to do one thing. I want you to stay in character." '

Once filming started, Kim dressed at her hotel rather than heading for the set in her casual clothes. She went on, 'They would pick me up totally dressed with my make-up on and my hair done. I was very unused to that. Shooting this film was like being out with a bunch of gypsies and a camcorder.'

Strangely enough, Kim had never done fashion shows when she was a model. She had gone to Milan in 1992 as a guest of designer Giorgio Armani but the Paris collections were new to her.

The film revealed the cattiness of the catwalk. Kim faced it in real life when she turned up for shooting in a 1980s' style 'power suit' with big padded shoulders, and the real fashion fanatics shuddered. The film had decidedly mixed reviews, with Duane Byrge in the *Hollywood Reporter* saying, 'It's a zippy undressing, aswirl with the *haute* drama of the fashion players. Undeniably it's a strange and savage blend and Altman has undressed the fashion world as a heap of dirty laundry. He has fashioned a super satirical send-up.' But *Daily Variety* was less flattering. Their reviewer wrote, 'While pic is eye-catching and fitfully amusing, net effect proves frivolous and ephemeral.'

While Kim was shooting *Prêt-à-Porter* — which was translated to *Ready to Wear* before it was released in the United States — she flew her father, Don, to Paris for a break. He was thrilled to meet stars he had loved when he was younger, like Lauren Bacall and Sophia Loren. Don had been with the American forces for the D-Day invasion of Northern France and had shown Kim and her brothers and sisters treasured pictures of himself in uniform, driving a Jeep, and carrying a little French boy on his shoulders. It was just before the 50th anniversary of the Normandy landings and Kim took him on a nostalgic pilgrimage to the beaches and to the little town of Ste Mère-Eglise, where he had taken his pictures.

Kim told an interviewer, 'We drive out to Normandy to see the cemetery and the beach. Everything is in my daddy's pockets, especially the pictures of the child. Now the most amazing thing is this: we go into a coffee bar and I say, "Daddy, where are those pictures of that little kid?" and we show them to this woman. She says, "Go next door. There's a family-owned shop that's been there for 50 years. If anybody around here knows, they will." We go next door, we bring out the picture and we show it to the woman. She looks at the boy then goes and gets another woman out of the back. She looks at the picture and says, "This is my father." He had just died of cancer, at 56. And my father and this woman sat in the store and cried together. After all the crying, they hugged each other and promised to keep in touch.'

Although *Prêt-à-Porter* was a chaotic film, Kim loved working with Altman again. She did not know what her character would be doing from day to day and found that nerve-wracking. She said, 'I come from the fashion world and had people coming up to me and I had to be rude to them because the camera was on me the whole time. I felt so horrible. I was doing everything but slapping these people in the face.' But she was confident that Altman knew what he was doing and added, 'I can tell you one thing about Altman: I trust him. I trust that he knows what's real.' So she was delighted when he offered her a role in his next film, *Kansas City*. But she had only been home from Paris for a few days when she called him to tell him she could not go ahead with it. He was delighted and so was she — because the reason she had to drop out was that she was pregnant.

Kim and Alec had made no secret of their desire to start a family. Kim was fit and healthy, but was ready to consider adoption if she could not conceive naturally once she was over 40. They were both from large families and talked happily about raising a brood. Alec even went into details about how they were trying to make babies. Months before she became pregnant, he said, 'My wife is telling me about what I should eat. I can't eat papaya because it kills sperm. I need beta-carotene. I can't go in the jacuzzi. And I can't wear tight underwear; I'm wearing boxer shorts.' He was even said to have had a clause written into his film contracts allowing him to fly home to Kim once a month, when she was most fertile. Ironically, he complained just before they learned the good news, 'I'd like to start a family soon. Kim is in Paris doing *Prêt-à-Porter*. We were supposed to be having a honeymoon but now it's delayed. I was planning on a honeymoon baby.'

Altman, who had cast Miranda Richardson in the *Kansas City* role meant for Kim, told her, 'Bring the baby to the première of *Ready to Wear*. And name it Robert or Roberta.'

They were delighted at the prospect of becoming parents, but Kim had a miserable pregnancy. She said, 'I was sick in bed for seven months. It was worse than being seasick. Every time I saw liquid being poured into a glass I'd puke. I didn't care what I looked like. I just wanted to feel well again. Everybody calls it morning sickness. I call it 24-hour-a-day sickness.' When she was out of bed she wore her usual baggy overalls, which made a perfect maternity outfit.

The baby was due on 5 November, but Kim awoke with labour pains early in the morning of 23 October. Alec rushed her to Cedars-Sinai Medical Centre in West Los Angeles, and she went into the delivery room at 8.15am. They had hoped for a natural childbirth but doctors recommended a Caesarean section.

Kim told *Movieline* magazine about the birth, 'My baby had been in the vaginal canal with her head down for four months. But three weeks before the due date she had completely turned. My doctor suggested a procedure where they try to turn the baby the right way. It was the most painful procedure I've ever dealt with in my life. Alec was holding my feet, two nurses were holding my hands. They moved the baby three-quarters down but they had to stop to give me a rest. Before they got out the door the baby had turned all the way back. I just burst into tears. I said, "I am not going home without this baby today. So schedule whatever you have to and get it out!" Two hours later, I was in the operating room.'

A hospital insider revealed later, 'Alec was very supportive of Kim and helped her through the Caesarean. He held her hand. He never left her side. They had both wanted to have a natural delivery and experience natural childbirth together. Kim was conscious during the surgery and she felt no pain.'

At 2.00pm, their daughter entered the world weighing in at a healthy 8lb 3oz. Both Alec and Kim were elated and Alec gushed,'Having a baby is the most exciting thing that has happened to me. I want to have 10 kids in all.' They had one moment of shock, however. They had refused to learn the baby's sex in advance but both assumed it would be a boy. So when the doctor commented, 'This one ain't got any balls,' they thought the baby was deformed.

After their experience during the Northridge earthquake the

year before, Kim and Alec did not want to put their precious daughter at any risk. When they decorated the nursery for her they paid $8,000 to make it earthquake-proof. But she had her first experience of the potential turbulence of life in Los Angeles before she even got through the front door, though obviously she didn't realise what was going on.

Kim and Alec brought their daughter home after three days. When they arrived back at Don Juan Place, they noticed a couple of strange vehicles parked in the street. One of them, a camper, was opposite their sloping driveway and through the tinted windows Alec could see a shadowy figure holding a video camera. He banged on the side of the van and shouted at the occupant to stop filming, hastily bundled Kim and the baby into the house, then came out and walked across the road to find out what was going on. He said to the man in the camper, whom he did not recognise, 'Look, I don't mind if you film me but I don't want you filming the baby.' To drive his point home, he held up an aerosol can of shaving cream and sprayed it over the windscreen and windows. The man inside, famed paparazzi photographer Alan Zanger, leapt out and was later to allege that Alec took a swing at him, knocking off his glasses, smashing them and also breaking his nose. When he bent down to pick up his spectacles, Alec kicked him and sent him sprawling.

Chaos broke out in the cul-de-sac as Alec dialled the emergency 911 number and the police soon arrived. So did helicopters from local television news stations, hovering over the house and filming the scene. Zanger, who was treated for his busted nose, made a citizen's arrest on Alec and he was taken to the local police station, booked on suspicion of battery and released on his own recognisance.

Alec said when he was released, 'Anyone with a shred of human decency knows there are times in your life when you want your privacy protected, whether you are a public figure or not. I do believe that bringing home your wife and three-day-old baby is one of those occasions. That Mr Zanger felt it was appropriate to videotape my home and my family for his own profit is unacceptable to me. I asked him repeatedly to stop filming us and he refused each request. I dispute his contention that I broke his nose or caused any other facial damage. I'm sorry for any problems caused and I look forward to Mr Zanger and I putting this behind us.'

It was not so easy to put the row behind them, however. The

next day, Zanger filed a million dollar civil suit against him, and a few weeks later Alec was formally charged with misdemeanour battery, which carries a possible six months in jail and a $2,000 fine.

The incident had an unusual postscript. In January 1995, a man called John Aquilino, whose five-year-old son, Johnny, was born with a serious heart defect, had written an open letter in the *Los Angeles Times* to Alec, stating that groups like People for the Ethical Treatment of Animals put children like his at risk by campaigning against medical experimentation on animals.

An organisation called Americans for Medical Progress Education Foundation bought a full-page advert in *Daily Variety* carrying another letter from Aquilino to Alec. In part it read, 'As you've discovered, your protective instincts for your daughter will astound you. You will do whatever it takes to protect her from every harm … Should she fall ill, you will move mountains to provide her with every medical treatment to restore her health … Today my son is quite healthy and happy. He is alive only because of generations of medical research which involved animals … Alec, as one very protective father to another, I have one request. Before you or your wife do one more public service announcement or raise funds for PETA, visit and get to know the medical researchers who work with animals.'

Alec pleaded 'not guilty' and was tried by a jury of eight women and four men — the same ratio as the jury that convicted Kim in the *Boxing Helena* trial — in Van Nuys Municipal Court. But unlike the *Boxing Helena* case, where Alec was often a comforting presence in the courtroom, Kim did not accompany him. The jury heard his emergency call, in which he said, 'The guy took my video, I wouldn't care. He took my wife's video, I wouldn't care. But he tried to take my baby. We don't want that. My name is Alec Baldwin. My wife is Kim Basinger. She's an actress. I only mention this because this is a relevant fact. Do you know my wife at all? Do you know who she is?'

The prosecution pointed out that Zanger was in a public street when he took his pictures, which is perfectly legal, and that when police arrived Alec admitted he was to blame and offered to pay any damages. Zanger insisted he had switched his camera off and had it pointed to the ground.

On the witness stand, Alec used all his acting skills, even mimicking Zanger's voice, which was very nasal because of his broken nose, and came down from the stand to demonstrate to the jury his version of events. He claimed he had been warned that someone might attempt to kidnap his daughter, and feared that Zanger was a stalker who was threatening to hit him with his camera. Alec's defence attorney suggested Zanger had deliberately provoked the confrontation, to make the event more newsworthy and to collect damages in a lawsuit. It took the jury just five days to acquit Alec, on the grounds that he reasonably felt he was being threatened. Zanger's civil lawsuit and a counter-suit brought by Alec were left in place to wend their long paths through the Los Angeles civil court system.

After his acquittal, Alec said, 'To me, this is something this guy invited. He wanted to have a confrontation. I could see it in his eyes. I really can't stand this guy. From now on, I will avoid these situations.' However, by this time lots of photographs of their daughter had been published, and Kim and Alec seemed much more relaxed about the idea.

It took nearly two years for the civil case to trial, and in July 1998 Alec was back in Van Nuys Superior Court, facing another jury. Zanger was claiming damages for $85,000 in medical expences and lost income, and punitive damages on top. There were actually two cases being heard simultaneously, because Alec had countersued, alleging invasion of privacy and stalking, assault, negligence and emotional distress, but not asking foe a dollar amount. This time the jury was made up of seven men and five women, who were quizzed, among other things, on their reaction to the death of Diana, Princess of Wales because of the involvment of photographers in the high-speed car chase through Paris which killed her and her lover, Dodi Fayed. Alec's lawyer, Philip Weiss, won a legal ruling that he could describe Zanger as a 'stalkerazzi' throughout the trial. In response, Zanger's attorney Leonard Steiner, pointed out that Zanger was a Vietnam veteran with a college education who had worked on the staff of the world-wide news agency United Press International for years and had had his work published in major newspapers and magazines around the world. 'We're not talking about someone who's not a member of the legitimate press,' he insisted. 'We're talking about someone who is an esteemed and established member of the legitimate press.' He also said that Zanger had been consistent in his version of events, whereas Alec had changed his story repeatedly.

The facts of the case, of course, were the same as they had been in the criminal hearing, but the jury was being asked to consider more than the simple question of whether Alec had struck the photographer, provoked or unprovoked. Zanger took the witness stand and said it was not his style to be confrontational. He preferred to take pictures of his celebrity subjects without them even knowing he was there. He said the incident had changed his life. 'I was a wreck,' he told the jury. 'I'm apprehensive every time I do somthing. I can't do my work like I used to.' He said Alec's punch had severely damaged his nose, deviating the septum, and that he was constantly dizzy as a result. He was backed by the ear, nose and throat expert who had treated him, who said he needed plastic surgery costing at least $10,000 to repair his septum. However, a second medical expert testifying for Alec said Zanger's nose was nearly normal, that any slight deviation existed before the incident and that Zanger had also complained of dizziness years earlier. Zanger also claimed his income had fallen from $276,000 in 1995 to $78,000 the following year. I don't know if that would have impressed the jury, however; even $78,000 is a healthy sum of money as far as most people are concerned.

Alec – this time without Kim in court – also gave evidence that he had been badly affected by the altercation and had been forced to intall a fence and security gate. 'This incident with Zanger changed everything in our lives,' he said. 'One of the reasons that we live in Woodland Hills is that people wouldn't expect us to live in Woodland Hills. Never, prior to this incident had anybody been hiding in a car in front of my house. I never thought anybody would be there bothering us. My wife was upset. I'll try not to get emotional about this, but my wife was crying. She was in incredible pain.' He also said he acted purely in self-defence, adding, 'If I had wanted to physically attack him, I think things would have been very different. With all due respect, he's not a very big guy.'

Zanger's attorney picked him up on that in cross-examination, reminding him that the records of his emergency phone call and his initial statement to the police when they arrived on the scene showed that he admitted hitting Zanger without mentioning that it was in self-defence. 'Mr Baldwin has changed his story every time he told it,' he said, dismissing the claims of self-defence. 'I think he made up this story. He belted Zanger and he panicked.' Alec appeared to gain the upper hand at one moment, when the jury was watching the video of the incident and he accused Zanger of editing the tape. 'There's a "jump cut" in this tape,' he blurted out spontaneously.

Legal experts predicted a victory for Zanger, because he was in a public place when he took his pictures. 'Anything a celebrity does in public can be filmed,' said lawyer Douglas Mirell, who specialises in issues involving the First Amendment to the United States constitution, which guarantees freedom of the press. 'I would say that it's an uphill battle for Baldwin.'

However, after a seven-day trial the jury reached their verdict – and decided both men were guilty of negligence. They awarded Zanger damages of $6,000, to pay for new glasses, treatment for his nose for a week and lost wages, and reduced the sum to $4,500 because they said he was 25 per cent at fault. 'What we had in essence, was one man's word against another,' said jury foreman Rodney Meyersberg, who admitted being one of the jurors who voted in favour of Alec's invasion of privacy claim. 'I personally saw it as a case that shouldn't have gone to trial at all. Basically we had a tough time with the credibility of Zanger on a number of issues, both with how the incident occurred and the existence of the injuries. We thought the negligence issue was the best way to come up with the best verdict.' Alec was not awarded any money, partly because because he had not asked for any but Meyersberg also explained, 'We though it was impossible to put an amount of money on what Mr Baldwin had suffered. How could you possibly recast that day for him and his child and his family?' As the court clerk read the verdict, Alec smiled and mouthed 'thank you' to the jurors.

Both sides claimed victory in the case. Alec's lawyer, Weiss, said, 'The message is that they – paparazzi – should be more respectful. We seem to have found a profession that's one step below attorneys. We're thrilled with the verdict all the way around. This was never about the money.'

Zanger's attorney, Steiner, who must have lost a lot of money on the case if he was representing the photographer free in return for a percentage of the damages, as is usual in civil cases of this nature in the USA, countered, 'The First Amendment is alive and well in California. We don't usually commence litigation to wind up at the end of the day with $4,500. On the other hand – hey, we won. We accept this verdict and will get on with our lives.'

From all accounts, Kim and Alec are devoted, hands-on parents, who took turns getting up in the night when their little girl was tiny. Naturally, she is being raised as a vegetarian and is certain to be an animal-lover. They want to raise her out of the Hollywood spotlight, but know they will not be able to protect her completely from their professional lives. Kim laughed, 'Alec and I always say that one day one of our kids is going to come home and say, "Dad, Freddy's daddy says Mommy was in a naked movie." Hey, if that happens, it's my career — that's what I did. There's nothing I'll ever hide from my daughter.'

Since the birth of their daughter, there have been rumours that Kim was expecting another child, but as she gets older that becomes less likely. But they have also talked about adopting. Alec told *US* magazine, 'I do think we'll have another one, hopefully. Adopt one or more. My wife and I had kids later in life and I just don't see it as possible for us to have as many kids as we might want, now. I'm happy with the way it worked out but I certainly would've liked to have six or eight or 10 kids'

However big a family Kim and Alec have, I hope they are all happy and healthy. I wish them all well.

Chapter 22

There can be no doubt that Kim finally gained from her peers the recognition that she has so long deserved in the highly critically-acclaimed, award-winning *L.A. Confidential*, a movie adaptation of James Ellroy's classic crime novel. Set in Los Angeles in the early 1950s, the film focused on the early days of tabloid journalism and exposed rampant police brutality and cops taking kickbacks.

In the film, Danny DeVito played the editor-manipulator of the fictional *Hush-Hush* magazine, based on the real life *Confidential* magazine, which wielded tremendous power in the booming Hollywood of that era. Kim portrayed Lynn Bracken, a high-class prostitute whose success lay in the fact that she was a Veronica Lake lookalike and her customers were prepared to part with big bucks to fantasise that they were actually making love to a movie star. The part was particularly appealing to Kim not just because it was a tremendous role, but also because the movie had a production schedule that gave its stars weeks between camera calls. That meant Kim had plenty of time to spend with her baby daughter, who was only a few months old when filming began. Danny DeVito, who was wrapping up post-production of his movie *Matilda*, was also delighted with the timing of the picture. Other stars in the film included Oscar-winner Kevin Spacey, Oscar-nominated James Cromwell and two relative newcomers to Hollywood movies, Australian actors Russell Crowe and Guy Pearce, all playing Los Angeles Police Department detectives at a period when the force was riddled with corruption.

Director Curtis Hanson, who also co-wrote the screenplay, wanted Kim right from the start.

'Kim could understand this part like few other actresses,' he explained. 'She knows all too well that having a glamourous, erotic image can be an asset and a liability. It sometimes hides the real person behind the gorgeous façade. Kim has the glamour of earlier actresses, but who else would know how much long, blonde hair can be a trap? She had this reputation after *The Marrying Man*, but I've always found her so appealing as a woman — not just as a knockout; she's so *accessible* on screen. She invites you in. That's not true of many of the great screen beauties. Before you meet her you think, "She's Kim Basinger! She's this goddess!" Then you realise she's very different from that Hollywood glamour-puss. She's tomboyish, she's slightly awkward, she clomps around on her heels. The reality is that the woman on the screen isn't her.'

Though Kim had not been in a hit movie since *Batman*, which was not her vehicle, Hanson offered her $3 million for the part.

In what would have been a truly tragic move, Kim nearly turned the role down. But she read the script at her agent's insistence, recognising that she had made some spectacularly disastrous career decisions in the past when choosing her films. She said, 'It was a lady of the night and that didn't intrigue me that much. I thought, "No way! I'm not playing a prostitute. Never!" I wanted something like Jane Eyre. I'm my own worst enemy sometimes when I pick projects. But after I read the dialogue, I said, 'That's not what this is about at all. She's very complex…'

She met Hanson for lunch at a legendary Hollywood hangout, the Formosa Café, which was used for a scene in the film, and admitted she was nervous. So she was delighted when he told her he had no doubt she was the one. 'There's nothing more wonderful for an actor than to be told, "You're the one I want to play this part," ' she recalled.

Kim prepared for the part by watching Veronica Lake films and reading everything about her she could lay her hands on. She could easily identify with her, having so often been dismissed as a blonde bimbo herself. 'She was an incredibly talented actress whose talents went unnoticed for all the years she was on screen because her hairdo was more famous than her abilities,' she said.

Although Hanson had no doubts about Kim's abilities, others connected with the film were astonished by her performance. Author James Ellroy said, 'I was flabbergasted by her performance. Kim became the character I had written in my head. She seduced me completely and I swear I'm entirely in the erotic thrall of my wife.'

Co-star Russell Crowe, who played a brutal cop who fell for Kim's charms but could not overcome his violent nature, said, 'She blew me away. In one scene I needed to slap her and she wanted me to make contact. It was scary for me but I remember thinking, "Wow, this woman has the real stuff." '

The critics were equally enthusiastic about Kim and about the movie as a whole. Todd McCarthy wrote in *Daily Variety*, 'Drenched in the tawdry glamour of Hollywood in the early 1950s and up to its ears in the delirious corruption of police and politics, *L.A. Confidential* is an irresistible treat with enough narrative twists and memorable characters for a half-dozen films.' Leah Rozen in *People* magazine said, 'Basinger, portraying an emotionally vulnerable call-girl who could double for movie star Veronica Lake is actually darn good here — a first.' In the *San Francisco Chronicle*, Mick LaSale wrote, 'With its glossy finish and sustained atmosphere of romance and desolation, *L.A. Confidential* is the movie that every picture set in post-war Los Angeles tries to be ... Kim Basinger is there to uphold the female principle. It's a poignant performance with Basinger functioning as both lover and mommy for damaged boy Russell Crowe.' *Drama-Logue's* critic Abbie Bernstein said, 'Kim Basinger brings shading and humour to Lynn.'

L.A. Confidential, which cost $36 million to make, took nearly four months to recover its costs. It stayed on general release much longer than most mainstream films — from its September opening until well after the Academy Awards ceremony at the end of March — and eventually became a box office success as well as an acknowledged piece of cinematic artistry. It was even voted the second-best film of all time about cops turned bad. The Orson Welles – directed 1957 classic *Touch of Evil* was first.

But director Hanson was unhappy with the way it was marketed by Warner Bros. He complained, 'The marketing people didn't listen to the audience. They took a glance at the movie, saw it was about cops and concluded that *L.A. Confidential* was a movie for males and should be sold accordingly. But in our test screenings we found that women liked the picture as much as men. The audience articulated very clearly what they liked — they liked the story, they were engaged by the characters, they found it emotionally moving. The original campaign not only didn't attract people, it kept them away. We had a trailer and TV spots featuring cops and guns. Thank goodness for the critics, who almost uniformly have described the movie as rich, rewarding entertainment.'

The fact that Kim was the only significant woman in a cast with more than 80 speaking parts proved to be great for her when voters at organisations like the Academy of Motion Picture Arts and Sciences and the Hollywood Foreign Press Association had to choose their favourites. Warner Brothers promoted Kim heavily as Best Supporting Actress. But while the five lead male characters all gave brilliant performances, they were so good that it was impossible to select any of them as best.

L.A. Confidential was, not surprisingly, shot in LA, using buildings and streets still surviving from the 1950s and earlier, so it was a convenient shoot for Kim and did not keep her away from her little girl too much. But the filming did present her with one major trauma — it cost her her hair. She was so enthusiastic about the role she agreed to go for a totally authentic look, even though that meant using harsh chemical dyes. She said, 'The part called for me to be a platinum blonde. And back in those days, all the women in movies, Grace Kelly, Marilyn Monroe, they couldn't just use highlights the way I usually do. They had to dye it solid. All the time. So I told Curtis I was willing to dye what was, at the time, my very long hair. "Wouldn't you rather wear a wig?" he asked me. I said, "No, it'd be like wearing a football helmet." Well, I'd never dyed my hair like that before and after a while it just started falling off. That stuff burns. It was falling off, not out, thank God. There was no damage to the roots. For four months we had to keep it wet, keep wrapping it up in braids. We saved just enough of it to maintain the look but in the end we used wigs. At the end of the movie I told my stylist to just cut it all off. But it was in such poor shape that I went ahead and shaved it off. I loved it. I wanted to look like a boy. It's been a dream. I feel like I've been hiding all my life.'

I laughed when I read that. She had obviously 'forgotten' having much the same reaction when she first had her hair cropped short to make The Man Who Loved Women and she'd also chosen not to remember the time in New York when all the dye started coming out of her hair in the shower just before she was going to be interviewed for her role in Nadine.

Kim was delighted by the critical acclaim but bristled when it was described as a 'comeback' movie for her.

'It's not like I vanished off the face of the earth,' she snapped at interviewers. 'I took time off to have a child. I didn't go anywhere. I was quite happy being a mom and waving to Alec, "Bye-bye, dear". I missed being in the movies but I enjoyed being a mother more.'

But she did acknowledge that her long absence from the screen made her even more nervous than usual about starting a new film, and was grateful to Hanson for giving her such a spectacular return to the limelight.

'Once you're away from the screen, you get insecure and wonder if you can go back and click in,' she went on. 'Will you know how to do it? Curtis just had such a vote of confidence in me. He just saw me as her. That's a great director, someone who believes in who they cast.'

Fuelled by the success of *L.A. Confidential*, and confident that she has finally overcome her image as a blonde bimbo who looks beautiful but causes trouble and makes unsuccessful films, she gained a new, more philosophical outlook on life. Looking back on the stormy years of the early 1990s, she said the bruising blows of the *Boxing Helena* trial, going bankrupt and the Braselton débâcle have actually taught her a lot.

'It's been open season on me, so to speak,' she said. 'I've lived in a glass bowl, people have seen my life, unlike other celebrities. They've seen the good and the bad, and the this and the that, and the other things I've been through, the trials, the ups, the downs, so I think many times that has hurt me somewhat. But I don't look back on it with any anger or resentment or anything in the world. I know this is weird, but I look at it as a great gift having been handed to me, because a lot of people in this life, they might be rich, they might be famous and have it all in the eyes of other people. But I don't think you can have it all until all of it has been taken away. And then you understand what all is, really. In that respect I've been given a gift.'

After *L.A. Confidential*, I am sure Kim could pick and choose her projects, and another collaboration with Curtis Hanson could be on the cards. Alec said, 'Finally, Kim has done something where it all adds up to success. She has had a lot of offers since this movie, and she is simply crazy about Curtis. So they may go places movie-wise together.'

When the annual film awards season rolled round at the end of 1997, it seemed that *L.A. Confidential* could not do anything wrong. It became only the third film in history — the others being *Terms of Endearment* and *Schindler's List* — to be named Best Picture by the National Board of Review, the New York Film Critics Circle and the Los Angeles Film Critics Association. It made more than 100 year-end top ten lists from critics around the United States. Other critical nods included the National Society of Film

Critics, the Boston Society of Film Critics, The Scripter award for best adapted screenplay and, of course, the Golden Globes, the Hollywood Foreign Press Association awards which often predict Oscar winners. The film got five Golden Globe nominations, for Best Picture, Director, Screenplay and Score — and Kim as Best Supporting Actress. She had had this nomination before, for *The Natural*, and I was holding my breath as I watched the televised ceremony to see if she would win. She was, in fact, the only winner for *L.A. Confidential* on a night when the epic *Titanic* won most of the glory.

Even better than the Golden Globe nominations, however, was the Academy Awards, the ultimate accolade for the movie industry because it is the only one where players, whether actors or on the technical side, are chosen by their peers. *L.A. Confidential* picked up nine nods, the most important one as far as I was concerned being Kim, for Best Actress in a Supporting Role.

When Kim's name was announced as the winner at the Golden Globes ceremony at the Beverly Hilton Hotel, I was overcome with emotion. I felt like crying right along with her. I could see her nervousness, which is so real and which we lived through always. I sensed she could barely go up to the stage, but somehow she did. As always, she pulled through and pulled it off. People love her because she acts like they would, real and surprised and overwhelmed. She always used to say, 'If I ever win anything, I'll probably pass out.' It looked to me as if she almost did. I was so happy for her. Just a few weeks later she won yet another Best Supporting Actress prize, tying with *Titanic* actress Gloria Stuart in the Screen Actors' Guild Awards, boosting my hopes that she would win the big one, the Oscar. I always told her she was terrific as an actress and one day would show Hollywood what she could do. She used to ask me, 'Am I really good? Will I *ever* win anything?' She must have asked me a hundred times 'Will I ever be great? Will I ever do anything great?' I always told her she was the greatest and, as far as I'm concerned, she always will be. Our ways had parted, but Kim Basinger will stay in my heart … Longer Than Forever …

Epilogue

With the exception of holding her daughter for the first time, winning the Oscar for her role in L.A. Confidential must have been the happiest moment of Kim's life. The sheer joy in her face – and in Alec's – when her name was announced could leave no room for doubt.

As soon as the nomination were announced I was convinced she would win, but during the final 10 days in the run-up to the 70th annual Academy Awards ceremony I became nervous about Gloria Stuart, also nominated as Best Supporting Actress for her role in Titanic, and a sentimental favourite as the oldest nominee ever.

I could hardly bear to watch the ceremony as it was broadcast live from the Shrine Auditorium in Downtown Los Angeles. I'd been for a long ride on Reno, through the canyons, trying to take my nervous mind off the awards by concentrating on the beauty of the spring flowers and the streams and waterfalls sparkling in the warm late March sun. If I was so anxious about the winner, what must Kim have been going through?

As it happened I got home just in time to switch on the television and actually missed the opening moments of the ceremony. I was all by myself because I've never remarried, though I usually have a girlfriend. Best Supporting Actress was the first category announced and I had to steel myself as presenter Cuba Gooding Jr read out the names. When he opened that white envelope and said: "And the Oscar goes to – *Kim Basinger*" I just bent forward yelled: "*Yes!*" at the top of my voice, clapped my hands and was close to tears. That was the end of the show for me.

Kim looked incredulous and terrified, as if she could not take it in all at once. Then she hugged Alec, and director Curtis Hanson, who was sitting behind her, and walked somewhat unsteadily on to the stage, holding up the full skirt of her pale green Escada gown.

"Oh, my God," she gasped as she took the gold statuette into her right hand. "*Yes!*" Thank you. Wait a minute. We did only get 30 seconds and to give a thousand thank yous... I just want to thank everyone I have ever met in my entire life. Curtis Hanson, Curtis Hanson, Curtis Hanson. The cast and crew for the movie. I couldn't have done it without you. Annet Wolf. My great friend Georgia. My sister Ashley. My husband Alec. My baby girl [...]. If anyone has a dream out there, just know I am living proof that they do come true. Thank you so much to the Academy. I am so grateful for this."

Then, raising the statuette above her head she added dramatically: "And Daddy, this is for you."

I was so happy for her. I felt elated for myself too, as if somehow I had helped her get there. And when she thanked everyone she had ever met, I thought she was thanking me too. So did the friends who started telephoning me as soon as she had finished her speech. Kim looked as if it really meant something to her and I know it does. She'd vindicated for her entire existence. Five years ago, after the Boxing Helena trial, she was practically untouchable. Now she's immortal. She always wanted to be and now she is for sure. Longer than forever...

Backstage she explained why she had dedicated her prize to her father. "My father was my very first acting teacher," she said. "I used to spend many night on the floor watching old '40s and '30s and '50s movies and he would question me about Humphrey Bogart and John Huston. So by the time I actually left home I had a pretty good background in film."

I was glad she thanked her daddy, because she would never have got there without him. But I did feel a bit sorry for her mother Ann and sister Barbara because Kim had singled out Don and Ashley for a mention. I felt even worse for them the next morning when I called Don Basinger to congratulate him and discovered he'd thrown an Oscar party for Ashley, Barbara and their husbands, as well as Kim's brother Skip. I thought that Barbara must have felt very uncomfortable being at the celebration and not getting a mention and, wherever Ann was, she would have felt left out as well. I told Don Kim would not have done it without him – and he told me that I had also helped her. Ann wasn't at the party, of course: although she and Don are not divorced they have been separated since 1980 and have no contact. Even since the birth of her daughter, Kim is not reconciled with her mother, who has never seen her granddaughter. Mother and daughter spoke briefly by telephone shortly after the baby's birth, when Kim and Alec visited Athens. They stayed at a hotel rather than with relatives, Ann revealed to an interviewer. "I was expecting them for dinner," she said. "I phoned them and Alec said Kim couldn't talk to me because she was bathing the baby. Finally she came to the phone for a minute. Then we both hung up. I never talked to her again." In an interview with top television personality Barbara Walters broadcast on American TV immediately after the Oscar ceremony, Kim said that she was "in love" with her mother but that they were hopelessly estranged.

Although Kim had not lined up her next film when she won the Oscar, I knew her professional future was guaranteed and that no longer would her beauty hide her talent, the talent I had always believed existed. As I watched the rest of the Oscar ceremony, not really concentrating, I kept getting flashbacks to the moment when she won, and burst out laughing.

Within a month Kim started lining up offers for her next project. She was in talks to play tough cop Jane Tennison in the film version of *Prime Suspect*, based on the British television series starring Helen Mirren, and Kukie Gallman, an Italian-born wildlife activist who lives in Kenya, in *I Dream of Africa*. In the end the *Prime Suspect* makers decided that Mirren, who had won two Emmy awards for her portrayal of the tough woman cop, would be a better choice, so Kim went with *I Dream of Africa*. That was to take her back to Nairobi, Kenya, where we had enjoyed an exotic holiday, after an initial shoot in Italy. The film would be a tragic love story, directed by Hugh Hudson, who made the Oscar-winning film *Chariots of Fire*. It co-starred French actor Vincent Perez, of *The Crow 2: City of Angels*. Alec and their daughter were due to join her on location for the four-month shoot.

It's still a little bit unbelievable, to flash back to the little girl I knew so long ago. So much has happened to her since we met. She has realised her dreams and made such a success of her life. It should make all of us who ever knew her struggles feel happy for her.

Time is a great healer and, although I know we will never be friends again, I wish her well in everything she does. The next morning, as Tinseltown rested – recovering from the most important night of the year – I sent her a note.

It read:

"Hi Kim:

"You did it

"Long ago you asked me: 'Will I be the best? Will I ever win anything?' I told you then: 'One day the world will know you are the best.'

"Luck to you and your new family.

"L T F... Ron"

Filmography

Hard Country (1981) Director: David Greene. Producers: David Greene, Mack Bing. Screenplay: Michael Kane. Photography: Dennis Dalzell. Editor: John A Martinelli. Music: Jimmie Haskell. Released by: Associated Film Distribution through Universal. Cast: Jan-Michael Vincent, Kim Basinger, Michael Parks, Tanya Tucker, Ted Neeley, Gailard Sartain, Michael Martin Murphy.
Fee: $125,000
US Box Office: N/A

Mother Lode (1982) Director: Charlton Heston. Producer: Fraser Clarke Heston. Screenplay: Fraser Clarke Heston. Photography: Richard Leiterman. Editor: Eric Boyd Perkins. Music: Ken Wannberg. Released by: Agamemnon Films. Cast: Charlton Heston, Nick Mancuso, Kim Basinger, John Marley.
Fee: $125,000
US Box Office: N/A

Never Say Never Again (1983) Director: Irvin Kershner. Producer: Jack Schwartzman. Screenplay: Lorenzo Semple Jr, based on an original story by Kevin McClory, Jack Whittingham and Ian Fleming. Photography: Douglas Slocombe. Editor: Ian Crafford. Music: Michel Legrand. Released by: Warner Bros. Cast: Sean Connery, Klaus Maria Brandauer, Max Von Sydow, Barbara Carrera, Kim Basinger, Bernie Casey, Alec McCowen, Edward Fox, Pamela Salem, Rowan Atkinson.
Fee: $175,000 + $75,000 overtime
US Box Office: $53,381,466

The Man Who Loved Women (1983) Director: Blake Edwards. Producers: Blake Edwards, Tony Adams. Screenplay: Blake Edwards, Milton Wexler, Geoffrey Edwards. Photography: Haskell Wexler. Editor: Ralph E Winters. Music: Henry Mancini. Released by: Columbia Pictures. Cast: Burt Reynolds, Julie Andrews, Kim Basinger, Marilu Henner, Barry Corbin, Cynthia Sikes, Jennifer Edwards, Sela Ward, Ben Powers, Elle Bauer, Denise Crosby.
Fee: $200,000
US Box Office: $6,706,412

The Natural (1984) Director: Barry Levinson. Producer: Mark Johnson. Screenplay: Roger Towne, Phil Dusenberry, based on the novel by Bernard Malamud. Photography: Caleb Deschanel. Editor: Stu Linder. Music: Randy Newman. Released by: TriStar Pictures. Cast: Robert Redford, Robert Duvall, Glenn Close, Kim Basinger,

Wilford Brimley, Barbara Hershey, Robert Prosky, Richard Farnsworth.
Fee: $250,000
US Box Office: $47,951,979

Fool for Love (1985) Director: Robert Altman. Producers: Menahem Golan, Yoram Globus. Screenplay: Sam Shepard, based on his play. Photography: Pierre Mignot. Editors: Luce Grunenwaldt, Steve Dunn. Music: George Burt. Released by: The Cannon Group. Cast: Sam Shepard, Kim Basinger, Harry Dean Stanton, Randy Quaid.
Fee: $208,000
US Box Office: $836,156

9¹/₂ Weeks (1986) Director: Adrian Lyne. Producers: Antony Rufus Isaacs, Zalman King. Screenplay: Patricia Knop, Zalman King, Sarah Kernochan, based on a novel by Elizabeth McNeill. Photography: Peter Biziou. Editors: Tom Rolf, Caroline Biggerstaff. Music: Jack Nitzsche. Released by: MGM/UA. Cast: Mickey Rourke, Kim Basinger, Margaret Whitton, David Margulies, Christine Baranski, Karen Young, William De Acutis, Dwight Weist, Roderick Cook.
Fee: $508,000
US Box Office: $5,873,580

No Mercy (1986) Director: Richard Pearce. Producer: D Constantine Conte. Screenplay: Jim Carabatsos. Photography: Michel Brault. Editors: Jerry Greenberg, Bill Yahraus. Music: Alan Silvestri. Released by: TriStar Pictures. Cast: Richard Gere, Kim Basinger, Jeroen Krabbe, George Dzundza, Gary Basaraba, William Atherton, Terry Kinney, Bruce McGill, Ray Sharkey, Marita Geraghty, Aleta Mitchell.
Fee: $1 million
US Box Office: $12,303,904

Blind Date (1987) Director: Blake Edwards. Producer: Tony Adams. Screenplay: Dale Launer. Photography: Harry Stradling. Editor: Robert Pergament. Music: Henry Mancini. Released by: TriStar Pictures. Cast: Kim Basinger, Bruce Willis, John Larroquette, William Daniels, George Coe, Mark Blum, Phil Hartman, Joyce Van Patten, Georgann Johnson, Sab Shimono, Momo Yashima.
Fee: $1 million
US Box Office: $39,321,715

Nadine (1987) Director: Robert Benton. Producer: Arlene Donovan. Screenplay: Robert Benton. Photography: Nestor Almendros. Editor: Sam O'Steen. Music: Howard Shore. Released by: TriStar Pictures. Cast: Jeff Bridges, Kim Basinger, Rip Torn, Gwen Verdon, Glenne Headly, Jerry Stiller.
Fee: $1.15 million
US Box Office: $5,669,831

My Stepmother Is an Alien (1988) Director: Richard Benjamin. Producers: Ronald Parker, Franklin R Levy. Screenplay: Jerico Weingrod, Herschel Weingrod, Timothy Harris, Jonathan Reynolds. Photography: Richard H Kline. Editor: Jacqueline Cambas. Music: Alan Silvestri. Released by: Columbia Pictures. Cast: Dan Aykroyd, Kim Basinger, Jon Lovitz, Alyson Hannigan, Joseph Maher, Ann Prentiss.
Fee: $1.25 million
US Box Office: $12,897,014

Batman (1989) Director: Tim Burton. Producers: Jon Peters, Peter Guber. Screenplay: Sam Hamm, Warren Skaaren, from a story by Hamm based on characters created by Bob Kane appearing in magazines published by DC Comics. Photography: Roger Pratt. Editor: Ray Lovejoy. Music: Danny Elfman. Songs: Prince. Released by: Warner Bros. Cast: Michael Keaton, Jack Nicholson, Kim Basinger, Robert Wuhl, Pat Hingle, Billy Dee Williams, Michael Gough, Jack Palance, Jerry Hall, Lee Wallace, Tracey Walter.
Fee: $3 million
US Box Office: $251,185,407 (No.11 on the top-grossing domestically of all-time list)

The Marrying Man (Too Hot to Handle) (1991) Director: Jerry Rees. Producer: David Permut. Screenplay: Neil Simon. Photography: Donald E Thorin. Editor: Michael Jablow. Music: David Newman. Released by: Buena Vista. Cast: Kim Basinger, Alec Baldwin, Robert Loggia, Armand Assante, Paul Reisner, Fisher Stevens.
Fee: $2.5 million
US Box Office: $12,454,768

Final Analysis (1992) Director: Phil Joanou. Producers: Charles Roven, Paul Junger Witt, Anthony Thomas. Screenplay: Wesley Strick, based on a story by Robert Berger and Wesley Strick. Photography: Joran Cronenweth. Editor: Thom Noble. Music: George Fenton. Released by: Warner Bros. Cast: Richard Gere, Kim Basinger, Uma Thurman, Eric Roberts, Paul Guilfoyle, Keith David, Robert Harper, Agustin Rodriguez, Harris Yulin.
Fee: $3 million
US Box Office: $28,590,665

Cool World (1992) Director: Ralph Bakshi. Producer: Frank Mancuso Jr. Screenplay: Michael Gras, Mark Victor. Photography: John A Alonzo. Editors: Steve Mirkovich, Annamaria Szanto. Music: Mark Isham. Conceptual Designer: Barry Jackson. Animation Supervisor: Bruce Woodside. Released by: Paramount Pictures. Cast: Kim Basinger, Gabriel Byrne, Brad Pitt, Michele Abrams, Deidre O'Connell, Carrie Hamilton, Frank Sinatra Jr. Voices: Charles Adler, Maurice LaMarche, Candi Milo, Michael David Lally, Joey Camen, Gregory Snegoff.
Fee: $1.7 million
US Box Office: $14,110,589

The Real McCoy (1993) Director: Russell Mulcahy. Producers: Martin Bregman, Willi Baer, Michael S Bregman. Screenplay: William Davies, William Osbourne. Photography: Denis Crossan. Editor: Peter Honess. Music: Bred Fiedel. Released by: Universal Pictures. Cast: Kim Basinger, Val Kilmer, Terence Stamp, Gailard Sartain, Zach English.
Fee: $3 million
US Box Office: $6,332,265

Wayne's World II (1993) Director: Stephen Surjik. Producers: Howard Koch, Lorne Michaels. Screenplay: Mike Myers, Bonnie Turner, Terry Turner. Released by: Paramount Pictures. Cast: Mike Myers, Dana Carvey, Christopher Walken, Tia Carrere, Ralph Brown, Kim Basinger.
Fee: N/A
US Box Office: $47,069,217

The Getaway (1994) Director: Roger Donaldson. Producers: David Foster, Lawrence Turman, John Alan Simon. Screenplay: Walter Hill, Amy Jones, based on a novel by Jim Thompson. Photography: Peter Menzies Jr. Editor: Conrad Buff. Music: Mark Isham. Released by: Universal. Cast: Alec Baldwin, Kim Basinger, Michael Madsen, James Woods, David Morse, Jennifer Tilly, James Stephens, Richard Farnsworth.
Fee: $4 million (split with co-star Alec Baldwin at their discretion)
US Box Office: $15,545,115

Ready To Wear (*Prêt à Porter*) (1994) Director: Robert Altman. Producer: Robert Altman. Screenplay: Robert Altman, Barbara Shulgasser. Photography: Pierre Mignot, Jean Lepine. Editor: Geraldine Peroni. Music: Michel Legrand. Released by: Miramax. Cast: Marcello Mastroianni, Sophia Loren, Tim Robbins, Julia Roberts, Kim Basinger, Anouk Aimee, Rupert Everett, Lyle Lovett, Georgianna Robertson, Michel Blanc, Tara Leon, Forest Whitaker, Lili Taylor, Linda Hunt, Sally Kellerman, Tracey Ullman. Stephen Rea, Lauren Bacall, Danny Aiello, Teri Garr.
Fee: N/A
US Box Office: $11,203,670

L.A. Confidential (1997) Director: Curtis Hanson. Producers: Arnon Michan, Curtis Hanson, Michael Nathanson. Screenplay: Brian Helgeland, Curtis Hanson, based on a novel by James Ellroy. Photography: Dante Spinotti. Editor: Peter Honess. Music: Jerry Goldsmith. Released by: Warner Bros. Cast: Kevin Spacey, Russell Crowe, Guy Pearce, James Cromwell, David Strathairn, Kim Basinger, Danny DeVito.
Fee: $3 million
US Box Office: $64,616,940

TELEVISION

Charlie's Angels (1976) Series – episode

The Six Million Dollar Man (1977) Series – episode

McMillan (1977) Series – episode

Dog and Cat (1977) Series

Vega$ (1978) Series – episode

The Ghost of Flight 401 (1978) TV movie

Katie: Portrait of a Centerfold (1978) TV movie

From Here to Eternity (1979) mini series

Killjoy (1981) TV movie

MTV's 10th Anniversary Special (1991)

Dangerous Game of Fame (1992)